Illustrator® 10 For Dummies

P9-DFJ-200

Cheat Sheet

Selecting and Moving Shortcuts

To Do This	Macintosh Shortcut Key	Windows Shortcut Key
Activate Selection tool last used (Select, Direct Select, or Group Select)	⌘+any tool (except Selection tools)	Ctrl+any tool (except Selection tools)
Toggle between Select and Direct Select (or between Select and Group Select)	None	Ctrl+Tab
Add to or subtract from selection	Shift+click with any Selection tool	Shift+click with any Selection tool
Select All	⌘+A	Ctrl+A
Deselect All	Shift+⌘+A	Shift+Ctrl+A
Move selection in one-point increments	Any arrow key	Any arrow key
Move selection in 10-point increments	Shift+press any arrow key	Shift+press any arrow key
Constrain movement to 45-degree angles	Shift+drag with any Selection tool	Shift+drag with any Selection tool
Lock selected artwork	⌘+2	Ctrl+2
Unlock all artwork	Option+⌘+2	Alt+Ctrl+2
Hide selected artwork	⌘+3	Ctrl+3
Show all hidden artwork	Option+⌘+3	Alt+Ctrl+3
Group selected artwork	⌘+G	Ctrl+G
Ungroup selected artwork	Shift+⌘+G	Shift+Ctrl+G

Painting Shortcuts

To Do This	Macintosh Shortcut	Windows Shortcut
Toggle between Paint Bucket and Eyedropper tools	Press Option while using Paint Bucket or Eyedropper tool (tool changes from one to the other when you do so)	Press Alt while using Paint Bucket or Eyedropper tool
Sample specific color from gradient	Shift+click with Eyedropper tool	Shift+click with Eyedropper tool
Add appearance of other object to Appearance palette of currently selected artwork	Shift+option+click with Eyedropper tool	Shift+Alt+click with Eyedropper tool
Swap Stroke and Fill colors of an object	Shift+X	Shift+X
Set Stroke and Fill colors to Black and White	Press D	Press D

Hungry Minds™

For Dummies: Bestselling Book Series for Beginners

Illustrator® 10 For Dummies®

Cheat Sheet

Path Editing Shortcuts

To Do This	Macintosh Shortcut	Windows Shortcut
Toggle between Pen tool and Convert Anchor Point tool	Option+Pen tool	Alt+Pen tool
Move anchor point while drawing	Click+Spacebar with Pen tool	Spacebar+Pen tool
Create closed path while drawing	Option+drag with Pencil tool or Paintbrush tool	Alt+drag with Pencil tool or Paintbrush tool
Connect path to end of another path (both paths must be selected)	⌘+drag with Pencil tool	Ctrl+drag with Pencil tool

Type Shortcuts

To Do This	Macintosh Shortcut	Windows Shortcut
Align text to left, right, or center	Shift+⌘+L, R, or C	Shift+Ctrl+L, R, or C
Justify text	Shift+⌘+J	Shift+Ctrl+J
Increase font size	Shift+⌘+. (period)	Shift+Ctrl+. (period)
Decrease font size	Shift+⌘+, (comma)	Shift+Ctrl+, (comma)
Reset Horizontal Scaling to 100 percent	Shift+⌘+X	Shift+Ctrl+X
Increase/decrease kerning/tracking	Option+right arrow/left arrow	Alt+right arrow/left arrow
Select entire word	Double-click word	Double-click word
Select entire paragraph	Triple-click a word in the paragraph	Triple-click a word in the paragraph

View Shortcuts

To Do This	Macintosh Shortcut	Windows Shortcut
Fit page in window	⌘+0 or double-click Hand tool	Ctrl+0 or double-click Hand tool
View at 100%	⌘+1 or double-click Zoom tool	Ctrl+1 or double-click Zoom tool
Change any tool into the Hand tool	Spacebar (when not editing text)	Spacebar (when not editing text)
Change any tool into the Zoom In tool	Option+⌘+Spacebar	Alt+Ctrl+Spacebar
Pixel Preview	Option+⌘+Y	Alt+Ctrl+Y
Outline View	⌘+Y (also toggles preview)	Ctrl+Y
Show/Hide Smart Guides	⌘+U	Ctrl+U
Zoom In	⌘++	Ctrl++
Zoom Out	⌘+-	Ctrl+-
Reposition Zoom marquee	Drag with Zoom tool; then press Spacebar and continue dragging	Drag with Zoom tool; then press Spacebar and continue dragging

For Dummies: Bestselling Book Series for Beginners

by Ted Alspach and Barbara Obermeier

Foreword by Shane Tracy

Hungry Minds™

Best-Selling Books • Digital Downloads • e-Books • Answer Networks • e-Newsletters • Branded Web Sites • e-Learning

New York, NY ◆ Cleveland, OH ◆ Indianapolis, IN

Illustrator® 10 For Dummies®

Published by
Hungry Minds, Inc.
909 Third Avenue
New York, NY 10022
www.hungryminds.com
www.dummies.com

Library of Congress Control Number: 2001092910

ISBN: 0-7645-3636-2

Printed in the United States of America

10 9 8 7 6 5 4 3 2 1

1B/RX/RQ/QR/IN

Distributed in the United States by Hungry Minds, Inc.

Distributed by CDG Books Canada Inc. for Canada; by Transworld Publishers Limited in the United Kingdom; by IDG Norge Books for Norway; by IDG Sweden Books for Sweden; by IDG Books Australia Publishing Corporation Pty. Ltd. for Australia and New Zealand; by TransQuest Publishers Pte Ltd. for Singapore, Malaysia, Thailand, Indonesia, and Hong Kong; by Gotop Information Inc. for Taiwan; by ICG Muse, Inc. for Japan; by Intersoft for South Africa; by Eyrolles for France; by International Thomson Publishing for Germany, Austria and Switzerland; by Distribuidora Cuspide for Argentina; by LR International for Brazil; by Galileo Libros for Chile; by Ediciones ZETA S.C.R. Ltda. for Peru; by WS Computer Publishing Corporation, Inc., for the Philippines; by Contemporanea de Ediciones for Venezuela; by Express Computer Distributors for the Caribbean and West Indies; by Micronesia Media Distributor, Inc. for Micronesia; by Chips Computadoras S.A. de C.V. for Mexico; by Editorial Norma de Panama S.A. for Panama; by American Bookshops for Finland.

For general information on Hungry Minds' products and services please contact our Customer Care Department within the U.S. at 800-762-2974, outside the U.S. at 317-572-3993 or fax 317-572-4002.

For sales inquiries and reseller information, including discounts, premium and bulk quantity sales, and foreign-language translations, please contact our Customer Care Department at 800-434-3422, fax 317-572-4002, or write to Hungry Minds, Inc., Attn: Customer Care Department, 10475 Crosspoint Boulevard, Indianapolis, IN 46256.

For information on licensing foreign or domestic rights, please contact our Sub-Rights Customer Care Department at 212-884-5000.

For information on using Hungry Minds' products and services in the classroom or for ordering examination copies, please contact our Educational Sales Department at 800-434-2086 or fax 317-572-4005.

For press review copies, author interviews, or other publicity information, please contact our Public Relations Department at 317-572-3168 or fax 317-572-4168.

For authorization to photocopy items for corporate, personal, or educational use, please contact Copyright Clearance Center, 222 Rosewood Drive, Danvers, MA 01923, or fax 978-750-4470.

Hungry Minds™ is a trademark of Hungry Minds, Inc.

Foreword

- -

Did you ever consider sending in a drawing of that little guy on the matchbook cover from one of those art school come-ons? Do you still remember how much fun you had finger-painting in second grade? Do you ever dream of using your computer to realize a new kind of creative freedom and expression, but you struggle even to draw a straight line?

If you're like me, you sometimes see in your mind's eye something that you wish you could share with others, but somehow you were standing in the snack line when God handed out raw drawing ability. Luckily, drawing-and-painting programs can help anyone draw a straight line — and a whole lot more — and Adobe Illustrator 10 is the best.

Illustrator's wealth of features may seem daunting at first. I know I was a bit intimidated. But with *Illustrator 10 For Dummies*, that feeling quickly disappears. Before long, the tools that made me nervous were opening my mind to a new creative freedom. In no time at all, I was using transparencies to create graphics for the Web; the Styles palette to create consistent artwork across related projects; and Pixel Preview mode to know right away whether the color I chose was going to look good on my Web page, rather than relying on trial and error.

Charting a clear path through the complexity of Adobe Illustrator, Ted and Barb have created a book that can help anyone get comfortable with the program. Step-by-step instructions and explanations on how to use the tools — along with tips that make using Illustrator easier — give you a boost in accomplishing the most with this software.

Illustrator 10 For Dummies won't overwhelm you with everything there is to know about Illustrator. Instead, this book gives you a reliable foundation upon which to build. And that, my friends, is the key. Whether you're an experienced graphic designer or a newbie, this book can help you realize and share your artistic vision.

Shane Tracy
Worldwide Product Support Manager, Illustration
Adobe Systems, Inc.

About the Authors

Ted Alspach is the author of more than 30 books on graphics, design, and Web publishing, including the *Illustrator 10 Bible* (published by Hungry Minds, Inc.), *PageMaker 7 for Windows and Macintosh: Visual QuickStart Guide,* and *PDF with Acrobat 5 Visual QuickStart Guide.* Ted is the Group Product Manager, Illustration Products, Adobe Systems, Inc.

Barbara Obermeier is principal of Obermeier Design, a graphic design studio in California. She's the revision author for *Photoshop 6 For Dummies, Photoshop 5 For Dummies,* and *CorelDRAW 9 For Dummies,* and the technical editor for the *Acrobat 5 PDF Bible* (all published by Hungry Minds, Inc.). Barb also teaches computer graphics at the University of California at Santa Barbara and at Ventura College.

Dedication

From Ted: To all the people who are experimenting with Illustrator for the first time — may this serve as a guide to the wonders of vector graphics.

From Barbara: To my mom, Fumiko, who always had endless faith and confidence in me.

Authors' Acknowledgments

From Ted: I would like to thank Barb Obermeier for her excellent work on updating this edition, as well as the folks at Adobe who worked to make Illustrator 10 the powerhouse application it is. They can never get enough kudos or praise. Great work, everyone!

From Barbara: I would like to thank: the great staff at Hungry Minds, Inc., especially Andy Cummings, Bob Woerner, Teresa Artman, and Amy Pettinella, whose patience and professionalism were much appreciated; Technical Editor, Tim Plumer, who politely and with good humor corrected my goofs; my friend, Ted Padova, who forced me to take breaks and dragged me to sushi lunches; my husband, Gary, who tolerated my ranting and raving every time the computer froze; and my daughter, Kylie, who patiently waited for everything because Mom was "working on a book . . . again."

Publisher's Acknowledgments

We're proud of this book; please send us your comments through our Hungry Minds Online Registration Form located at www.dummies.com.

Some of the people who helped bring this book to market include the following:

Acquisitions, Editorial, and Media Development

Project Editor: Teresa Artman

Acquisitions Editor: Bob Woerner

Copy Editors: Amy Pettinella, Nicole Laux

Technical Editor: Tim Plumer

Editorial Managers: Leah Cameron, Constance Carlisle

Senior Permissions Editor: Carmen Krikorian

Media Development Coordinator: Marissa Pearman

Media Development Manager: Laura VanWinkle

Media Development Supervisor: Richard Graves

Editorial Assistant: Amanda Foxworth

Production

Project Coordinator: Nancee Reeves

Layout and Graphics: Jackie Nicholas, Gabriele McCann, Jacque Schneider, Betty Schulte, Brian Torwelle, Julie Trippetti, Jeremey Unger, Erin Zeltner

Proofreaders: John Greenough, Andy Hollandbeck, Carl Pierce, Linda Quigley, TECHBOOKS Publishing Services

Indexer: TECHBOOKS Publishing Services

Special Help: Jean Rogers

General and Administrative

Hungry Minds, Inc.: John Kilcullen, CEO; Bill Barry, President and COO; John Ball, Executive VP, Operations & Administration; John Harris, Executive VP and CFO

Hungry Minds Technology Publishing Group: Richard Swadley, Senior Vice President and Publisher; Mary Bednarek, Vice President and Publisher, Networking; Joseph Wikert, Vice President and Publisher, Web Development Group; Mary C. Corder, Editorial Director, Dummies Technology; Andy Cummings, Publishing Director, Dummies Technology; Barry Pruett, Publishing Director, Visual/Graphic Design

Hungry Minds Manufacturing: Ivor Parker, Vice President, Manufacturing

Hungry Minds Marketing: John Helmus, Assistant Vice President, Director of Marketing

Hungry Minds Production for Branded Press: Debbie Stailey, Production Director

Hungry Minds Sales: Michael Violano, Vice President, International Sales and Sub Rights

Contents at a Glance

Foreword v

Introduction 1

Part 1: Driving People Crazy — Illustrator's Bum Rap 7
Chapter 1: Introducing the World of Illustrator 9
Chapter 2: Following the Righteous Path 31
Chapter 3: Doing Everyday Things with Illustrator 45

Part 11: Drawing and Coloring Your Artwork 63
Chapter 4: Shaping Up, Basically 65
Chapter 5: Getting Your Fill of Fills and Strokes 81
Chapter 6: Selecting and Editing Paths 103
Chapter 7: Wielding the Mighty Pen Tool 117
Chapter 8: Wielding the Versatile Pencil, Line Segment, and Arc Tools 135
Chapter 9: Creating Magnificent Brushstrokes 149
Chapter 10: Extreme Fills and Strokes 169
Chapter 11: Keeping Up Appearances, with Style(s) 187

Part 111: Taking Your Paths to Obedience School 203
Chapter 12: Pushing, Pulling, Poking, and Prodding 205
Chapter 13: Taking Images Out of the Realm of Reality 221
Chapter 14: Organizing Efficiently 235

Part 1V: Practically Speaking: Type, Print, and Files 249
Chapter 15: Introducing Letters and Such (Type 101) 251
Chapter 16: Printing Your Masterpiece 267
Chapter 17: Putting Your Art on the Web 277
Chapter 18: Moving Files into and out of Illustrator 309

Part V: The Part of Tens 327
Chapter 19: Ten Production-Enhancing Tips 329
Chapter 20: Ten (Or So) Ways to Customize Illustrator 341

Index 351

Cartoons at a Glance

By Rich Tennant

"Are you sure that's the best way to apply a stroke to a path?"

"I COULDN'T SAY ANYTHING — THEY WERE IN HERE WITH THAT PROGRAM WE BOUGHT THEM THAT ENCOURAGES ARTISTIC EXPRESSION."

page 63

"OK, TECHNICALLY, THIS SHOULD WORK. JUDY, TYPE THE WORD 'GOODYEAR' IN ALL CAPS, BOLDFACE, AT 700-POINT TYPE SIZE."

page 249

Illustrator's awesome! I can finally drag and drop a spleen into my memos.

INTERNAL ORGAN BANK

page 7

Jeez — that's impressive! Let's see that airbrush effect again.

page 327

Cartoon Information:
Fax: 978-546-7747
E-Mail: richtennant@the5thwave.com
World Wide Web: www.the5thwave.com

Table of Contents

Foreword v

Introduction 1
About This Book 1
What You Don't Need to Read 2
Foolish Assumptions 2
How This Book Is Organized 3
    Part I: Driving People Crazy — Illustrator's Bum Rap 3
    Part II: Drawing and Coloring Your Artwork 3
    Part III: Taking Your Paths to Obedience School 3
    Part IV: Practically Speaking: Type, Print, and Files 3
    Part V: The Part of Tens 4
    But that's not all!: Bonus chapters 4
About All Those Little Icons 4
Road Signs along the Way 5
Where to Go from Here 5

Part 1: Driving People Crazy — Illustrator's Bum Rap 7

Chapter 1: Introducing the World of Illustrator 9
From Humble Origins to Master of the Graphics Universe 9
    A brief history of Illustrator 10
    Illustrator's place in the cosmos 10
Starting Up Illustrator and Revving It a Little 11
    What's in a Name (field)? 12
    Page size, units, and orientation 12
    CMYK or RGB? 13
Exploring the Illustrator Workspace 15
    A graphic handyman's Toolbox 16
    Palettes to suit any artist 17
    Menus with the finest cuisine 19
    Mac and Windows issues spring eternal 20
Defining the Document Area 21
Opening Existing Documents 23
Viewing Illustrator Documents 23
    Zooming in and out of artwork 24
    Scrolling around your document 26
    Using the Navigator palette 27
    Looking at the guts of your artwork 28
Saving Illustrator Documents 28
Changing Your Mind 29
Printing Illustrator Documents 30
Closing Documents and Quitting Illustrator 30

Chapter 2: Following the Righteous Path **31**

Whether Paths or Pixels Are Better 32
    Paths: The ultimate flexibility in graphics 33
    Pixels: Detail and realism to spare 33
How Paths and Pixels Compare 36
    A comparison of path and pixel documents 36
    The big limitations and upcoming solutions 38
    When to use paths and when to use pixels 39
Paths and the PostScript Language 40
    Which is faster — a square or a square? 40
    PostScript: The evolution of Bézier curves 40
    What's my vector, Victor? 41
Gray's Anatomy of a Path 41
    In Illustrator, it's polite to point 41
    You can handle the truth 42
Drawing Basics 44

Chapter 3: Doing Everyday Things with Illustrator **45**

Picking Up Stuff and Moving It Around 45
    Discovering Selection tools 46
    Moving and transforming objects 48
    Distorting paths 48
    Organizing objects 50
Using the Fun Stuff 51
    Transparency 52
    Blends 52
    Masks 54
    Compound paths 54
    Flares 56
Entering the Wide World of the Web 58
Saving the World 59
    Save 59
    Save As 60
    Save a Copy 60
    Save for Web 61
    Export 61
Using Illustrator for What It Does Best 61

Part II: Drawing and Coloring Your Artwork **63**

Chapter 4: Shaping Up, Basically **65**

Creating Basic Shapes 65
    Drawing rectangles and squares 66
    Drawing ellipses and circles 67
    Creating polygons, stars, and spirals 68

Putting Shapes Together 71
   Compound Shapes 73
   Pathfinders 75
Creating Objects Using the Pathfinder Palette 77
   Crescent moon 77
   Sunrise 78

Chapter 5: Getting Your Fill of Fills and Strokes **81**
Understanding Fill and Stroke 81
   Filling and stroking paths with color 83
   Making a bold stroke 84
   Filling crossed and open paths 85
The Swatches Palette 86
   All the colors in the rainbow and then some 86
   Swatch Options for super colors 88
   Swatch libraries 89
The Color Palette 90
   Parts of the palette 90
   Modes and models 92
Filling with Patterns and Textures 94
   Applying patterns to paths 95
   Making patterns 95
Using the Gradient Fill 96
   The Gradient tool 98
   The Gradient palette 98
   Gradient-mania: Color-tweaking made simple 99
   The secret Gradient 100

Chapter 6: Selecting and Editing Paths **103**
Selecting with Different Methods 103
   Natural selection 104
   Direct selection 105
   Group selection 106
   Selecting more or less of what you have 108
   Freeform selections 108
Selecting Magically with the Magic Wand 109
   Working wizardry with the Wand 109
   Magic Wand options 109
Selecting without Tools: The New Select Menu 110
   A giant vat of really sticky stuff 110
   Specialized selection functions for important occasions 111
Editing and Adjusting Points 112
   A relocation bonus for points 113
   Fine-tuning curves with direction points 113
   Converting anchor points 114
   Adding and subtracting points (path math) 115

Chapter 7: Wielding the Mighty Pen Tool 117

Performing with the Pen, the Path, and the Anchor Points 118
    Smooth anchor points 118
    Straight-corner anchor points 119
    Curved-corner anchor points 120
    Combination-corner anchor points 121
Creating Straight Lines with the Pen Tool 123
Open and Closed Paths 125
Creating Super-Precise Curves with the Pen Tool 125
    Taming the draggin' 126
    Following the one-third rule 128
    Following rules for the other two-thirds 129
    Drawing the tricky anchor points with the Pen tool 130
Drawing Shapes with the Pen Tool 131
    Drawing a sad, lumpy circle with the Pen tool 132
    Drawing a heart 133

**Chapter 8: Wielding the Versatile Pencil,
Line Segment, and Arc Tools** 135

Using the Pencil Tool as a Pencil 136
    Minimal effort and hefty stress reduction 136
    A few unexpected exceptions to all this bliss 137
Cherishing the Multipurpose Pencil Tool 138
    Making the Pencil tool work just for you 139
    Changing the path not penciled 143
    Working with the all-natural "Smoothie" tool 144
Using the Pen with the Pencil 145
    Swapping one tool for another 145
    Precision versus speed: You make the call 145
Lines Made Quick and Easy 146
    Working with the Line Segment tool 146
    Setting the tool options 146
Getting Curvy with the New Arc Tool 147
    One-step Bézier curves 147
    Getting the arc you want 147

Chapter 9: Creating Magnificent Brushstrokes 149

Brushing Where No Stroke Has Gone Before 149
    Embracing your inner artist 151
    The Paintbrush tool options 153
Creating a New Brush 153
Working with the Different Brush Types 155
    Art brushes for times when you're a bit wacky 155
    Scatter brushes for times when you're a bit wacky 158
    Pattern brushes — too cool and utterly wacko 159
    Calligraphic brushes for formal occasions 167

Chapter 10: Extreme Fills and Strokes 169

Messing Around with Meshes 169
Making Objects Partially Transparent and Blending Colors 173
    Fade away with opacity 174
    Big fun with math! Blending graphics with Blend Modes 175
Discovering How Strokes Work 176
Caps, Joins, and Dashes 177
    Caps 178
    Joins 179
    Dashes 179
The Effect Menu 181
    Applying live effects to objects 181
    Removing and changing effects 183
    Here's the catch . . . rasterization! 184
Clipping Masks 185

Chapter 11: Keeping Up Appearances, with Style(s) 187

The Appearance Palette 188
    Reading the Appearance palette 188
    Adding fills and strokes 190
    Changing the appearance of groups and layers 192
    Applying effects to strokes and fills 194
    Going back to adjust settings 195
    Removing appearances 195
    Killing live effects until they're dead 196
Figuring Out Styles 196
    Applying styles to objects 197
    Creating and editing styles 197
    Spotting the difference between graphic and text styles 200
    Applying graphic styles to text 200

Part III: Taking Your Paths to Obedience School 203

Chapter 12: Pushing, Pulling, Poking, and Prodding 205

Understanding the Five Transformation Sisters 205
    Move 206
    Scale 207
    Rotate 210
    Reflect 210
    Shear 212
Additional Transformation Tidbits 213
    The Transform palette 213
    Copying while transforming 214
    Transform Each 215
    Transform Again 215
    Partial transformations 216
Blending: The Magic Transformation 217

Chapter 13: Taking Images Out of the Realm of Reality 221

Applying Simple Distortions 221
    Pucker & Bloat 221
    Roughen and Scribble & Tweak 222
    Zig Zag 223
    Free Distort and Twist 223
Creating Graphic Ooze with Live Distortions 223
    Liquifying without a blender 224
    Liquify options 225
Pushing the Envelope 228
    At warp speed 228
    What a mesh 229
    Pathways 230
Inflicting Warps without Harm 232
    Applying a warp 232
    Warped beyond belief 232

Chapter 14: Organizing Efficiently 235

Stacking Illustrator Artwork 235
    Stacking order 236
    Moving art up (front) or back (down) in the stacking order 237
Managing the Mess 238
    Using the Layers palette 238
    Lock and Unlock, View and Hide 241
    Copying layers (quickly and completely) 241
    Viewing objects and groups 241
    Using your options on layers, groups, and objects 242
Imposing Slavish Conformity with Groups 244
Lining Up 244
    Electronic graph paper 245
    Guides that are truly smarter than most of us 246
    Let the rulers guide you 247
    I'm a path, I'm a guide 247
    Alignment 248

Part IV: Practically Speaking: Type, Print, and Files 249

Chapter 15: Introducing Letters and Such (Type 101) 251

Using the Word Processor from Outer Space 252
    Controlling type in Illustrator 252
    The Type tool 252
    The Character palette 254
    The Paragraph palette 254

Introducing the Strange Land of Type 256
    Fonts, typefaces, and font families 256
    Serif and sans serif 258
    The biggest Don't Do It that we can think of 259
Exploring Size, Leading, and Other Mysterious Numbers 259
    Measuring can be just plain odd 260
    Measuring can be just plain annoying 261
    Spacing out while staring at type 262
    Putting type on the rack 262
    Moving on up and down 264
Adjusting Entire Paragraphs 264
    Changing the alignment of a paragraph 264
    Changing the space around the paragraph 265

Chapter 16: Printing Your Masterpiece **267**
Printing Quickly 267
What You See Is Roughly What You Get 268
Setting Up Your Page to Print (You Hope) 268
    Printer type and page size 269
    The only options you need to care about 270
Printing Mechanics 271
    Printing composite proofs 271
    Important printing options 271
All about Way-Scary Separations 273
    Remember, separations are not in color 275
    Looking at Separations Setup 275

Chapter 17: Putting Your Art on the Web **277**
From Illustrator to the Web 277
    Using Web colors only 278
    Working in Pixel Preview mode 280
    Choosing a file format 281
    So which file format is best, already? 283
Creating Web-Specific Pixel Graphics 284
    Saving a graphic as a GIF file 286
    Saving a graphic as a JPEG file 289
    Saving a graphic as a PNG-8 or PNG-24 file 291
Creating Web-Specific Vector Graphics 291
    Saving a graphic as a Macromedia Flash file 291
    Saving a graphic as a SVG file 294
Legal Graffiti 299
    Using the Symbol Sprayer 300
    Creating a custom Symbol 301
    Editing your Symbols 301
    Setting the Symbolism options 302
Slicing and Dicing Your Graphics 304
    Creating slices 304
    Cascading Style Sheet layers 307

Chapter 18: Moving Files into and out of Illustrator 309

Bringing Files into Illustrator 310
    Which is better, linking or embedding? 312
    Managing links 313
Getting Files out of Illustrator 315
Working with Illustrator and Photoshop 317
    Making life easy: Copy and paste, drag and drop 317
    Placing files 319
    Now opening in an application near you 320
    Exporting a graphic 321
Using Adobe Illustrator with Nearly Everything Else 323

Part V: The Part of Tens 327

Chapter 19: Ten Production-Enhancing Tips 329

Punching Holes 329
Whoa! Don't Use That Photoshop Filter! 331
When White Isn't Nothing 332
Expanding for Simplicity 334
Quick! Hide! 335
Taking a Tip from Illustrator 336
Changing Your Units Whenever You Want 337
Reusing Your Brushes, Swatches, and Libraries 338
Avoiding Russian Dolls 338
Selecting Type When You Want 339

Chapter 20: Ten (Or So) Ways to Customize Illustrator 341

Positioning Palettes 342
Changing the Items on the Menu 342
The Flexible Toolbox 344
The Start-up Document 344
Changing the Default Settings 345
Changing Hidden Commands You Never Knew About 346
Using a Master Document 346
Action Jackson 347
Sticky Settings 349

Index 351

Introduction

Welcome to *Illustrator 10 For Dummies.* You're reading this book because you want to find out more about Adobe Illustrator. That's a very smart move because Adobe Illustrator is the industry-standard drawing tool for print and the Web. Not only does it outsell all its competitors, it's also one of the most powerful graphics-creation tools ever created. With Illustrator, all you need to produce graphics like the best you've seen in print or on the Web is knowledge and artistic ability. Artistic ability is a challenge that you can handle on your own. The other half — knowledge — is what this book is all about.

Like a tragic hero, Illustrator's great power is also its terrible curse. With its 25+ palettes, 70+ tools, and scores of menu items, its sheer depth is enough to make the most hardened graphics expert go shaky in the knees. Don't be fooled by Illustrator's vastness, however, because you will find a unique, consistent logic underlying it all. After you master a few basics, all the rest falls nicely into place.

In this book, our mission is to get you past Illustrator's intimidation factor and into its Wow! factor. We take you from being befuddled and mystified by Illustrator's nigh-infinite options to creating the kinds of graphics that others look at and say, "Wow, how did you do *that*?"

About This Book

This book is written to make your journey into Adobe Illustrator flexible and self-paced. Each chapter is as self-contained as possible. You can hop in anywhere you want, with a minimum of flipping to other parts of the book to find out what you missed. If your goal is to find out more about the Pencil tool, for example, you can skip everything else and go directly to Chapter 8 without getting hopelessly lost. On the other hand, if you're determined to find out as much about the program as possible, you can read the book from cover to cover. We organized the book so that the chapters move from simple to more complex concepts. The early chapters make a good base for understanding the latter ones.

Use this book as both a reference book and an on-site trainer for Adobe Illustrator. To find out more about a specific feature, look for it in the index or Table of Contents. To get a more in-depth feel for the feature, follow the step-by-step instructions that accompany the information on the major features.

By and large, people get more out of doing than out of reading about doing. Adobe Illustrator is a classic case-in-point. Don't bother to memorize anything in this book. Instead, pick up a concept, work with it in Illustrator for a while, and then come back to the book when you're ready for something new. Above all, have fun with it! Adobe Illustrator is one of the coolest programs on the planet. With a little practice, you can be creating illustrations that knock your socks off.

Note: Because we realize that some folks use PCs and some folks use Macs, we try to offer commands for both Windows and Macintosh platforms. Occasionally we offer information specific to one platform or the other, including keyboard shortcuts. While you journey through this book, you'll see that many figures (those that show you what you see onscreen) are a mixed bag of all things Mr. Gates and Mr. Jobs.

What You Don't Need to Read

We'd love to think that you'll pore over each and every word we've written. We also realize that you have a life. Feel free to skip any information that seems far afield from what you need to know. The stuff that no one should ever *really* have to know (but which is nonetheless utterly fascinating) is clearly labeled with a Technical Stuff icon. You'll also run across some bonus material placed in a sidebar — a gray shaded box — that we fill with cool-to-know-but-not-imperative stuff.

Foolish Assumptions

We're going to make just the following two basic Foolish Assumptions about you, Gentle Reader:

- ✔ **You have time, patience, and a strong desire to learn Adobe Illustrator 10.** Illustrator has a steep learning curve at the start; but after you get the basics, you find the program pretty straightforward. Getting over that first hump is going to take a little endurance and can get pretty frustrating at times. Be patient with yourself and the program. All shall be revealed in the fullness of time. Until then, this book is intended to help you get over that initial learning hump.

- ✔ **You have access to a computer with Adobe Illustrator 10 on it.** This hands-on book isn't meant to be read like a novel. If this is your very own copy of the book, attack it with highlighters and sticky notes, scribble in some marginalia, or even force it open until it lies flat on your desk. Then — after you collect all the loose pages and glue 'em back in — you can have both hands free to work at the computer while you follow along.

How This Book Is Organized

In this book, you find 20 chapters organized in five parts. Each part reflects a major Illustrator concept; each chapter chomps a concept into easily digestible morsels. The whole thing is arranged in a logical order, so you can read straight through if you're so inclined. Or you can jump in at any point to find the exact information you need. To help you do that, here's an overview of what you can find in each of those five parts.

Part I: Driving People Crazy — Illustrator's Bum Rap

Here's where you get the absolute basics of Illustrator. What it is, what it does, and why it's worth the effort. The wonders of blank pages, paths, and the beguiling Pen tool all make their debut here. By the time you finish this part, you have a good overview of the entire program.

Part II: Drawing and Coloring Your Artwork

This part is where the fun begins — you roll up your sleeves and start creating illustrations. Whether or not you can draw using old-fashioned paper and pencil (ewww — how twentieth century), wait'll you see what you can create with Illustrator!

Part III: Taking Your Paths to Obedience School

With Illustrator, you can really unleash your creativity. Unfortunately, unleashed creativity often results in an unruly mess. This part looks at how to tame the mess through changing parts of graphics, organizing graphics into separate layers, and using many other techniques that prove that organization and creativity are not mutually exclusive. You don't even need a smock.

Part IV: Practically Speaking: Type, Print, and Files

Illustrator is truly a wondrous modifier of written characters, so we devote this part to working with type, and then getting your creations to print.

We cover everything from the most basic formatting to complex type treatments. Stick around here, too, for the skinny on posting your art to the Web and moving files in and out of Illustrator.

Part V: The Part of Tens

No *For Dummies* book is complete without its Top Ten lists, and this book is no exception. Here are lots of tips to help you use Illustrator more effectively, and ways to customize Illustrator (chrome hubcaps optional). Save this part for dessert.

But that's not all!: Bonus chapters

We tried and we tried but no matter how hard we squeezed, we just couldn't fit everything we wanted into this book. (Kind of like how some people pack a steamer trunk for a weekend getaway lark.) Rather than try to skimp on all we wanted to show you, we put two extra-cool chapters on the Web for you. These two chapters cover advanced typography and ten techniques for creating some killer effects. Check 'em out at `www.dummies.com/extras/ Illustrator10/`.

About All Those Little Icons

Scattered throughout this book you find some nifty little icons that point out bits of information that are especially useful, important, or noteworthy.

This bull's-eye points out information that can help you do something faster, easier, or better; save you time and money; or make you the hero of the beach. Or at least make you a little less stressed during a production crunch!

Watch out! This impending-explosion icon means that danger lurks nearby. Heed it when directed to those things you should avoid and what things you must absolutely never do.

Look to these icons for utterly fascinating technotrivia that most people never need to know. This information is the kind you can drop into a conversation at a party to remind people how much smarter you are than everyone else. (Assuming that you plan to go home alone, that is.)

Remember helps you remember to remember. The information you find at these icons is stuff that you use on a regular basis in Illustrator. Write it down on your hand so that you can refer to it at any instant. Just don't wash that hand! Or better yet, bookmark the page or remember the advice you find there.

Check out these special guys for the scoop on what's new in Illustrator 10. The sky's the limit when you follow these hot air balloons with the numeral 10.

Road Signs along the Way

You will see some special ways we make text look in this book, such as bold print or shortcut keys or paths for how to find things. Here's a quick legend for the road signs you should watch for.

When we ask you to type (enter) something — in a text box, for example — **we make it bold**. When you see a construction like this — Choose Edit➪Paste — that means to go to the Edit menu and choose Paste from there. To show you words like they appear onscreen, such as a text box name or a warning, It Shows Up in Text Like This. Keyboard shortcuts look like Ctrl+Z (Windows) or ⌘+Z (Mac).

Where to Go from Here

Illustrator is a graphics adventure waiting for you to take it on. This book is your guide for that adventure. If you're ravenous to know everything now, you can rush through the text as fast as you can, starting with Chapter 1 and charging right through to the end. Or you can take your time, pick a point that interests you, explore it at your leisure, and then come back to a different place in the book later. Whatever works best for you, this book is your ready-willing-and-able guide for the journey. All you have to do is start your computer, launch Illustrator, turn the page, and let the adventure begin.

Part I
Driving People Crazy — Illustrator's Bum Rap

The 5th Wave · By Rich Tennant

In this part . . .

Here you meet the main character of the book: Adobe Illustrator 10. You get a look at its illustrious past, its remarkable powers, its place in the universe, and (most importantly) what it can do for you. You probe the difference between vectors and pixels. You hover above the various parts of Illustrator and watch what they do. By the end of this part, you uncover a straightforward and easy-going program behind the complex, sometimes intimidating exterior of Illustrator.

Chapter 1

Introducing the World of Illustrator

In This Chapter

▶ Getting a look at how graphic artists use Illustrator

▶ Becoming familiar with the Illustrator interface

▶ Noting some Mac and Windows differences

▶ Creating new documents

▶ Saving your artwork

▶ Printing Illustrator documents

▶ Bailing out of a document (and Illustrator itself)

*1*f there were any truth in advertising (or at least in product naming), Adobe *Intimidator* would be a more appropriate name for Adobe Illustrator. The program's dozens of tools, hundreds of commands, and more than 25 palettes can transform confident, secure individuals into drooling, confused, and frustrated drones.

The situation doesn't have to be that way, of course. Sure, all that stuff is scary. Even more frightening to some is the prospect of facing the giant white nothingness of the document window — the endless possibilities, the confusion over where to start. This chapter helps you get past that initial stage and move forward into the mystical state of *eagerly awaiting* (instead of fearing) each new feature and function.

From Humble Origins to Master of the Graphics Universe

As its box proudly proclaims, Adobe Illustrator is the "Industry Standard Graphics Creation Software for Print and the Web." But the software didn't always enjoy that standing. Illustrator evolved from a geeky math experiment into the graphics powerhouse it is today.

A brief history of Illustrator

Until the mid-1980s, computer art was limited to blocky-looking video games, spheroid reflections, and the movie *Tron*. Then something happened to change all that — PostScript, a computer language created especially for printers. Adobe created PostScript specifically to help printers produce millions of teeny-tiny dots on the page, without running out of memory. (Graphics files *are* notoriously huge.)

In 1987, Adobe released Illustrator 1.1, which was designed primarily to be a *front end* for PostScript — a way to make its capabilities actually usable. At that time, the concept of artwork that is scalable to any size *without loss of quality* (one world-beating advantage of creating art within Illustrator) was brand new. Illustrator gave companies the opportunity to have electronic versions of their logos that could be printed at *any* size.

In the 10-plus years since Version 1.1, Adobe Illustrator has become the Web-ready, giant application that it is today. Millions of people around the world use Illustrator, and its *thousands* of features, big and small, meet a wide variety of graphics needs. Oddly enough, the one aspect of Illustrator that *hasn't* changed is the intimidation factor. Version 1.1 had several tools, many menu items, a neurosis-inducing Pen tool, Bézier curves, and that way-scary blank document when you started it up. Version 10 still has nearly every feature that 1.1 did and adds a staggering array of new features — Liquify, Envelope, Warp, Symbolism, and on and on. Illustrator 1.1 was a playful little kitten compared with the tigerish Illustrator 10!

Illustrator's place in the cosmos

Professional graphic artists have a toolbox of programs that they use to create the books, magazines, newspapers, and Web sites that you see every day. Any professional will tell you that you need the right tool for the job to do the job well. The right tools (in this case) are software products — drawing programs, paint programs, and products for page layout and Web-authoring. *Drawing programs,* such as Adobe Illustrator, are the best tools for creating crisp, professional-looking graphics (such as logos), working with creative type effects, and recreating photographs from line drawings. *Painting programs* (often called *image editing programs*), such as Adobe Photoshop, provide tools to color-correct, retouch, and edit digital photographs and recreate "natural media" effects, such as hand-painting. Page layout programs, such as Adobe PageMaker, InDesign, or QuarkXPress, enable you to combine graphics that you create in drawing and paint programs with text for print publishing. You can use Web-authoring tools (such as Macromedia Dreamweaver or Adobe GoLive) to combine graphics, text, sound, animation, and interactivity for presentation on the World Wide Web.

Although each tool performs a fairly specific (if wide-ranging) task, there is some cross-over between applications. For example, Illustrator has some limited image editing capabilities, but very few people ever use them. Because you can edit images with complete control and freedom in Photoshop, why use the wrong tool for the job? QuarkXPress enables you to run type along a curve, but Illustrator has so many tools for creative type effects that you'd be silly to do them anywhere else.

By using Illustrator on its own, you can create an astonishing variety of graphics and type effects. When you combine it with paint, page-layout, and Web-authoring programs, you have the tools you need to create print and Web publications that match the quality of anything you see in the stands or onscreen today.

In the field of professional graphics and publishing, each software program has to perform only a few basic functions: graphics creation, image editing, page layout (for print), or Web layout.

Illustrator is the *de facto* standard in graphics creation. Adobe has products in the other categories (two in the page-layout category). One benefit of using Illustrator is that it works very well (as you may expect) with the other Adobe products, most of which have a similar interface and way of working. If you know one Adobe product well, chances are you'll have an easy time of figuring out other Adobe products.

Illustrator excels at creating and editing artwork of all types. In fact, you can use Illustrator to create and edit nearly anything that isn't a photograph. (For more about the differences between photographs and artwork created with Illustrator, see Chapter 2.)

Starting Up Illustrator and Revving It a Little

To get Illustrator running, either choose Illustrator from the Start menu (in Windows on a PC) or double-click the application's icon (on a Mac). (The latter method also works in Windows, if you're a Mac user who happens to be using Windows. Don't worry; we won't tell a soul. Honest.)

The Illustrator startup process displays the *splash screen* — an image to look at while the program is cranking up. You're in luck; this one is a lovely picture of Venus, from Botticelli's famous painting, rendered by using Illustrator. Look at her enigmatic smile — she's inviting you to enter the creative and exciting world of Illustrator! To accept her invitation, choose File⇨New and answer the riddles of the New Document dialog box, shown in Figure 1-1.

Figure 1-1:
The New
Document
dialog box.

Before you start a new document, you have to answer a few questions in the New Document dialog box about the name, page size, units of measurement, orientation, and color mode that you plan to use.

What's in a Name (field)?

You can give your new document a name in the Name field. If you don't, Illustrator names it Untitled-1, and every new document you create is titled sequentially — Untitled-2, Untitled-3, and so on, until you quit the program. When you re-launch, you'll be right back at Untitled-1. If you don't give a name to the new document, you get another chance when you save it. The advantage to naming your document is that if you accumulate a whole bunch of unsaved files (*not* recommended!), you can tell them apart.

Page size, units, and orientation

You set your page size by either choosing a predefined size from the new Size pop-up menu or typing values into the Height and Width fields. Your page size truly matters only when you're printing your document directly out of Illustrator. Otherwise, it just exists as a point of reference — a guide to show you how far things are apart from each other. One great thing about Illustrator: For the most part, size doesn't matter. When you create graphics for the Web, you can determine the size of the graphic when you save it. When you're creating graphics for print, most of the time you'll be creating graphics to be imported into page layout applications, such as QuarkXPress, PageMaker, or InDesign. In the latter case, although it's always best to size your image in Illustrator, you can scale the graphic to the size you need it in your page layout. In either case, the Web browser or page-layout application recognizes your Illustrator drawing, ignoring the page size.

Page size is good for two things: proofing and conceptualization. Often you'll want to print your artwork on paper directly from Illustrator to get an idea of what it looks like. In this case, set the Size to the size paper you've loaded in your printer. While creating graphics, keep in mind the size of the page or browser window that you're creating for — in this case, set the Height and Width to whatever the target output is. For example, if you're creating for the Web, you may want to set the size to 640 pixels x 480 pixels, which is a fairly standard size for computer screens. This is just to help you visualize the final artwork. Actually, you can change the size of the artwork to be anything you want, and that's one of the great things about creating in Illustrator.

By default, Illustrator measures image size in *points* (1 point = ½₂ inch). If that unit of measurement is unfamiliar to you, be sure to select a different unit from the new Units pop-up menu. This will also change your ruler (when you choose View⇨Show Rulers) units to the type you selected. And although it won't change the ruler units, you can also type the unit of measurement along with the number when you specify values for page size in the Height and Width fields. When you open a new document, it comes up showing a width in points — say, for instance, 612 pt. If you want to specify a width of 10 inches or 30 centimeters, just type (respectively) **10 in** or **30 cm** in the Width field. If you don't know the standard abbreviation for a unit of measurement, you can type the whole word out (for example, **10 inches** or **30 centimeters**). Illustrator understands what you mean and does the conversion for you. And it will do so wherever you enter a unit of measurement, not only in the New Document dialog box. Smart, very smart!

Illustrator has now provided an orientation option in the New Document dialog box. Simply choose your desired orientation — Portrait or Landscape.

CMYK or RGB?

CMYK or RGB? In Illustrator, this question is a bit more significant than the ubiquitous question, "Paper or plastic?" To understand why you have to answer Illustrator's question, you need a little more history and some technobabble. (Sorry, we'll try to keep this brief.)

Illustrator has been around for a long time, back when putting color images on the Web was impossible and interactive multimedia was little more than a buzzword. In those days, the main reason for creating documents in color on the computer was so you could print them out in color. Color printing almost always uses a *CMYK* process — for *C*yan, *M*agenta, *Y*ellow, and blac*K* inks (the *K* stands for black because RGB has dibs on *B,* which stands for *blue*). These four colors, blended in different amounts, produce the full range of colors you see in printed material. So back then, Illustrator used only CMYK colors because nobody needed to do anything in color besides print.

Then along came interactive multimedia — in effect, the "lights, camera, sound, and action" for computer users. Shortly after that came the Web. Because images used for multimedia and the Web appear only on the computer screen, a need emerged for RGB images. *So what's RGB, already?*

Okay, we're getting to that: Computer screens create the colors you see by using electrons to make a coating of phosphors glow *R*ed, *G*reen, or *B*lue (hence RGB) in different intensities. If you're creating content for multimedia applications or for the Web, you need RGB images that look good onscreen. You probably don't give two hoots about CMYK. So Illustrator, trying to please everyone, added the capability to create colors in RGB.

Unfortunately, this new feature didn't quite please *everyone*. In fact, it upset some people quite a lot. And left a wake of money wasted, deadlines blown, marriages ruined, lives lost. (Well, okay, that's a little exaggeration, but *only* a little.) CMYK and RGB just didn't get along.

Some side effects of a typical CMYK/RGB goof were minor. If you accidentally used CMYK colors for an image displayed on the Web (for example), your colors would look a little different from what you expected, but that's all. The mistake wouldn't cost you anything. Printing out that image, however, was an entirely different matter.

Printing in color meant using the standard four-color printing process: Every image had its own percentage of cyan, magenta, yellow, and black, so four sets of films were made (one for each of those colors); the final printed image combined the colors. Each set consisted of only four single-color plates (C, M, Y, and K) — and that's all you'd expect to print out. But if your Illustrator file contained any RGB elements (even a few pixels' worth), you had big trouble: Three additional films would print out — frequently at a cost of $100 or more per film — for *every* page that contained *any* RGB colors. If you weren't paying attention, one mistake like that could cost thousands of dollars. And a lot of people weren't paying attention because they'd never had to worry about RGB colors in an Illustrator file before. (You can bet they did after that!) To prevent this sort of uproar from happening again, Adobe wisely removed the capability to combine CMYK and RGB colors in the same document. That's why you have to specify CMYK *or* RGB before you start a new document. Sure, it's a hassle, but you're *so much* better off having this hassle now, rather than spending money for it later!

So which do you choose, CMYK or RGB? You may think it safe to assume that RGB is for multimedia or the Web and CMYK is for print. Okay, that's a *safe* assumption, but not necessarily the *best* assumption. For the sake of your creativity, choose RGB when

- ✔ **You're creating for the Web or for multimedia:** In this situation, you're always creating work that's going to be viewed in RGB and you've no practical reason whatever to use CMYK.

- ✔ **You're creating for print BUT do not need precise CMYK colors:** If you don't have to specify exact CMYK values while you work, choose RGB. (You can convert to CMYK by using the File⇨Document Color Mode command *before you print* — just don't forget to, okay?) We know that approach sounds like asking for trouble, but we can give you three good reasons for using RGB this way:

- Some of Illustrator's coolest features (including many Effect commands) only work with RGB color.

- When you work in RGB, you can use the full range of colors — *millions* of them — that are possible on the computer. (CMYK only supports mere *thousands* of colors.) If you're creating content for both print and the Web, creating the image in RGB gives you the maximum color range possible in both CMYK *and* RGB.

- Some desktop inkjet color printers print well in RGB. For example, Epson six color printers print a wider range (gamut) of colors in RGB than in CMYK.

For the sake of accuracy, choose CMYK when

✔ **You need precise CMYK colors:** Some artists who create for print use a swatch book of printed CMYK colors. They use only the specific CMYK colors they see in the book because they feel (and rightly so) that this is the only way to get a good idea of what that color will look like when it finally prints. If your designs have to meet such specific requirements, you should always work in CMYK. Some companies specify the exact CMYK colors they want in their publications. If you're working on a project for one of those companies, use CMYK.

✔ **You're creating for grayscale or black and white print:** In RGB, shades of gray exist by default as blends of red, green, and blue. If you're printing with black ink, this blending is a hassle because you always have to work with three colors instead of one. In CMYK, however, you can create shades of gray as percentages of black ink, ignoring all other colors (which you may as well do if they won't be visible anyway).

After you answer the three magic New Document questions (name, page specs, and color choice), click OK and behold: A blank page opens, inviting you to realize your creative potential. You're ready to start illustrating. If blank-page syndrome doesn't faze you and you want to dig into the good stuff right away, thumb over to Chapter 2.

Exploring the Illustrator Workspace

Between figuring out what the 250+ menu items actually do and rearranging palettes (until you have a tiny little area on your document in which you can actually work), you may find the Illustrator environment a bit daunting. (If you do, you're far from alone.) The next sections are an overview of all the stuff that's preventing you from getting any work done. (That stuff is what the geeks call the *UI* — pronounced *you eye* — for *user interface*.)

A graphic handyman's Toolbox

The Illustrator Toolbox (that alien artifact in Figure 1-2) is the place that most people start when they use Illustrator. After showing you 24 tools, 6 odd-looking buttons, and a gang of giant square things, the Toolbox pretends that's all there is to it. Actually, the Toolbox has over 50 hidden tools. Call up most tools in Illustrator by clicking (once) the tool you want in the Toolbox. The cursor then changes to either something that looks like the tool, or in the case of special tools (Rectangle, Ellipse, and others) a cross-hair cursor.

The tools live in *toolslots,* which are subdivisions within the Toolbox. Many toolslots contain more than one tool, as indicated by a small black arrow in the bottom-right corner of the toolslot. To access a hidden tool, click and hold the mouse pointer on a tool in its toolslot. You then see a bunch of other (usually related) tools materialize by the toolslot that you clicked (as shown with the Pen tool in Figure 1-2). Use those other tools by dragging to the tool you want to use and releasing the mouse button.

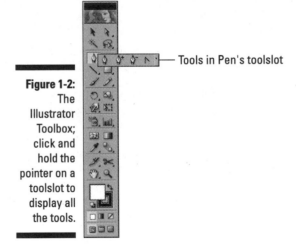

Tools in Pen's toolslot

Figure 1-2: The Illustrator Toolbox; click and hold the pointer on a toolslot to display all the tools.

Drag over to the little bar to the right of the hidden tools in the toolslot and let go of the mouse button when the little bar becomes highlighted (refer to Figure 1-2). A separate little window appears containing all the tools from the toolslot. You can place this window anywhere on the screen. This procedure can save your sanity if you're constantly switching between two tools that share a toolslot. To get rid of this toolslot window, click the X (Windows) or the tiny white Close box (Mac) in its upper-left corner.

As you gaze at the Toolbox, notice that it doesn't have a Close or Expand box along its top. One possible explanation for this is that you go to the Toolbox for just about everything you do in Illustrator, and it's almost impossible to work without it. If you really want to, though, you can hide the Toolbox by selecting Hide Tools from the Window menu at the top of the screen. To bring back the Toolbox, go to the Window menu again and select Show Tools.

You can hide the Toolbox temporarily — along with everything else but your artwork and menus — by pressing the Tab key. Although this feature can be unsettling if you don't know about it (if you hit the Tab key by accident, everything disappears except your graphics and the menu bar!), it's still mighty useful — especially if you're working on a small computer screen. You can work with everything hidden, hit the Tab key when you need to, select the tool or palette item you need, and get back to work unfettered by the things you aren't using. This approach is a lot faster than selecting Show or Hide from the Window menu whenever you want to do something different.

When you pause the mouse pointer over any tool, the name of the tool appears, followed by a letter. Well, no, the letters aren't grades given to the tools for their usefulness; the letters let you know which keys to press if you want quick access to the tools. (For instance, press the **P** key on your keyboard to get the Pen tool or **R** to get the Rotate tool.)

Palettes to suit any artist

Illustrator has a ton of palettes. You may think of a palette as something more closely associated with a painter than an Illustrator, but nonetheless, Illustrator has 25 or so of them. As with a painter's palette that holds the paints she uses most, an Illustrator palette provides quick access to the most frequently used commands and features. The contents of palettes are organized according to what they do. The Character palette contains commands to format text, and the Color palette lets you create and change colors. Although Illustrator has dozens of palettes, you rarely need to have them all open at once. When entering text, for example, you want the Character palette open, but you probably don't need the Gradient palette open because the Gradient palette controls only gradients.

You open a palette by choosing it as a menu item. Most of these are under the Window menu (such as Window➪Colors) but more are hiding under other menus. To close a palette, click the X (Windows) or the tiny white box (Mac) in its upper-left corner.

Fortunately, Illustrator can both tab and dock palettes to keep them more organized, giving you a wee bit of space in which you can actually draw and edit your artwork. *Tabbing* lets you stack palettes in one area so they overlap like index cards. *Docking* connects the top of one palette to the bottom of another so that both palettes are visible but take up as little space as possible.

By default, Illustrator displays the palettes shown in Figure 1-3. Notice that some of the palettes are grouped into sets and offer you several tabs. (For instance, the Styles, Swatches, Brushes, and Symbols palettes are tabbed together in one set.) Initially, you see only the Styles palette; the Swatches, Brushes, and Symbols palettes are hidden behind the Styles palette. To see either of those palettes, click the tab for the one you want to view.

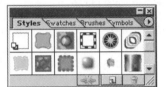

Figure 1-3:
Palettes are tabbed together in a set.

You can combine palettes by any method that you feel works for you. To move a palette from one set to another, click and drag that palette's tab from one set into another — or out by itself (which creates a new set). Illustrator doesn't limit you; you can combine any palette with any set. You can even put all of Illustrator's palettes into one set if you really want to — but we don't advise doing so. The tabs all overlap so you can't tell what's what.

Another way to combine palettes is by docking them together, as shown in Figure 1-4. Unlike tabbed palettes, docked palettes are all out there in plain sight; you can see more than one palette in a set at the same time. To dock one palette to another, drag the tab of the first palette to the bottom of the other palette. A dark line appears on the bottom of the second palette when it's in docking position. When you release the mouse button, the first palette docks with the second one.

Figure 1-4:
The Layers palette docked to the Styles palette.

Many Illustrator palettes have their own menus, which you access by clicking the triangle in the upper-right corner of the palette, as shown in Figure 1-5.

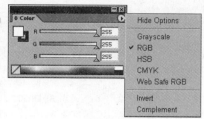

Figure 1-5:
Palettes
also have
their own
menus.

Items in the palettes' pop-up menus relate specifically to each palette. This makes them easy to ignore and easy to figure out — after you master the individual palette.

Menus with the finest cuisine

Illustrator menus are organized fairly well. Some menus are immediately obvious. You find commands having to do with type under the Type menu and commands for viewing your document under the View menu. Other menus are a little less intuitive and make sense only after you start using them. For instance, after you realize that *any one onscreen "thing" in Illustrator is an object,* you discover that items in the Object menu relate to objects (see Figure 1-6). Other menus take a little more work and experimentation to understand. For instance, the Filter menu and the Effects menu have many items that appear identical, yet do very different things. Believe it or not, all these menus are arranged to make figuring out and using Illustrator as easy as possible.

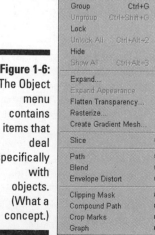

Figure 1-6:
The Object
menu
contains
items that
deal
specifically
with
objects.
(What a
concept.)

To use an item in a menu, drag down to that item and release. Something should happen when you do that (no explosions or tsunamis — as far as we know), depending on which menu item you select. Even the way a menu item appears on a menu can be a handy tip — for example, consider the following characteristics:

- **Submenus:** Many of Illustrator's menus have several submenus in them, indicated by a little triangle to the right of the menu item. To access a menu item in a submenu, drag down to the title of the submenu and then over to the item you want to use. (See Figure 1-7.)

- **Keyboard commands:** Most menu items in Illustrator have keyboard shortcuts (key combinations listed at the right) that can activate them.

- **More info needed:** An ellipsis (. . .) indicates that when you click the item, a dialog box appears, requesting additional input from you.

- **Unavailable commands:** A grayed-out menu item means Illustrator won't let you do anything with that item just now.

Figure 1-7:
The Path submenu in the Object menu.

Mac and Windows issues spring eternal

Okay, we know some loyalties in this area are fierce — can't we all just get along for a while? Regardless of which system you use or like, you work in Illustrator pretty much the same way. A few little differences are important enough to mention, however, especially if you jump between the two systems:

- **The .ai extension:** Windows users often need filename extensions after their filenames or the system refuses to look at the files. The Illustrator file extension is .ai. That's right, as in *aieee!* but without the *eee!*. Most file types (on Windows systems) have three-letter extensions; Illustrator uses two. (Think of the situation this way — they could have used .ill.) Windows folks should save Illustrator documents with the .ai extension for maximum compatibility with all flavors of Windows. Having the wrong extension on the file can cause problems. If you were to put .aif on there, for example, Windows would try to open the file as a sound file, fail, and give you an error message!

Windows users are accustomed to using two- and three-letter filename extensions. Mac users don't have to, but they really should get in the habit of doing so. For starters, that keeps the peace when you send files and lets you instantly identify what the file is. Illustrator lets you save files in an alphabet soup of file formats, such as PDF (.pdf), TIFF (.tif), EPS (.eps), or JPEG (.jpg). Each of these formats has its own unique properties and purposes. When you see .eps on a file, chances are good that it's a graphic created for use in a page-layout program. When you see .gif, you know it's a graphic created for display on the Web. File extensions can tell you a lot about your files even before you open them.

✔ **Right-click versus Ctrl+click:** While in Illustrator, Windows users can right-click most places in Illustrator to display a context menu (see Figure 1-8). Mac users, who don't have a right mouse button, press the Ctrl key while clicking the mouse button. Context menus (clever creatures!) are context-sensitive: They recognize what the mouse is near when you click and give you options you can apply . . . the following, for example:

- Right-click (or Ctrl+click) the Ruler, and a context menu shows up, offering to help you change the Ruler's unit of measurement.

- Right-click (or Ctrl+click) text, and you can change the font, size, and a slew of other options.

- Click a path, and up come the options related to paths, and so on.

Figure 1-8:
A Context menu appears when you Ctrl+click (Mac) or right-click (Windows).

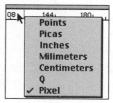

All the items found in context menus appear in the regular menus, too, so you never really *have* to use context menus. They're among those little luxuries (like a steering-wheel-warmer on a cold day) that make Illustrator so nice to use.

Defining the Document Area

Illustrator uses a traditional art table as metaphor; it's what you see when you create a new file (shown in Figure 1-9). You have the page you're working on (the Artboard), and the table the page sits on (called the Scratch area, but traditional artists will recognize it as a Pasteboard). When you create a new document, the Artboard appears as a rectangle in the middle of a white expanse. (The actual size and shape of the Artboard depends on what you enter for height and width when you create a new document.)

Artboard   Scratch area

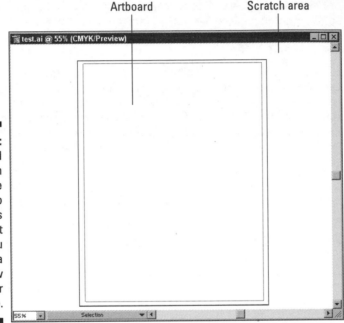

Figure 1-9:
Artboard and Scratch area — the first two wiseguys you meet when you create a new Illustrator file.

The Artboard serves as a guide to show how large your artwork is (relative to the page size you chose when you created the document). Many people find it easier to create with a specific page size in mind. If you come from a traditional graphic arts background, you may find the idea of an Artboard and Pasteboard (or Scratch area) reassuring. You can create elements and leave them in the Scratch area, ready for you to grab and add to the artwork you're creating on the Artboard. As to how the Artboard affects your art — well, it doesn't. It's only a guide to help you get your bearings. Elements in the Scratch area still print if you print to large enough paper. If you save your Illustrator artwork as an EPS (Encapsulated PostScript) to bring it into a page-layout program (or as a GIF to use on the Web), anything in the Scratch area is saved with it.

If you don't find the Artboard useful as a guide, you can hide it altogether by choosing View➪Hide Artboard.

For printing a document, you may find the Page Tiling feature a little more significant than the Artboard. Illustrator smartly recognizes the printer that your document is currently selected to print to and creates a Page Tile (a rectangle), which is the size and shape of the largest area that the selected printer can print. You can recognize the Page Tiling feature by a thin, dotted line that appears just inside the Artboard if you set page size to the size of your printer paper.

Most printers show a printable area slightly smaller than the page size. Anything outside these guides doesn't print. Even so, remember that this guide is based on *your* printer; what's inside someone else's printable area may not be the same.

Opening Existing Documents

To open any existing Illustrator document, choose File⇨Open and then select the document you want (using the Open dialog box shown in Figure 1-10, Mac dialog boxes will look a little different).

Another way to open a document is by double-clicking the file itself. If you double-click an Illustrator file when Illustrator isn't running, the program launches for you automatically. (Glad it's not a missile.)

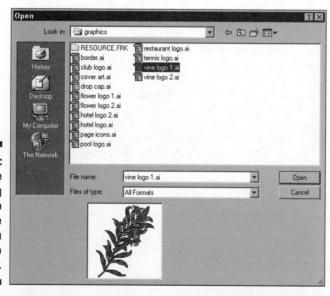

Figure 1-10:
Use the
Open dialog
box to
select the
file you
want to
open.

Viewing Illustrator Documents

Illustrator provides versatile options for viewing documents — including controls for zooming, scrolling, and hiding (or showing) certain document features. You can get close-up to the smallest areas of your artwork and make changes so minute that they aren't visible to the human eye — but you feel better knowing that your graphic is microscopically perfect. Or, to get a good feel for your artwork's effect in the real world, view your document at the actual size it prints at. Or you can view your onscreen objects as their "skeletons" of essential points and paths, with no strokes or colors to distract you from the true essence of your artwork. A view of any phase is available, from points-and-paths to perfect printout. Bottom line: You have to see what you're doing to know what you're doing. Illustrator offers that capability.

Zooming in and out of artwork

You can view your artwork at actual size (approximately its size when it prints), much larger, or much smaller. Changing the zoom amount changes only the image's onscreen appearance — not the image's actual size, the way it prints, or its appearance in another application. Zooming is like using binoculars to watch a neighbor violate the bylaws of the homeowners' association. Those unapproved maple saplings (and the sap who's planting them) don't actually change size; you just zoom in on them from a discreet distance.

The Zoom tool

The Zoom tool is the magnifying glass in the lower-right corner of the Toolbox. When you click the Zoom tool and move it over the document, a plus sign appears in the center of the magnifying glass. Clicking the Zoom tool makes the details of your artwork appear larger in the document window. You can click until you zoom in to 6,400 percent (64 times larger than actual size). Figure 1-11 shows a document viewed at actual size and zoomed in to 400 percent.

The Zoom tool is actually two tools in one. When you hold down the Alt key (Windows) or Option (Mac), the magnifying glass contains a minus sign. Holding down the Alt or Option key and clicking your image with the Zoom tool causes your image to appear smaller. You can zoom out as far as 3.13 percent (where everything is really tiny). Figure 1-12 shows the art from Figure 1-11 as it would look at 25 percent of its actual size.

Speed zoom ahead

Zooming is something Illustrator users do often enough to warrant the multitude of keyboard commands associated with this function. In order of usefulness, the following items represent some of the most useful speed-zoom techniques:

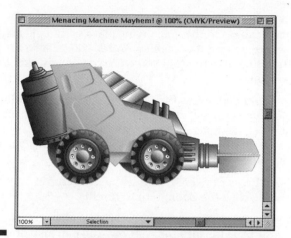

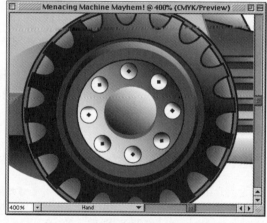

Figure 1-11: Two views of the artwork: actual size and zoomed to 400 percent. If you print while zoomed in, the image still prints at actual size.

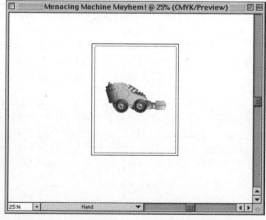

Figure 1-12: The artwork from Figure 1-11 at 25 percent of its actual size.

- ✔ **Use any tool to Zoom In:** Press Ctrl+Space (⌘+Space on a Mac) and the tool you're using changes to the magnifying glass with a plus sign in it. Click the area where you want to zoom in. After you release the keys, the Zoom tool switches back to the tool you were previously using. This shortcut is *really* handy.

- ✔ **Use any tool to Zoom Out:** Press Ctrl+Alt+Space (⌘+Option+Space on a Mac), and the tool you're using changes to the magnifying glass with a minus sign in it. Click the image to zoom out. After you release the keys, the Zoom tool switches back to the tool you were previously using. This shortcut is as handy as the temporary Zoom In tool.

- ✔ **Go to Actual Size:** Press Ctrl+1 (⌘+1 on a Mac) to return to actual size. You can also double-click the Zoom tool to do this.

- ✔ **Go to Fit In Window view:** Press Ctrl+0 (⌘+0 on a Mac) to zoom to the level at which your page fits into the window. You can also double-click the Hand tool to do this.

- ✔ **Zoom in and out:** Press Ctrl++ (plus) (⌘++ [plus] on a Mac) to zoom in one level or Ctrl+- (minus) (⌘+- [minus] on a Mac) to zoom out one level.

- ✔ **Activate the Zoom In tool:** Press Z to change to the Zoom In tool. If you actually read to the bottom of this list, geekiness from someone you know is starting to rub off on you. We strongly advise taking a few days off — away from your computer (and from said geek).

Scrolling around your document

You can use the scroll bars to move around your document, but they limit you to moving horizontally or vertically — and only one of those directions at a time. If you're really cool (and you know you are), you can use the Hand tool to move around your document in any direction.

To use the Hand tool, choose it from the Toolbox. Then click and drag anywhere in the document. The artwork moves in the direction you drag. At first, this action may seem slightly awkward — but power corrupts. After a few minutes of pushing your art around, you'll never want to go back to those nasty scroll bars.

You can use any tool as the Hand tool. To change a tool into the Hand tool, hold down the spacebar while you click the tool. Then click and drag just as you would with the Hand tool. Let go of the spacebar, and the tool you were using returns to its original form. This trick works with any tool except the Text tool. (If you try it with that tool, you just type space after space after space.)

Using the Navigator palette

Illustrator's handy Navigator palette (see Figure 1-13) helps you move about
your document. If the Navigator palette isn't showing, choose Window⇨Show
Navigator. The Navigator palette displays your entire document in a tiny
window. A red rectangle indicates where the edges of the document window
are, relative to the artwork. This rectangle corresponds exactly to the
document window. If you change the shape of the document window,
the red rectangle changes shape correspondingly.

Figure 1-13:
The
Navigator
palette,
displaying
the artwork
from
Figure 1-11.

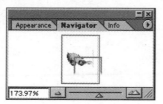

Don't confuse the view rectangle with the Artboard (represented in the
Navigator by a black rectangle around your artwork, even after you choose
View⇨Hide Artboard).

Drag the red rectangle around in the Navigator, and the part of the image
that's inside the rectangle miraculously appears inside the main document
window, as if you'd moved it there with the Hand tool. Hold down the Ctrl key
(⌘ on a Mac) and click and drag inside the Navigator palette to drag out a
new view rectangle. When you let go, that area fills the document window, as
though you'd used both the Zoom tool and the Hand tool simultaneously.

You can also zoom by dragging the Zoom slider in the lower-right corner of
the Navigator palette or by typing a different viewing percentage into the
readout box at the lower-left of the palette. In addition to zooming, the
Navigator palette is scalable. If the preview you have is too small to provide a
useful degree of detail, click and drag the Resize tab in the lower-left corner
of the palette. The thumbnail changes scale accordingly.

The Navigator palette can slow down your system if you have a slow system
or complex artwork. Every time you make a change to your artwork, zoom, or
view a different part of your artwork, the Navigator needs to update its
thumbnail image. Hiding the palette eliminates the slowdown.

Looking at the guts of your artwork

Typically, what you see in your document window is pretty much what's going to print (the view in Preview mode). However, what you see isn't what the printer and Illustrator look at. Instead, they see all your Illustrator artwork and objects as a series of outlines, placed images, and text (the view in Outline mode). If you want to view your document in this skeletal form, choose View⇨Outline. Outline mode is a great diagnostic tool; it helps you understand how a document was made. Figure 1-14 shows artwork in both Preview and Outline modes. Outline mode also makes it easier to select objects that are very close together.

Figure 1-14:
Art in
Preview
mode and
Outline
mode.

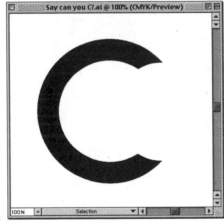
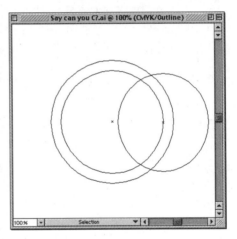

Notice that in Preview mode, the artwork appears to be the letter *C*; Outline mode shows the three circles (two white circles on top of a black circle) that create that appearance. Graphics like this can be tricky to work with; if you don't know how the object is made, you may assume (mistakenly, but logically enough) that you actually have a C-shaped object instead of three circles. As soon as you start making changes to it as though it were really a C, Illustrator starts acting completely illogical. Jumping into Outline mode lets you see the secret truth behind the graphic, helping you to understand how the graphic was made.

Saving Illustrator Documents

The instant you accomplish something you like, you should save it. And you should save every few minutes, even if you haven't done something you like because if you don't, you'll lose all the work and have to recreate it if you crash, accidentally quit, or accidentally shut off the power supply to your computer. Unlike applications such as Microsoft Word or Adobe InDesign, Illustrator has no auto-save feature. Anything you don't save is lost. Just remember that old TLA (three-letter acronym), SOS: Save Often, Silly! Saving only takes a second, and it saves not only your artwork but also your time and sanity.

To save a document, choose File⇨Save. If you haven't previously saved the document, the Save As dialog box (shown in Figure 1-15) appears; reward its promptness by naming your file something appropriate, witty, and deep. Or type something hurried-but-meaningful, such as **gasdfoiu** or **jkl23**, so you can challenge yourself later to figure out what that @#*! document is. (Just kidding.)

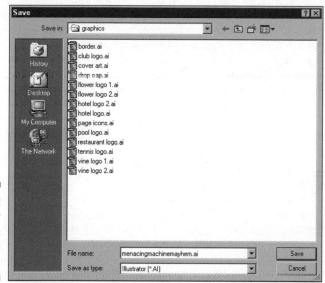

Figure 1-15:
Name your masterpiece in the Save dialog box.

If you've already saved your document, the Save command updates the existing file. If you're not sure whether you previously saved, look at the title bar. If it reads Untitled-1, you probably haven't saved (only someone with a creepy sense of humor would pick *Untitled-1* as a title just to befuddle the rest of us).

Changing Your Mind

One of Illustrator's most powerful features may be strikingly familiar: the Edit⇨Undo command that gives you a way to take back the goof you just made. But that's so common these days; in Illustrator, Edit⇨Undo is a multiple undo — it makes you the Master of Time! You can take your artwork back through time, step by step, all the way to when you first opened the document!

If you make a mistake (or several), just choose Edit⇨Undo (or press ⌘+Z on a Mac) repeatedly, until you get back to the way things were before they went so wrong. To redo the last thing you undid, select Edit⇨Redo (or press ⌘+Shift+Z on a Mac). (A time machine with a reverse gear — way cool.)

Imagine creating with wild abandon — moving points, changing colors and line thicknesses, running filters — because in Illustrator, you can change your mind after the fact. Think of what you could obliterate from time — the misplaced stroke that looks like a bad tattoo, the missed goal that kept your team from the playoffs, the blind date that went so horribly wrong — well, okay, it only works in Illustrator. At least it works somewhere.

You can take a graphic back to the way it was when you first opened it, with one exception: If you close a file and then open it again, you can't go back to anything you did before you closed the file. You can, however, save a file and then go back to things that happened before you saved it — if you left the file open after you saved it. In that case, the only thing that can't be undone is the Save command: You still have a file on your hard drive that exists exactly as it did when you hit Save. This method can be useful if you have to create multiple revisions of the same document.

Printing Illustrator Documents

If your computer is hooked up or networked to a printer, you can print just about anything you create in Illustrator. Before you print, however, make sure that your artwork is within the Page Tiling boundaries (that dotted gray rectangle that shows up when you select View⇨Show Page Tiling). Only items within these boundaries print. The dotted lines on the page indicate the trim area; if your image is outside the dotted lines, it won't print.

To print your artwork, choose File⇨Print. The Print dialog box appears. Click OK; soon a sheet of paper emerges from your printer with your artwork on it.

Closing Documents and Quitting Illustrator

To close an Illustrator document, choose File⇨Close. The document closes without a fuss. If you haven't saved before closing, a dialog box appears, asking whether you want to save changes made to your artwork. To quit Illustrator, choose File⇨Exit (Windows) or File⇨Quit (Mac). If you haven't saved before quitting, a dialog box appears and asks whether you want to save your changes. (Consistent good manners — aren't they wonderful?)

Chapter 2

Following the Righteous Path

In This Chapter

▶ Understanding how paths and pixels work

▶ Knowing the differences between paths and pixels

▶ Determining when to use paths and when to use pixels

▶ Using PostScript printing and paths

▶ Creating paths

*B*eing new to Illustrator typically means being new to paths. Paths are the heart and soul of Illustrator — its primary way to create graphics. Nearly all computer-generated graphics are either pixel-based or path-based (also known as vector-based — more on that later). Getting a firm grip on the differences between the two graphics types can help you create graphics of any type.

Pixel-based images (created in Adobe Photoshop, Corel Painter, as well as by scanners and digital cameras) use a fixed grid of tiny colored squares (kind of like a tiny mosaic tile) to create images on your screen. Your computer monitor's *resolution* is a measure of how detailed an onscreen image can be, based on how many pixels the screen can provide per square inch. To give you an idea of how small these pixels are, every square inch of the average monitor contains 5,184 pixels. Even so, monitors have a relatively low-resolution; they don't use many pixels per inch compared with high-resolution printing, which can require 90,000 pixels in a square inch or more.

In spite of their astonishing quantity, pixels work just like mosaic tiles (or like the dots in a Seurat painting). Because images are a bit less distinct from farther away, putting squares of different colors together results in a continuous picture when seen from a distance; the individual squares are (in effect) invisible. The more squares used to create a square inch of the image (that is, the higher the resolution), the more continuous and realistic the picture is.

In addition to their staggeringly small size, the range of colors pixels can have is equally astonishing. A single pixel can display only one color at a time, but that color can be any of 16.7 million.

Path-based (often called *vector-based*) graphics are much simpler — and in some ways, easier to comprehend — than their pixel-based cousins. Think of an image in a coloring book: A shape is defined by a line. Inside the line you can add color. By using this simple method of shapes and color, you can create just about any picture you can imagine. In Illustrator, the shapes can be any size and complexity, and the lines can be as thick or as thin as you want, or even invisible. And the shapes can be filled with an astonishing variety of colors, even patterns and gradients (even pixel-based images), but the same basic coloring-book principle applies.

Whether Paths or Pixels Are Better

You choose between paths and pixels for different reasons. Paths are better for some things and pixels for others, and each approach has its strengths. The key to determining whether to use paths (which Illustrator creates) or pixels (from a program, such as Photoshop) is to be familiar with the capabilities of each method. Figure 2-1 shows path-based artwork next to pixel-based artwork.

Figure 2-1:
Path-based artwork (left) and pixel-based artwork (right).

 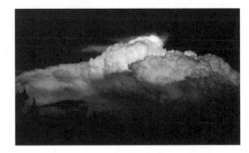

Paths are generally better for type, logos, and precision graphics. Pixels are generally better for photographs, complex backgrounds, textures, and simulated lighting effects. Quite often, however, the proper combination of paths and pixels results in the best final illustration possible. Determining what combination to use is a lot easier when you're hip to the advantages and drawbacks of both paths and pixels.

Paths: The ultimate flexibility in graphics

Paths are used to define any shape from a simple square or circle to the shape of South America. Because paths are the outline of these shapes and not the shapes themselves, they take up very little storage space. A path-based square that measures 15 x 15 feet takes up no more room in your computer than a 1 x 1-inch path-based square.

How can such a large square and such a tiny one accompany the same amount of computer memory? Through math, mostly. Looking at how Illustrator draws a square can help you make sense of all this information. To Illustrator, a square is simply a set of four locations — one for each of four points (the corners) — as well as any Fill or Stroke information (what color the square is). Where the points are doesn't matter; what matters is that you've got four of 'em and they make a square when you connect the dots.

What about complex outlines? A semi-accurate representation of South America with a limited amount of detail probably needs dozens of points to define the shape of the continent. In this case, there's nary a straight line anywhere — from point to point, it's nothing but curved lines. And because they need more information to describe them, those curved lines take up about twice as much disk space as straight lines do. Even so, a tiny little 1-inch-high illustration of South America could be enlarged to 15 feet tall and still have exactly the same file size because the illustration still has exactly the same number of points. Only the math that determines the location of those points has been changed to put them farther apart.

Figure 2-2 shows South America next to a square that physically appears to be about three times as large as South America (well, three times as large as the illustration of South America). Which one is bigger in terms of file size? South America is. It has more detail and, therefore, more points.

What's so cool about paths is something we previously alluded to: You can make paths much larger or smaller in physical dimensions without increasing the file size or losing image quality. You can rotate a path, flip it (*reflecting*), skew it (*shearing*), or distort it in a number of ways without changing the file size or detail. (Here's the secret: *All you're really changing is the location of the points.*) This near-effortless scalability makes Illustrator the perfect choice for creating logos that appear on business cards, letterhead, Web pages, various documents, banners, billboards, or signs.

Pixels: Detail and realism to spare

Pixel-based images are used for photorealistic illustration because photorealism is virtually impossible to create in a path-based image. Digitized photographs represent about 75 percent of the pixel-based images in use today. Most of the rest are Web graphics and other onscreen images.

Figure 2-2:
The South
America
shape is
actually
a larger
Illustrator
file than the
square
because
more points
are used to
define the
continent's
shape.

Even a low-resolution pixel-based image can have 5,184 squares of color per square inch, each of which can be any of 16.7 million different colors. In a path-based image, every different color (with a few exceptions) must be defined by a separate path. To equal the number of different colors that you can create in a pixel-based image you'd have to draw so many paths that . . . well, imagine covering a basketball with confetti, one piece at a time. For this reason, pixel-based images are the hands-down choice over path-based graphics if you're creating incredibly detailed images — or recreating the continuous tones found in nature, such as the smooth darkening of the skin as you follow the line from someone's cheek to the shadow under the chin. To portray realistically in Illustrator all the colors you find in someone's face, you'd have to draw so many paths that . . . well, imagine covering a mannequin's face with confetti, one piece at a time.

On the other hand, paths are far superior to pixels if you want to maintain the quality of a graphic image despite enlarging and reducing its size. Think what you have to do to increase the size of artwork made with mosaic tiles. You have to increase the number of tiles unless you can enlarge the tiles that are already there. But if you did that, the tiles would be obvious from a distance. Same deal with pixel images. You have to add more tiles (pixels), or you see the pixels you already have showing up onscreen as big squares. And when you add pixels, you make the file size larger while reducing the quality (worst of both worlds) because you can't get away with just tossing in any old pixels. An artisan might be able to add tiles to her mosaic and preserve its image quality, but the computer is just guessing about what tiles to add (in geek speak, a process called *interpolation*). There's just no way to enlarge a pixel-based image without reducing the quality, as shown in Figure 2-3. Likewise, shrinking the image means throwing away pixels, which degrades the image because it then has fewer pixels available for showing detail. In technical circles, changing the number of pixels in an image is called *resampling*.

Original

Reduced to 900 pixels

Figure 2-3:
The effects
of reducing
and
enlarging
the image.

Re-enlarged

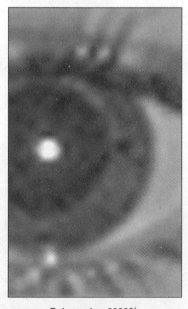

Enlarged to 2000%

An image with thousands of pixels can be displayed onscreen or printed much larger with high quality than an image with only 900 pixels. Of course, all those pixels take up a whole lot more storage space on your hard drive. Path-based images have no such limitations.

How Paths and Pixels Compare

This is it — the definitive answer you've been looking for: Use pixels to create graphics that are very complex, such as photography. File sizes are large but smaller than if you tried to create the same quality of graphic using paths. Pixel-based graphics that need to print or display at large sizes require larger file sizes than the same graphics printed or displayed at smaller sizes. Use path-based graphics to create fairly simple graphics; their file sizes are typically much smaller than their pixel-based counterparts. A path-based graphic can be displayed or printed at any size, from microscopic to billboard, without any change in file size, yet always at maximum quality.

A comparison of path and pixel documents

The best way to show advantages of each format is to take a look at the same graphic created with both paths and pixels. The illustration shown in Figure 2-4 is a logo, created with paths, for the country of Oddland to use on all its manufactured goods, as well as on signs, brochures, and other places.

Figure 2-4:
A logo for Oddland, created with paths and weighing in at 188K.

One thing you notice right away is that the logo is text-heavy. Paths represent text fairly well. A big advantage in creating this logo with paths is its scalability; you can enlarge or reduce it to virtually any size without changing the image quality. Compare Figure 2-4 with Figure 2-5, which shows a pixel-based version of the logo. (Looks like a clone, doesn't it? Looks can be deceiving.)

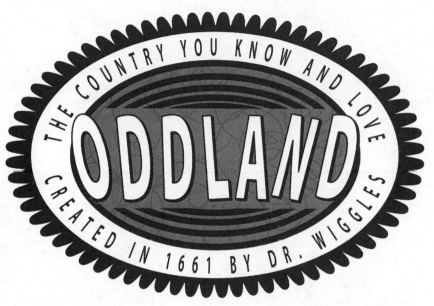

Figure 2-5: The same Oddland logo, created with pixels and tipping the scales at 1.2MB.

If you use a high enough resolution, the pixel-based logo looks as good as the path-based — but its file size is 1.2MB (almost ten times the size of the path-based logo). Maybe that isn't a problem if you have a hard drive the size of New Jersey, but watch what happens when you change the size of the logo. If you enlarge the path-based version, you get the image on the left in Figure 2-6.

All we had room for in Figure 2-6 was a smidgen of the logo — the whole thing would be over 20 inches square — but note how the edges remain perfectly smooth and crisp in the path-based version. And the file size is still only 188K! On the other hand, if you enlarge the pixel-based version, you get the image on the right. Notice the dreaded jagged edges. Worse, the whole logo at this size would become the Giant File That Ate New Jersey — over 25MB in size — more than 100 times the file size of the path version!

Just for laughs, consider what happens when you try to use Illustrator to create photographic reality. Figure 2-7 is a photograph of a little girl, one of the residents of Oddland. This document was created entirely with pixels.

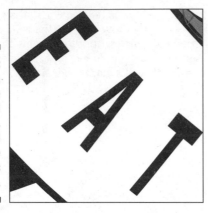

Figure 2-6:
A section of the Oddland logo, enlarged to five times its original size.

Path-based

Pixel-based

 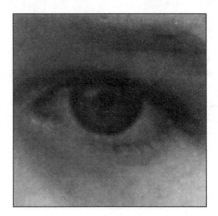

Figure 2-7:
She looks good in all pixels. In the close-up of her eye, you see blurring but only when you get this close.

The path-based illustration is a different matter entirely. To recreate this image as paths, it was necessary to trace the pixels with Adobe Streamline (software that recreates pixels as paths that can be used in Illustrator). A graphic like this would take weeks to create in Illustrator by hand. As Figure 2-8 shows, paths are hard-pressed to achieve the look of the pixel-based original, so they give up in despair.

The big limitations and upcoming solutions

From the preceding figures, you can see some limitations of both pixels and paths. Depending on the type of artwork, detail is lost if you use the inappropriately based method to create images. Fine detail is present in pixel-based images only at very high resolutions (many, many pixels) and in path-based images only with an unreasonably large number of paths.

Figure 2-8: Now she's in a path-based file (trying to match pixel-based detail); note the same close-up of her eye.

As computer processing power increases, however, paths are likely to find more use in graphics tasks that used to be pixels-only affairs. For instance, new technologies enable paths to contain smooth, flowing gradations (such as Illustrator's Gradient Mesh). Although the sheer number of paths needed to create the continuous tones of photographs is prohibitive — even today — look for that capability to emerge as computers get faster and can deal more quickly with larger numbers of paths.

When to use paths and when to use pixels

In Table 2-1, check out some attributes that are best created with paths and some that are best created with pixels.

Table 2-1	What Paths and Pixels Are Especially Good For
Use Paths if Your Artwork Contains	*Use Pixels if Your Artwork Contains*
Large amounts of type	Photographs
Geometric shapes	Complex textures
Thin lines	Soft-edged details

Often, for best results, you may have to combine pixels with paths (or vectors) in the same artwork. Fortunately, Illustrator is a perfect tool for doing that. The File⇨Place command enables you to bring pixel-based artwork into Illustrator to combine it with vector-based artwork.

Paths and the PostScript Language

The PostScript printing language, present on many printers, uses paths to print smooth-edged images. This happy circumstance is one reason that Illustrator can make such good-looking artwork; most printers are designed specifically for printing out path-based images.

Dot-matrix printers of the '80s gave way to laser printers and inkjets, and with them came a dramatic increase in speed (not to mention blessed quiet). When you add PostScript to the mix, the printing process is even faster.

Which is faster — a square or a square?

For basic shapes, path-based artwork prints much faster than pixel-based artwork. For instance, a 5 x 5-inch path-based square prints in a fraction of the time that it takes to print the same pixel-based square. Why? The printer needs only the four corner locations for the path-based square. For the pixel-based square, the printer needs to see each and every pixel that's on the way to the printer. (Imagine trying to count sand grains with tweezers, really fast.)

PostScript: The evolution of Bézier curves

The PostScript language handles paths in much the same way that Illustrator does — using points connected by lines. Think of a Connect-the-Dot game you did as a kid. Instead of processing each pixel, the PostScript code says, "Connect this point to that point, that point to this one over here, and so on." All it takes is another bit of code to say, "Now fill that shape with solid red" or some other color.

This approach works well for objects with flat sides, but curves are another matter entirely. You'd need to connect an infinite number of dots to make a perfect curve. Here's where PostScript (and Illustrator) get really clever. Instead of using straight lines between points, PostScript uses curves between points: *Bézier curves,* named after their creator, world-famous mathematician Pierre Bézier (pronounced *BEZ-zee-AY*).

The idea behind Bézier curves is that you need no more than four points to define any curved line: One point to say where the path begins, one point to say where the path ends, and two control points in between. Where you put each control point (relative to the end points) determines how much the line curves — and in what direction — on its way to meet the end point.

Fortunately, Illustrator spares users the headache of having to work out the math; you have a little magnet-like handle onscreen (the Bézier control point) that changes the direction of the curve. Okay, actually using it may be far from intuitive, but it does give Illustrator the capability to generate complex shapes with curves — using the PostScript language, no less.

What's my vector, Victor?

You often hear the words *vector graphics* used to describe the kind of art created in Illustrator. In mathematics, a *vector* is a quantity, such as a force or velocity, having direction and magnitude and a line representing such a quantity drawn from its point of origin to its final position. In artists' terms, a *vector* is a line of a specific size drawn in a specific place. Hmm, vector graphics are simply graphics made with lines! The basic building blocks of every Illustrator graphic are just a bunch of lines. Those lines may have other information attached to them (such as color and width), but no matter how fancy they get, underneath they're still just lines.

So why not call such graphics line art? Unfortunately, that term is already taken. Line art is a specific type of pixel-based graphic. We could call such illustrations *Illustrator illustrations,* but that term is a little alliterative (is there an echo in here?) and not quite accurate. You can also create vector graphics in CorelDRAW and Macromedia FreeHand. So this book follows convention, using *vector graphics* to describe the kind of graphics you create in Illustrator. Pretty soon you'll be doing the same!

Gray's Anatomy of a Path

Paths can be a thorn in your side while you're getting up to speed with Illustrator. At first, points may seem like a necessary evil (with *evil* the key word here) — but the more you know about how they're constructed, the easier it is for you to modify them. Eventually you may even stop cursing at your poor, defenseless monitor.

In Illustrator, it's polite to point

Each path consists of a series of points. These are called *anchor points* because they anchor the path. Another type of point is called a *direction point* (a point that determines the direction and distance of a curve), but when most people refer to a point in Illustrator, they mean an anchor point, which appears only in a curved path. A path has at least two anchor points to determine where it starts and where it ends. Figure 2-9 shows a path and the locations of its anchor points.

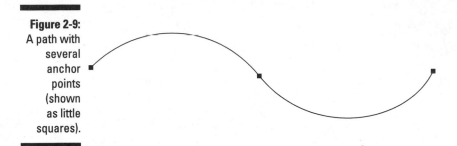

You can handle the truth

For basic shapes with straight lines, points are all that paths need. But as soon as you want curves on a path, you need *direction points* (also known as *handles* among Illustrator insiders). Direction points are connected to anchor points by *direction lines*. They control how a path curves. Figure 2-10 shows the same path but with direction points showing.

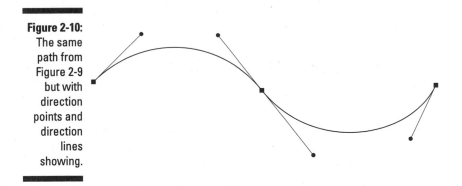

Handles work like magnets for the paths that extend from points. The farther you drag a handle away from the path, the more that path curves toward the handle. Figure 2-11 shows a few variations of a path between two points. In each of these variations, only the handle on the left has been moved.

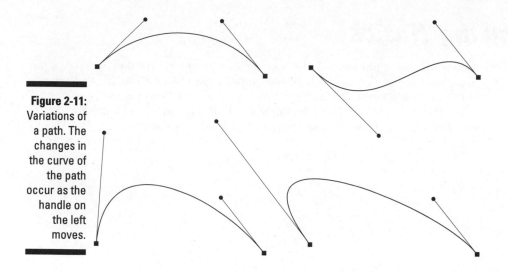

Figure 2-11:
Variations of
a path. The
changes in
the curve of
the path
occur as the
handle on
the left
moves.

You can move the handles of paths by using the Direct Selection tool (the hollow arrow at the top of the Toolbox). Click the curve you want to adjust to select it. This action makes the direction points visible. Direction points are invisible unless the curve is selected with the Direct Selection tool. After the direction point is visible, click and drag the handle. Figure 2-12 shows a circle with handles showing. Even basic Illustrator shapes use handles to create curves.

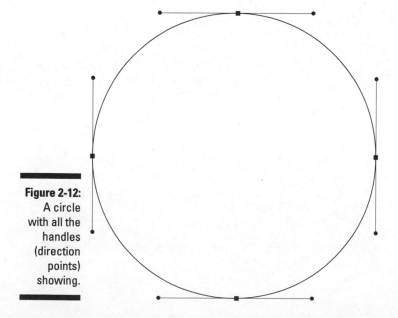

Figure 2-12:
A circle
with all the
handles
(direction
points)
showing.

Drawing Basics

Illustrator has a full arsenal of drawing tools, ready to take on any illustration task imaginable. But with this power comes a wee bit of difficulty. Well, okay, a fair bit of difficulty. Illustrator's drawing tools (the Pen in particular) can be a hassle to use at first. However, after you nail the concept of paths (which we discuss in the previous section) and follow a few simple rules, you'll be able to use Illustrator's tools just as they were meant to be used — in next to no time. (Check out Part II for a guided tour.)

Chapter 3

Doing Everyday Things with Illustrator

In This Chapter

▶ Selecting objects so they can be changed

▶ Moving objects in a document

▶ Rotating and resizing documents

▶ Looking at all the really fun stuff in Illustrator

▶ Using Illustrator with the Web

▶ Taking Illustrator documents into other programs

▶ Zeroing in on what Illustrator does best

*T*he hard part for new users of Illustrator is figuring out just what it does. The program is so vast and has many capabilities that aren't immediately obvious or self-explanatory. Even seasoned Illustrator veterans often discover that they use many convoluted steps to accomplish something they can do with a single hidden command. This chapter is a tell-all exposé of everything that you can do in Illustrator (at least as much as we can in a single chapter). You'd need an entire book to cover such a complex program! By the end of this chapter, you should have a good overview of the features of Illustrator and know where to look to find the things you need to get the job done.

Picking Up Stuff and Moving It Around

Any time you want to do something to an Illustrator object, you must select it first. After you get the whole select-then-do thought lodged in your brain, many of Illustrator's functions come to you much more easily.

Illustrator has a wide variety of ways to select things, including six tools, a bunch of keyboard commands, and several menu items. Fortunately, even if you know only one or two of these methods, you can be off and running with Illustrator selections in no time, just like a pro. Using the selection tools enables you to select virtually anything in your document.

In Chapter 6, we detail the process of selecting paths and objects. In this chapter, you discover the basics — all the ways of selecting, from tools and commands to menu items.

Discovering Selection tools

Illustrator has six Selection tools. You choose a tool according to the type of object(s) that you want to select. The Selection tools are as follows (we love a parade):

✔ **Selection tool:** This solid black arrow is the regular Selection tool. Use the Selection tool to select entire paths or groups by clicking them or dragging around them. If the object you click or drag around is part of a group, all the paths and objects in that group are selected as well. The Selection tool, located at the top left of the Toolbox, is plain but powerful.

✔ **Direct Selection tool:** Also known as the hollow arrow, the Direct Selection tool enables you to select portions of paths — single points or segments — by clicking or dragging said points or segments. You can also use the Direct Selection tool to select other objects, such as placed images or text. The Direct Selection tool, located at the top right of the Toolbox, selects only the portions of the path that you click or drag.

✔ **Group Selection tool:** This tool looks like a hollow arrow with a + symbol beside it. It selects "up" through paths and groups. The first click selects the entire path you click. Click the selected path again and you select the group that the first path is in. If you keep clicking, you continue to select groups of groups, all containing the group that the first group is in. The Group Selection tool shares a tool slot with the Direct Selection tool. Just click and hold on the Direct Selection tool, and the Group Selection will spring out from behind it.

✔ **Lasso tool:** This tool selects any objects that are partially touched by (or included within) the area you drag. The Lasso tool is the flexible version of the Selection tool. You can find the Lasso tool in the upper left of the Toolbox, directly beneath the Selection tool.

✔ **Direct Select Lasso tool:** This tool looks like an anemic loop of string — until you use it to select points and path segments within an area you designate by dragging the mouse pointer. The Direct Select Lasso tool is a go-anywhere version of the Direct Selection tool.

✔ **Magic Wand tool:** Photoshop users will recognize this much-beloved tool. The Magic Wand tool selects multiple objects with similar attributes — fills, strokes, transparency — within a specific tolerance range. For example, you can select all objects that have a stroke weight of between five and ten points. The Magic Wand palette controls the various attributes and tolerance settings. For more on the Magic Wand, see Chapter 6.

Illustrator provides two primary ways of using the Selection, Direct Selection, and Group Selection tools: by clicking-and-releasing the object or group you want to select, or by dragging a marquee around the objects you want to select. *Marquee* is techno-speak for the dotted line that's created when you drag with these tools (and all this time you thought it had to do with movie theaters).

The new Select menu also provides a handy way to make selections. All the Illustrator selection commands are centralized within this new menu. Find more on the Select menu in Chapter 6.

You can tell when an object is selected in Illustrator: Any selected object shows its "guts" onscreen — the path used to create the object, as well as any points needed to create the path. Text and placed images also show points (and sometimes paths) when they're highlighted, even though they aren't made up of paths and points (weird, isn't it?). Figure 3-1 shows a pair of star illustrations; the star on the left is unselected, and the one on the right is selected.

Figure 3-1:
The left object is unselected; the right object is selected. Note the points and paths that appear on a selected object.

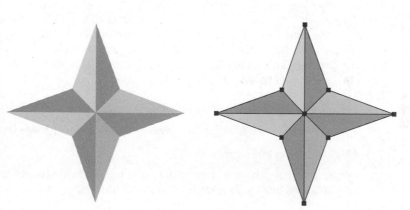

After an object is selected, you can do any number of things to it, such as change its color, move it, transform it, or even delete it. You may want to consider which tool you use to make the selection. One key difference between the arrow-shaped selection tools and the Lasso and Magic Wand selection tools is that the arrow tools also move objects that are selected; the Lasso and Magic Wand tools do not. If you're attempting to use an arrow tool to drag a marquee around an object and happen to click the object first, you move the object instead of selecting it. No marquee appears.

Moving and transforming objects

To move a selected object (or objects), just follow these steps:

1. **Select the object you want to move by using one of the selection tools.**

2. **Using the Selection tool or the Direct Selection tool, click and drag the selected object to the position you want to move it to.**

   Using the Selection or Direct Selection tools to click and drag an object that's already selected doesn't add to the selection or release the selection, but this action does enable you to move what's currently selected.

3. **Release the mouse button after the object is in position.**

   The object is all settled in at its new location.

Instead of dragging with the mouse, you can use the arrow keys to nudge anything that is selected a little bit at a time. This trick works no matter what tool you've selected in the Toolbox.

Illustrator power-users call the other things you can do to an object *transforming* it. These actions include rotating, resizing, reflecting, and skewing objects. Illustrator puts all these transformation tools together in the middle of the Toolbox. Regardless of which transformation tool you use, the process, shown in Figure 3-2, is much the same as for moving objects. Just follow these steps:

1. **Select the object you want to transform using one of the selection tools.**

2. **Choose the Rotate tool (or any transformation tool) from the Toolbox.**

3. **Click the selected object and drag.**

   While you drag, the outlines of the object show how the object will be transformed after you release the mouse button.

4. **Release the mouse button when the object's preview appears how you want to change the object.**

   As soon as you release the mouse, the object is transformed.

For more in-depth information on transforming objects, see Chapter 12.

Distorting paths

Moving and transforming paths makes them look different, but you can tell that the moved or transformed path is pretty much the original path in a different position, at a different angle, or maybe at a different size. Distorting paths, however, can make them look drastically different from the way they look originally.

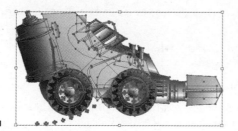
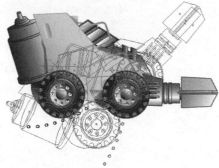

Figure 3-2:
Rotating an
object.

Illustrator provides a number of different ways that paths can be distorted, but the majority of these fall into the category of filter-based distortions. These distortions, found in the Filter⇨Distort menu, can create all sorts of interesting (and some downright ugly) effects. Figure 3-3 shows how an innocent path can become grossly distorted in a number of ways by using some of the different distortion filters.

Figure 3-3:
The original
path (left) is
(to the right)
Puckered,
Scribbled,
Zig-Zagged,
and
Roughened.

Because Distortion Filters have no "right" settings, they produce immediate and profound changes to your artwork. They also all have *previews,* which show you what's going to happen to your artwork before you make any permanent change to it.

To use a Distortion Filter, follow these steps:

1. **Select your artwork using any selection tool.**

2. **Choose Filter⇨Distort⇨Pucker & Bloat (or any of the other Distort filters).**

   A dialog box opens, showing a Distort filter that has a Preview check box. Put a check mark in this box to make the filter show you what it's going to do to your artwork.

3. **Using the slider (a little triangle under a straight line), set the amount of the distortion.**

   Drag the slider to the left; watch what happens to the artwork. Drag it to the right and look again.

4. **When you get something you like, click OK.**

   If the filter doesn't produce effects that you like, click Cancel to exit the filter without changing your artwork.

For more information on distortions and other ways to mess up — er, *enhance* — your artwork, see Chapter 13.

Organizing objects

Illustrator provides many tools to help you organize your artwork. You can move objects above or behind each other, group objects together, and distribute objects to layers for heavy-duty organization.

To move an object behind all the other objects in a document, as shown in Figure 3-4, follow these steps:

1. **Use any selection tool to select the object that you want to move behind another object.**

2. **Choose Object➪Arrange➪Send to Back.**

   The selected object moves behind all the other objects in the document.

Figure 3-4:
Moving an
object
behind other
objects.

Selecting Object➪Arrange➪Bring to Front moves the selected object in front of all the objects in the document. Use Send Backward and Bring Forward to move the selected object just one level to the back or front of a stack of three or more objects.

The new Send to Current Layer command moves the selected object to the active layer in the Layers palette. (For more on layers, see Chapter 14.)

These commands are the basic movement of objects back and forth in a document. You can also group a set of objects so that they always stay together (and are all selected at once, all the time). To group a series of objects, follow these steps:

1. **Select the objects that you want to group together.**

   To select more than one object, either drag a marquee around the objects or hold down the Shift key and click each object you want to include in the group.

2. **Choose Object⇨Group.**

   The objects are grouped together. The next time you click any one of them with the Selection tool, all are selected.

You can group two or more groups together to form a bigger group, and you can select paths along with a group (or several groups) and create a group out of them.

The next step up from grouping is putting related paths and objects in layers. Using layers is like placing your artwork into separate sheets of clear plastic. A single layer can have as many pieces of artwork on it as you want. You can select all the pieces of artwork in a layer at the same time. You can lock the layers to keep them from being selected while they still remain visible. You can hide a layer (and everything on it) to get rid of artwork as if you'd deleted it but still have the option of bringing it back whenever you want. Layers are created, selected, and hidden (and that's just for starters) by using the Layers palette. See the Layers palette in Figure 3-5.

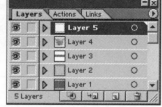

Figure 3-5:
The Layers
palette.

You can do all sorts of amazing things by organizing your artwork into layers, so we devote a big section specifically to layers in Chapter 14.

Using the Fun Stuff

Have you ever looked at an illustration and scratched your head and thought, "How did they do *that*?" Here's a secret. Chances are that it wasn't that hard. A slew of features in Illustrator let you do really cool things with little difficulty.

The only catch is that you must walk before you can run. In Illustrator, this means being able to create simple shapes, color them, and move them in front of or behind one another (which we cover in Chapters 4, 5, and 6).

After you have those things down, you're ready to move on to the fun stuff. You'll be amazed at the things you can do with a simple command or two.

Transparency

When you draw a shape in Illustrator that's filled with a solid color or a gradient, the shape covers up any objects beneath it. You can move the object behind other objects in the document by selecting it with the Selection tool and using Object⇨Arrange⇨Send to Back, but you can't see through that shape to the objects behind it.

Transparency breaks those rules by enabling you to fade an object away (from 0%, or completely transparent; to 100%, or completely opaque; or any degree in between) to reveal the objects hidden beneath it. Figure 3-6 shows this basic transparency at work with a partially transparent ellipse appearing above a logo.

Figure 3-6:
The ellipse
on top of the
logo is set to
be partially
transparent.

Transparency is used to see through one part of a shape more than another part or to blend the colors of a shape with the colors beneath it in strange and interesting ways. Thumb through Chapter 10 for more on transparency.

Blends

In the 1990s, morphing was all the rage in movies and TV shows. *Morphing* combines (averages) two images together in a series of steps so that the first image appears to be magically turning into the second. In Illustrator, you're able to use a similar technique — *blending* — to transform one object into another in as many steps as you want.

Blending lets objects change color, shape, and size, resulting in exciting effects. Illustrator's blends are "live:" You can blend between objects but still edit them after you create the blend. The objects in between change automatically to match the changes you make to the original objects, which allows you to tweak the way the blend looks without having to start over. The top figure in Figure 3-7 represents a step blend occurring between a small black circle and a larger gray triangle. Only the rightmost and leftmost objects were created by hand. The other objects are an average of the two created by the Blend tool. The bottom figure in Figure 3-7 shows a smooth color blend between the large and small circles. We cover blends in more detail in Chapter 12.

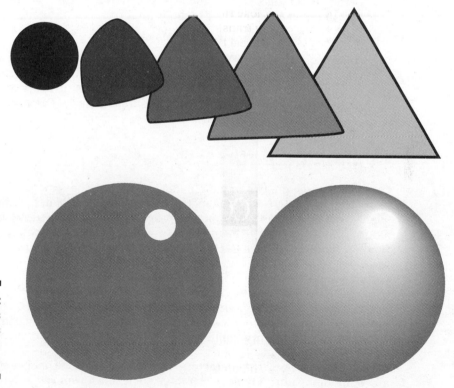

Figure 3-7:
Examples
of blends
between
two objects.

Masks

An Illustrator *mask,* now called a *clipping mask* in Illustrator 10, is a path used to hide objects outside itself. For instance, you can mask out everything in an Illustrator drawing except for the area inside the path so only the area shows. Creating a clipping mask is quite simple, as shown in Figure 3-8, with the following steps:

1. **Create a path to use as a mask on top of some other art.**

   The fill and stroke of the path don't matter because the path itself becomes invisible, along with anything outside the path.

   The art beneath the clipping mask can be as complex and have as many parts as you want. The top path masks all paths beneath it. You can use any tool to create this path (such as the Pen, Pencil, or Rectangle).

2. **Using any of the selection tools, select both the path you just created and the object(s) you want to mask.**

3. **Choose Object⇨Clipping Mask⇨Make.**

   Anything selected that's outside the masking path is hidden, and the masking path itself becomes invisible. Nothing is deleted when you make a mask; it's just hidden. You can restore your artwork to its unmasked state by selecting Object⇨Clipping Mask⇨Release.

Compound paths

Compound paths join two or more paths together so that one path makes part of another invisible. Compound paths may sound complicated, but if you've ever typed anything in any computer program, you've been using them all along without knowing — many letters are really compound paths! Any letter that has a hole in it (such as *B* or *O*) is a compound path. If you want to place text over something else and see things through the holes in the text, use compound paths, as shown in Figure 3-9.

A figure-8 is a single compound path, made up of three paths. The two paths in the middle are *holes* — areas made transparent so you can see the background artwork through them.

As you may imagine, text characters have lots of holes in them — so they're all compound paths. A typical character, such as a lowercase *a,* is made up of two paths; the hole in the middle is one of those paths. If you want to magically transform a bit of text into a graphic object made of paths, select the text with a selection tool and choose Type⇨Create Outlines. The text changes from a text object to a series of compound paths (which you can then edit as you edit any other path).

Figure 3-8:
Masking
artwork.

Figure 3-9:
A compound
path is laid
over a
piece of
background
art (which
is visible
through the
two round
holes).

You can make any number of overlapping paths into a compound path by selecting them and choosing Object⇨Compound Path⇨Make. If you want to turn the compound path back into two (or more) individual paths, select the compound path and choose Object⇨Compound Path⇨Release. Figure 3-10 shows what happens when you release compound paths that were originally text objects. When you release the compound paths, the hollow part of the letter fills in, because the purpose of the compound path in the letter is to make those hollow parts of the letter transparent.

Figure 3-10:
Text as text (left), as compound paths (middle), and as compound paths after release (right).

Compound paths work best when you keep things simple. If you stack too many objects on top of each other and try to make a compound path, holes may appear where you didn't expect them. But if you try to keep things to a minimum (only use a few objects, and try not to have more than two objects overlapping in any one place) you'll get splendid results from the Compound Paths command.

Illustrator has also gone one step better, providing you with an easy way to create better compound paths — by using compound shapes. Check them out in all their glory in Chapter 4.

Flares

No longer are cool effects, such as flares, reserved to Photoshop territory. The new Flare tool allows you to create effects, such as lens flares and reflections, that are photo realistic yet totally vector-based (as shown in Figure 3-11). That is, the effects can be easily edited — moved and scaled — to produce just the right look. The Flare tool is equipped with numerous options that can be adjusted to produce a multitude of variations.

Figure 3-11:
A boring
sun gets
transformed
into a
dazzling star
of rays
and rings.

To create your own lens flare, first create some interesting art and fill with the colors of your choice; then follow these steps:

 1. Select the Flare tool.

It shares a toolslot with the Rectangle tool.

2. **Double-click the Flare tool to bring up the Flare Options palette. Play with the various settings and then click OK.**

   These are the settings used for Figure 3-11:

Center	100% Opacity and 50% Brightness
Halo	Growth 20% and Fuzziness 0%
Rays	Number 15, Longest 300%, and Fuzziness 100%
Rings	Path 100 pt, Number 10, Largest 41%, and Direction 42%

3. **Place your cursor over the place on your art where you want to establish your light source; click and drag.**

   You should see the appearance of some funky lines and circles. These are the rays and the halo.

   Use your up or down arrow keys to interactively increase or decrease the number of rays.

4. **Place your cursor over the place on your art where you want to center your rings. Click and drag. The distance you drag will also determine the length of the flare.**

   You should see the appearance of some circles of varying size and opacity. Your sun should now be decked out with a bright and beautiful lens flare.

5. **Deselect the flare and admire the results. If you're not quite happy, delete the flare and try again with different settings.**

Entering the Wide World of the Web

Illustrator is a Web-happy application. Anything that you create in Illustrator can make an appearance on the Web in one form or another. Illustrator gives you mighty powers to create both vector-based and pixel-based images for use on the Web.

We devote an entire chapter (Chapter 17) to the Web. Illustrator does all sorts of Web-specific tasks, such as creating animations, optimizing pixel-based images, and providing a preview of how your artwork looks when viewed in a Web browser.

The following is a laundry list of Web-happy things you can do with Illustrator at no extra charge:

✔ **Create images without resolution headaches:** When you use a pixel-based graphics program, you must continually worry whether your graphics have enough resolution to display with the quality you want. In Illustrator, you can always create Web graphics with optimum quality because you decide on the resolution after you complete the image instead of when you start creating it.

- **Optimize artwork as pixel-based images:** You can save your art as JPEG, GIF, or PNG images, using the Save for Web command to preview how various color reductions and compressions affect the artwork.

- **Export artwork as Flash or SVG vector graphics:** Flash and Scalable Vector Graphic format (SVG) are new technologies that enable you to display vector (path-based) graphics on the Web. Before Flash and SVG, only pixel-based artwork could be displayed. Vector graphics on the Web are smaller and look better than their pixel-based counterparts.

- **Preview artwork as pixel-based graphics:** If you plan to save your artwork as GIF, JPEG, or PNG files, you can turn on the Pixel Preview mode while you create it. This makes Illustrator show you your artwork as close as possible to how it'll look after it's on the Web. With this mode turned off, the artwork displays as close as possible to how it'll look in print.

- **Apply object-based slicing:** Simply put, slices enable you to divide your image into pieces so that you can later apply separate loading or optimization settings or other HTML features, such as animation. However, rather than slicing an entire image based on a square grid, as in Photoshop or ImageReady, Illustrator enables you to apply slices to objects, groups of objects, or layers.

For more information on any of these topics, see Chapter 17.

Saving the World

Well, maybe saving the world is a little bit of an overstatement, but saving your work is arguably the most important thing you can do in Illustrator. And you may feel as if you have saved the world when your client mentions — 40 hours into the job — that she needs the graphics to work in AutoCAD, and you say, "Sure, no problem!" instead of breaking down in tears. Or when your graphics look every bit as good on the Web as they do in print. Or when your computer crashes and you laugh it off because you didn't lose any work. The key to all these heroic scenarios is Illustrator's massive Save features, all found under the File menu: Save, Save As, Save a Copy, Save for Web, and Export.

Save

Choosing the Save command writes the document that you're working on to the hard drive, which is the fastest way to save a file. However, using Save is limited because it can be used only on files that were already saved. If you're working on a brand new document, you can't just save it using the Save command. Doing so doesn't change the format; the file is saved in a format as close as possible to the format it had when it was opened. If you open an

Illustrator 9 file and hit Save, even if you're working in Illustrator 10, the file is saved as an Illustrator 9 file — in the exact same location as when you opened it. To change the file's format (or to save it to a different location on your hard drive), use the Save As command.

Save As

Use the Save As command to change the file format of the open document and save it to a different location from where it was originally. Using the Save As command also saves new documents that haven't been saved before. When you create artwork for print, Save As is the command to use 90 percent of the time; it allows you to save in the EPS (Encapsulated PostScript) format. The EPS format is supported by every major page-layout application, PC or Mac. When you save a file in this format, you're assured almost universal compatibility in the world of print. Save As also gives you the option of saving files in the formats of earlier versions of Illustrator, all the way back to the decade-old version 3.0. This is handy for sharing your files with other Illustrator users who don't have the latest and greatest version of the program, as you do.

You also have the option of saving your file as a PDF (Portable Document Format). PDF is a great for exchanging files for review and approval processes because it only requires that the recipient have Adobe Acrobat Reader (a free download from Adobe, www.adobe.com) installed. The recipients don't need Illustrator or any graphics program. They don't even need to have any fonts you may have used in the file. If you save your file as a PDF, select the Preserve Illustrator Editing Capabilities option in the Adobe PDF Format Options dialog box. Then you can later open the file as an Illustrator file with access to edit the elements, fonts, colors, patterns, and type blocks.

For more information on the Save As command and file formats, see Chapter 18.

Save a Copy

Save a Copy has all the features of the Save As command but adds a twist: You can also use it to save all the information in your current document as a different file on your hard drive — at a different location and sporting a different file format — without changing anything in the current file. You can save multiple versions of the same file (say, one for printing and one for the Web). Moreover, if you need to restore the file to the way it was the last time it was saved using Save or Save As, you have a handy way to do so: the File⇨Revert command. Revert breezes right past the Save a Copy command, allowing you to make a completely different series of changes.

Save for Web

The improved Save for Web command, as you probably guessed, enables you to save Illustrator graphics for display on the Web. Even better, you can use this command to save your files in any of the three most commonly used Web graphics file formats: JPEG, GIF, or PNG, and now with Version 10 — Flash (SWF) and SVG. Best of all, the Save for Web dialog box provides a preview of what the file will look like after you save it, as well as what the file size and download time will be, so that you can manage the delicate balance between graphic quality and short download time. You use this feature most when you save graphics for the Web. You can find a whole lot more information on the Save for Web command in Chapter 17.

Export

The Export command could be called "Save for Everything Else." Use it to save Illustrator files in an astonishing variety of formats — from the commonplace (Photoshop) to the obscure (Pixar). Use the Export command when you need to save a graphic in a specific format that you can't find under the Save As or Save for Web command. Here's where to find every other file format you can use when you save an Illustrator file.

The most commonly used formats found here are Flash (a format for displaying vector graphics on the Web), SVG, and Adobe Photoshop. Flash (SWF) files can be opened and edited in Flash-savvy applications, such as Macromedia Flash. Photoshop format recreates your Illustrator file as a Photoshop file, maintaining the features of the original file (such as Layers and Transparency) as closely as possible. Chapters 17 and 18 provide further information on using Illustrator with these formats.

Using Illustrator for What It Does Best

Illustrator is a powerful tool, but it's limited to certain types of tasks. Knowing what Illustrator does best is key to getting the most out of the software.

Illustrator does anything having to do with path-based artwork extremely well and performs the basics with pixel-based artwork. You can use Illustrator for page layout, but it really isn't designed for documents longer than a single page. You can also use Illustrator for some basic image adjustment, but that sort of thing is easier with Photoshop.

Any time you want to create art or graphics pieces that need to serve multiple purposes, consider Illustrator. Illustrator's flexibility in transforming artwork is second to none — with equal ease, you can create artwork to appear on a business card, a bottle label, a poster, a billboard, television or film, or on the Web.

Illustrator isn't limited to portraying the way things are in the real world. You can use it to create things that may have no real-world equivalents. Give light bulbs spikes. Create a monster out of eyeballs. Whatever you imagine, Illustrator can help you create an image of it. And after you create your image, Illustrator gives you the means to edit it by adjusting the original or cooking up batches of variations.

Part II

Drawing and Coloring Your Artwork

The 5th Wave   By Rich Tennant

"I COULDN'T SAY ANYTHING—THEY WERE IN HERE WITH THAT PROGRAM WE BOUGHT THEM THAT ENCOURAGES ARTISTIC EXPRESSION."

In this part . . .

In this section, we cover the essentials of creating new graphics in Illustrator. You meet the various tools that create new graphics:

- ✔ The basic **shape tools** that you use to whomp up stars, rectangles, ellipses, and so forth in a jiffy

- ✔ The **Pencil tool**, your handy friend for drawing free-form lines (get it? — hand-y?)

- ✔ The **Line** and **Arc tools**, which enable you to create quick and easy lines and curves

- ✔ The **Pen tool**, which gives you the power to create lines and shapes with astonishing precision

- ✔ The Brush tool for painting complex objects onscreen with ease

You also discover how to add solid colors, patterns, and gradients to your graphics. Finally, we slide you the skinny about some cool effects that you can create in Illustrator, such as fading out your artwork by using Transparency; coloring a single piece of artwork with multiple colors, gradients, or patterns; and making your viewers' eyes bug out with cool-factor envy.

Chapter 4

Shaping Up, Basically

In This Chapter

▶ Creating objects the easy way

▶ Customizing basic objects

▶ Combining objects to create other objects

A regrettably large number of people avoid Illustrator because they find the whole point/path thing so intimidating. This situation is unfortunate but not surprising. When most people look at artwork, they see it as complete shapes, not as the lines that form the shapes. Working with points and paths forces you to see your artwork in a way that many people have never thought of before, which creates enough of a hurdle to scare people away from Illustrator.

Fortunately, Illustrator offers the shape-creation tools as a way to get a running start to clear that hurdle. The shape-creation tools are six tools that let you create basic shapes, such as rectangles, ellipses, stars, and polygons. With the shape-creation tools, you can create graphics without even thinking about points and paths! (Don't be fooled — the points and paths are still there, but the tools create them all for you with just a single click-and-drag. Ah, progress.)

In this chapter, you discover how to use the shape-creation tools, which offers you a good foundation for understanding and using the more complex features of Illustrator. You also find out how to combine simple shapes. Although the shape-creation tools create basic elements, they are by no means limited, especially when used in conjunction with the Pathfinder palette. Some people discover that they can create such an astonishing variety of graphics with the shape-creation tools that they can bypass more complex tools, such as the Pen and Pencil, altogether!

Creating Basic Shapes

Illustrator has six tools for creating shapes. Although you could create all those shapes with the Pen tool, you'd torment yourself if you did so. The specialized tools in Illustrator make the shapes easy to create. The six tools are named for (and look like) the shapes they create, as follows:

- ✔ **Rectangle:** Use this tool to make rectangles and squares. Hold down the Shift key when using this tool to get a perfect square.

- ✔ **Rounded Rectangle:** As you may expect, you get rounded corners on your rectangles and squares when you use this tool. Of course, if you recall high school geometry, you know that a round rectangle is a contradiction in terms. By definition, a rectangle is a four-sided polygon with each corner forming a 90° angle. Oh, well. So much for Euclid.

- ✔ **Ellipse:** This tool makes ellipses and circles. Hold down the Shift key when using this tool to get a perfect circle.

- ✔ **Polygon:** This tool makes objects with any number of sides — from 3 to 1,000 — each side the same length. You can use this tool for triangles, pentagons, hexagons, and so forth.

- ✔ **Star:** This tool makes stars with any number of points between 3 and 1,000.

- ✔ **Spiral:** This tool makes spirals with any number of winds (that's long *i*, as in *whines*) between 360 and 3,600 degrees (360 degrees is equal to one wind). If you're looking for the Spiral tool among the shapes tools and can't find it, don't bother. It moved into the toolslot next door, which it shares with the new Line Segment, Arc, Polar Grid, and Rectangular Grid tools.

- ✔ **Flare:** This new tool creates effects, such as lens flares and reflections, which are photo realistic, yet entirely vector-based. See Chapter 3 for the complete low-down on this new and exciting tool.

The shape-creation tools are located in a single row in the Toolbox, as shown in Figure 4-1. The rectangles reside in the Rectangle toolslot; the others hang out in the Ellipse toolslot.

Figure 4-1: The six shape-creation tools.

Drawing rectangles and squares

To draw a rectangle, select the Rectangle tool in the Toolbox, and then click and drag where you want the rectangle to go. After you release the mouse button, a rectangle appears. To draw a square, you follow a slightly different procedure, as we describe in the following steps:

1. **Choose the Rectangle tool from the Toolbox.**

2. **Click and drag with the tool. (Don't release the mouse button yet.)**

3. **Press the Shift key.**

   The rectangle snaps into a square.

4. **Release the mouse button (but don't release the Shift key until after you release the mouse button).**

   A square appears. (If you release the Shift key before you release the mouse button, the square snaps back into a rectangle.)

You can draw a rounded-corner rectangle by choosing the Rounded Rectangle tool (hidden in the toolslot with the Rectangle tool) and draw with that instead of the regular Rectangle tool.

If you want to create a rectangle with exact dimensions (for example, 28 points x 42 points), select the Rectangle tool and click and release your mouse, but don't drag. A dialog box appears, as shown in Figure 4-2.

Figure 4-2:
The
Rectangle
dialog box.

Type in height and width and then click OK. Illustrator draws a rectangle to those exact specifications.

Illustrator places the rectangle's upper-left corner at the spot where you click with the Rectangle tool. If you hold down the Alt key (Option on a Mac) at the same time, Illustrator places the rectangle's center at the spot where you click with the Rectangle tool.

Drawing ellipses and circles

To draw an ellipse, choose the Ellipse tool and click and drag in the document window. After you release the mouse button, an ellipse appears. To draw a perfect circle, hold down the Shift key while you draw with the Ellipse tool.

If you hold down the Alt key (Option on a Mac) at the same time that you click (but don't drag) with the Ellipse tool, Illustrator places the ellipse (or circle) from its center instead of from its upper-left edge.

Like with the Rectangle tool, clicking (without dragging) causes the Ellipse dialog box to appear, as shown in Figure 4-3. Here you can type in an exact height and width for the ellipse. These values represent the distance across the ellipse at its widest and narrowest points.

Figure 4-3:
The Ellipse
dialog box.

Creating polygons, stars, and spirals

Illustrator has tools designed specifically for creating polygons, stars, and spirals. Like rectangles and ovals, these shapes can be drawn with the Pen tool, but having a tool for creating them makes the process much easier, faster, and more accurate. Using these tools is fairly straightforward. As with the Rectangle and Ellipse tools, just click and drag and then release the mouse button when the shape is the size you want. Also like with the Rectangle and Ellipse tools, just clicking (without dragging) with the Polygon, Star, or Spiral tool opens a dialog box, which you use to specify the shape's exact size (and other attributes).

Need to create stars at various sizes with a certain number of points? Or different sized polygons with the same number of sides? The dialog boxes for the Polygon, Star, and Spiral tools remember the number of sides, points, and winds you enter and use those settings for each subsequent shape you draw, even if you click and drag.

Pulling polygons

To create a polygon, click and drag with the Polygon tool. When the polygon is the size you want, release the mouse button. The new polygon appears. Because polygons are more complex than ellipses or rectangles, you can get all sorts of special capabilities by pressing certain keys as you draw. To customize the polygon as you create it, hold down any of the following keys as you drag:

- **Shift:** Constrains one side of the polygon so that it's parallel to the bottom of the page.
- **Up/Down Arrow:** Adds or deletes sides of the polygon while you draw it.
- **Spacebar:** Moves the polygon around as you draw it.
- **Tilde (~):** Creates multiple polygons while you draw. At times you can have so many polygons that they look like one solid figure, but each one is a separate entity that you can separate and move wherever you want. This feature can create quite astounding effects, as shown in Figure 4-4. To use this feature, you must release the mouse button before you release the key or all duplicates disappear. This works when you draw any of the other shapes, too! By the way, to get the swirly effect, move your mouse either clockwise or counterclockwise as you draw.

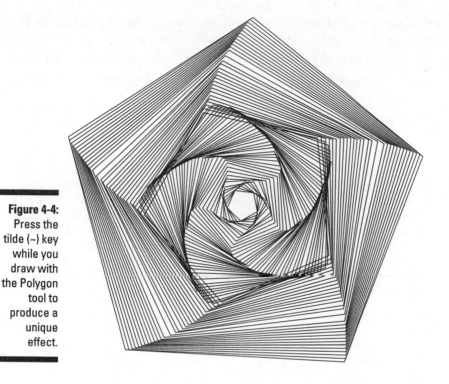

Figure 4-4:
Press the
tilde (~) key
while you
draw with
the Polygon
tool to
produce a
unique
effect.

Clicking (without dragging) with the Polygon tool opens the Polygon dialog box, as shown in Figure 4-5. Polygons use a Radius value instead of height and width. All sides of the polygon are the same distance from the center; this distance is the Radius value. To create a polygon of a specific width, type in half the width you want in the Radius field. You can type in any number of sides, from 3 to 1,000.

Figure 4-5:
The Polygon
dialog box.

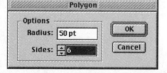

Seeing stars

To create a star, click and drag with the Star tool. After you release the mouse button, a star is born. Stars are even more complex than polygons. Fortunately, you also have more keys for customizing options. To customize a star, use the following keys as you drag:

- ✔ **Shift:** Constrains one side of the star so that the bottom two points of the star are parallel to the bottom of the page.

- ✔ **Up/Down Arrow:** Adds/deletes points of the star while you draw it.

- ✔ **Ctrl (⌘ on a Mac):** Constrains the middle points (the inner radius) of the star; the outer ones still move.

- ✔ **Spacebar:** Moves the star around as you draw it.

- ✔ **Tilde (~):** Creates multiple stars as you draw.

Clicking (without dragging) with the Star tool opens the Star dialog box, as shown in Figure 4-6. Stars have two radii that you can set in the Star dialog box. The first radius determines how far the inner points of the star are from the center. The second radius determines how far the outer points are from the center. In the Star dialog box, you can also set the number of points the star has. After you make your settings, click OK to create the star you specified. After you create a star using the Star dialog box, each star you create by clicking and dragging uses the same specifications, more or less. Regardless of each star's size, it has the same number of points (unless you change them using the up and down arrows), and the first and second radii maintain the same proportions, if not the same size. If you enter two inches for the first radius and one inch for the second, the second radius is 50 percent smaller for every star you create after you establish the settings in the dialog box, regardless of the star's size.

Figure 4-6:
Use the Star dialog box to set the quantity and length of its points.

Spiraling out of control

Spirals have fewer keyboard options associated with them than polygons or stars, but the Spiral dialog box is far less intuitive than any other shapes' dialog boxes. You're probably better off doing what you can by dragging and using the keyboard. Nonetheless, the Spiral dialog box is worth a look.

To customize a spiral, you can hold down one of the following keys as you drag:

- ✔ **Up/Down Arrow:** Adds or deletes the winds of the spiral as you're drawing it.

✔ **Ctrl (⌘ on a Mac):** Winds or unwinds the spiral (the outside moves, but the center stays where it is, making the spiral tighter or looser), which changes the number of winds.

✔ **Spacebar:** Moves the spiral around as you draw it.

✔ **Tilde (~):** Creates multiple spirals as you draw.

Click with the Spiral tool (instead of clicking and dragging) to open the Spiral dialog box, as shown in Figure 4-7. In the Spiral dialog box, the Radius option is the distance from the center of the spiral to its outermost point. The Decay option determines how much larger or smaller each coil of the spiral is from the previous coil. Values close to 100% result in a tight spiral, and 100% results in a perfect circle. The Segments option determines how many coils make up the spiral. Each wind of the spiral is made of 4 segments; if you want 5 coils in the spiral, type **20** in the Segments field.

Figure 4-7: Use options in the Spiral dialog box to set the spiral's tightness.

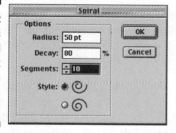

Putting Shapes Together

The basic shape-creation tools are great starting points for creating more complex illustrations because most complex shapes are simply many basic shapes put together. You may be astonished at what you can create simply by combining one basic shape with another. One of the quickest and easiest ways to do so in Illustrator is by using the Pathfinder palette.

The Pathfinder palette has a misleading name. All it really does is combine or separate two or more shapes in a variety of ways. You can use the Pathfinder palette to join two or more objects into one object, remove the shape of one object from another, cut apart two shapes where they overlap, or combine objects in many other ways.

To access the Pathfinder palette, choose Window⇨Pathfinder. The Pathfinder palette appears, as shown in Figure 4-8.

Veteran Illustrator users may notice that the Pathfinder palette has been slightly revamped. The Pathfinder palette is divided into two sections — Shape Modes and Pathfinders.

Add to shape area

Subtract from shape area

Intersect shape areas

Exclude overlapping shape areas

Figure 4-8:
Use the
Pathfinder
palette to
work with
complex
shapes in a
variety of
ways.

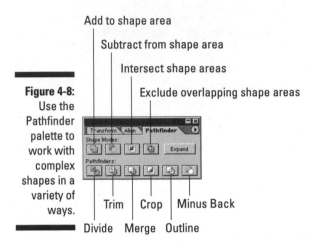

Trim | Crop | Minus Back

Divide | Merge | Outline

Using the Pathfinder palette is simplicity itself: Just overlap two or more objects, select them all by clicking them with any selection tool (to select multiple objects, hold down the Shift key while clicking each object), and click the button that does the operation that you desire.

Knowing which button to click isn't always obvious, but don't worry about that. Simply keep in mind that when you want to combine or separate two or more objects, you're likely to find a button to help you in the Pathfinder palette. Click a button; if it doesn't give you what you want, choose Edit⇨Undo and try a different button.

The results of the Pathfinder palette depend heavily on which object is in front and which object is behind. To change the stacking order of objects, select a single object with the Selection tool and choose Object⇨Arrange. In the Arrange submenu, you can send the object to the back, bring it forward, or move it backward and forward one level at a time. To get a better idea of how the Pathfinder palette functions, you can use it on two basic objects (in this case, a circle and a star), as shown in Figure 4-9.

Figure 4-9:
Two basic
shapes are
overlapped
from the
Pathfinder
palette.

Compound Shapes

Illustrator 10 enhanced part of the old Pathfinder palette, adding support for producing compound shapes. Not only does it enable you to create complex artwork from basic shapes, all the artwork you create remains fully editable. The Shape Modes portion of the palette is also easy to use. Overlap two or more objects, select them all, and click the button of the effect you want. The commands under the Shape Modes consist of the following:

- **Add to Shape Area:** Groups multiple objects so they're selectable as a unit but can also be selected individually with the Direct Selection or Group Selection tools. The resulting objects use the fill and stroke of the object that was on top before the objects were added together. By clicking the Expand button or by choosing Expand Compound Shape from the Pathfinder palette menu, the added objects are joined into a single physical object. See Figure 4-10 for an example.

  In all Shape Modes, the Expand Compound Shape command flattens the compound shape into a single path.

  You can add additional shapes in a compound shape at any time. Also, use the Direct Selection tool to edit any path or anchor point on the compound shape.

- **Subtract from Shape Area:** Cuts away all selected objects in front of the backmost object, leaving a hole in the backmost object in the shape of whatever was in front of it. In Figure 4-11, Subtract from Shape Area cuts away the star in front of the circle but also leaves the portion of the path that makes up the star tips which did not overlap the circle. By clicking the Expand button or choosing the Expand Compound Shape command, those star tips will be shaved off.

- **Intersect Shape Areas:** Cuts away all parts of the objects that don't overlap. The resulting object uses the fill and stroke color of the object that was on top before the objects were intersected. Here, Intersect Shape Areas joins the circle and star, using the fill and stroke color of the star (which was on top before the objects were intersected). Intersect also works on more than two objects. Clicking the Expand button or choosing the Expand Compound Shape command further simplifies the objects and deletes the remaining nonintersected portions of the paths of the original objects, as shown in Figure 4-12.

- **Exclude overlapping shape areas:** Removes all parts of the objects that overlap and unites what's left into a single object (the opposite of Intersect). The remaining object uses the fill and stroke of the object that was on top before the objects were united. In Figure 4-13, Exclude overlapping shape areas cuts away all parts of the circle and star that overlap, uniting what is left into a single object that uses the fill and stroke color of the star (which was on top before the objects were united). Clicking the Expand button or choosing the Expand Compound Shape command eliminates any unnecessary anchor points.

Figure 4-10:
The results
of using the
Add to
Shape Area
command,
and then
with
Expand.

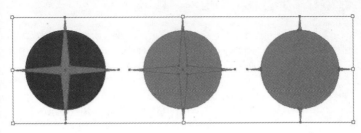

Figure 4-11:
The results
of using the
Subtract
from Shape
Area
command,
and then
with
Expand.

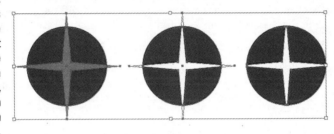

Figure 4-12:
The results
of using the
Intersect
shape areas
command,
and then
with
Expand.

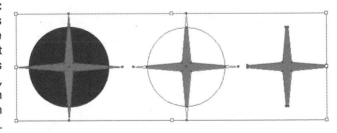

The Shape Modes effects can be combined, so knock yourself out. Unlike the Pathfinders commands, if you want to undo your compound shapes, simply select the Release Compound Shapes from the Pathfinder palette pop-up menu. By clicking the Expand button or selecting the Expand Compound Shape command from the Pathfinder palette pop-up menu, you can further clean up or simplify your paths by eliminating unnecessary anchor points. The compound shapes are flattened and condensed into a new simplified shape. But be warned: After you use the Expand Compound Shape command, you can no longer release your compound shape by using the Release Compound Shapes command. The Expand feature permanently fuses your effect, so there's no going back.

Figure 4-13:
The results
of using the
Exclude
overlapping
shape areas
command,
and then
with
Expand.

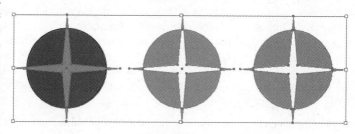

Pathfinders

The commands under the Pathfinders portion of the Pathfinder palette are a mixed bag of effects. Divide and Minus Back achieve results by cutting away specific parts of the image. Figure 4-14 demonstrates the results of applying these two commands: Minus Back and Divide. Trim, Merge, Crop, and Outline provide the means for tidying up your artwork before sending your creation out into the world. In Figure 4-15, this cleanup crew takes a bow.

Figure 4-14:
The results
of using
Minus Back
(left), and
Divide (two
images on
the right).

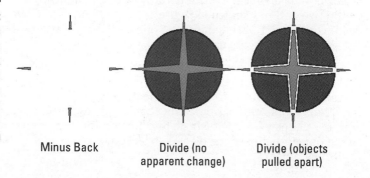

Minus Back   Divide (no   Divide (objects
       apparent change)   pulled apart)

Here's a quick rundown of the Pathfinder commands found under the Pathfinder palette:

- ✔ **Divide:** Breaks two overlapping objects into separate objects. This operation may look as though it hasn't done anything after you first apply it (left, Figure 4-14). However, after you divide an object, you can move or color each piece individually (middle, Figure 4-14). After the Divide button first breaks the overlapping star and circle into separate objects, they look as if you've done nothing to them. However, the star and circle can be individually moved or colored (far right, Figure 4-14).

✔ **Trim:** Removes any parts of objects hidden by other objects and also removes any strokes. As with Divide, this command may not produce visible results immediately (it affects only hidden items). However, when you start changing the affected objects, you see a big difference, such as the pie slices (right, Figure 4-15) that seem to change position. Here, the Trim button removes any parts of the circle hidden by the star and also removes any strokes. At first, the command's results aren't visible (left) until you start changing the position of the pie slices of the circle (right) — and they move as separate objects.

✔ **Merge:** Removes any parts of objects hidden by other objects, removes strokes, and merges overlapping objects that have the same fill colors. This option functions almost the same way as the Trim option does, with the key difference being that this option merges objects of the same color together into a single object while trim leaves them as separate objects. Here, the Merge button removes any parts of the circle hidden by the star, removes strokes, and merges overlapping objects that have the same fill colors (which the star and the circle do not).

✔ **Crop:** Divides two overlapping objects into separate objects where they overlap and then deletes everything outside the boundaries of the topmost object. Here, the Crop button divides the star and circle into separate objects where they overlap and then deletes everything outside the boundaries of the star (the topmost object).

✔ **Outline:** Breaks objects into separate line segments with no fill colors. Of the two outlines shown in Figure 14-15, the one on the left shows the visible effects of the command; the one on the right shows the now-separate line segments moved apart.

✔ **Minus Back:** Cuts away from the frontmost object all selected objects that are behind the frontmost object. The remaining object uses the fill and stroke color of the frontmost object. This option is the opposite of the Minus Front option. Here Minus Back cuts away the circle from the star and unites what's left (those four forlorn-looking points) into a single object that uses the fill and stroke color of the star (which is the frontmost object).

If you stumble upon the Pathfinder commands under the Effects menu, don't confuse them with those found under the Pathfinder palette. The commands under the Effects menu change the appearance of an object without changing the underlying object itself. The Pathfinder commands found under the Effect menu are designed to be applied to groups of objects, layers, and type objects. They usually have no effect on a few overlapping shapes. For more on appearances and effects, see Chapter 11.

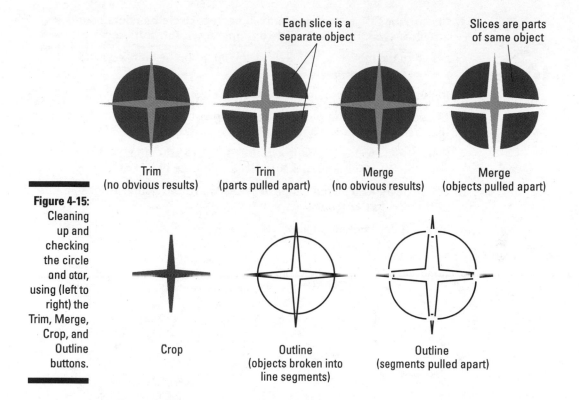

Each slice is a
separate object

Slices are parts
of same object

Trim
(no obvious results)

Trim
(parts pulled apart)

Merge
(no obvious results)

Merge
(objects pulled apart)

Figure 4-15:
Cleaning
up and
checking
the circle
and star,
using (left to
right) the
Trim, Merge,
Crop, and
Outline
buttons.

Crop

Outline
(objects broken into
line segments)

Outline
(segments pulled apart)

Creating Objects Using the Pathfinder Palette

By combining basic shapes, you can create just about anything you can imagine. So, how do you actually use the Shape Modes and Pathfinders commands to create such complex shapes? (Details, details.) Consider a couple of examples — a crescent moon and a sunrise.

Crescent moon

A crescent moon seems fairly simple to draw, but if you try to draw one accurately by hand, you get frustrated. The Pathfinder palette, however, makes drawing a crescent moon almost as easy as smiling and saying, "Green cheese." Just follow these steps:

1. **Choose the Ellipse tool and draw a perfect circle by clicking and dragging the Ellipse tool while holding down the Shift key.**

   Let go of the mouse button before you let go of the Shift key, and a perfect circle appears.

2. **Repeat Step 1, except make the second circle smaller than the first.**

3. **Choose the Selection tool and use it to position the second circle over the first, as shown in Figure 4-16.**

4. **Select both circles. (Hold down the Shift key and click each circle with the Selection tool to select more than one object at a time.)**

5. **Click the Subtract from shape area button in the Shape Modes portion of the Pathfinder palette.**

   Presto! A crescent moon appears!

Figure 4-16: Creating a crescent moon.

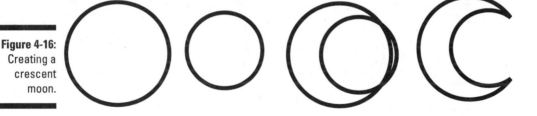

Sunrise

What better way to follow a crescent moon than with a beautiful sunrise? Just follow these steps:

1. **Click and drag with the Rectangle tool to create a box.**

2. **Click and drag with the Star tool to create a star. As you drag with the Star tool, repeatedly press the up-arrow (↑) key.**

   A many-pointed star appears.

3. **Choose the Selection tool and use it to position the star over the rectangle so the two objects overlap, as shown in Figure 4-17.**

4. **Select both the star and the rectangle. (Hold down the Shift key and click each object with the Selection tool so both objects are selected.)**

5. **Click the Minus Back button in the Pathfinders portion of the Pathfinder palette.**

   Voilà — a beautiful sunrise! (Well, almost. Still needs colors and a pot of fresh coffee.)

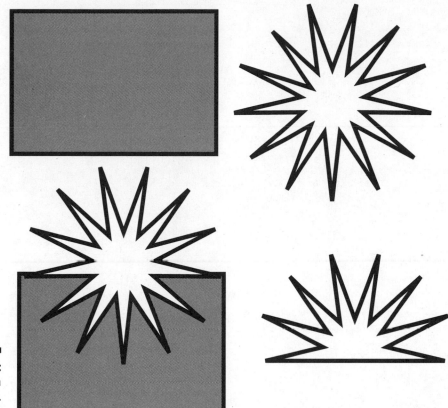

Figure 4-17:
Creating a
sunrise.

Chapter 5

Getting Your Fill of Fills and Strokes

In This Chapter

▶ Filling open paths

▶ Discovering how to use strokes

▶ Getting to know the Color and Swatches palettes

▶ Using and creating patterns

▶ Applying textures to paths

▶ Working with gradients

*F*ills and strokes give life to your artwork. If Illustrator were a coloring book, the fills and strokes would be the biggest, best box of crayons ever (only better because these colors always stay inside the lines). Better still, they're magic colors. You're not limited to a single solid color within an area. You can have gradients and patterns as well. And not only can you color inside the lines, you can color the lines themselves, make them thinner or thicker, or hide them altogether. Best of all, unlike crayons, these don't make a mess when your big sister grinds them into the carpet because you ran to show Mom your new artwork and forgot to clean up after yourself.

In this chapter, you discover the different boxes of crayons Illustrator has to offer, such as the Color palette and Swatches palette, and how to color your artwork with them by using the Fill box and Stroke box. You find out how to create your own colors. Rounding things out, you get to know the special colors, gradients, and patterns in Illustrator, which stretch the meaning of what color really is.

Understanding Fill and Stroke

A *fill* is a color enclosed by a path. A *stroke* is a line of color that precisely follows a path. To run the coloring book metaphor into the ground (carpet?), the stroke is the line, and the fill is the inside-the-line that you aren't supposed to color outside of (but you did anyway because you weren't about to let your parents stifle your creativity!). *Color* is a loose term here; it can mean a solid color, a pattern, or (in the case of fills) a gradient. In Figure 5-1, you can see a variety of paths with different strokes and fills applied to them.

2-point 100% black stroke
around a 35% black fill

Rainbow Gradient
fill, with a Stroke
value of None

25-point Brick
Pattern stroke, with
a Fill value
of None

Figure 5-1:
Paths with
different fills
and strokes
applied to
them.

2-point gray (22% black) stroke
around a 100% black fill

Although a stroke can be any thickness, it always uses a path as its center. You can stylize your strokes with solid colors or patterns but not with gradients. (*Patterns* and *gradients* are special combinations of colors; read more about them in the upcoming section "All the colors in the rainbow and then some.") A *path* surrounds the area where you put the color. This area is the *fill* because, um, it's filled (with color).

Fills and strokes can obscure the boundaries of your paths, especially when you have very thick strokes on your paths, such as the S-shaped bricks in Figure 5-1. To temporarily hide all fills and strokes, choose View➪Outline. This shows your artwork as just the paths, with all strokes and fills hidden. You can still edit the artwork like you would any other time. The only difference is that you can't see fills and strokes. To show all the colors again, choose View➪Preview.

You have many ways to create and modify fill and stroke color in Illustrator, but the quickest and easiest way to apply them is by using the Fill and Stroke box in the Toolbox, which looks remarkably like what you see in Figure 5-2.

You can change a fill or a stroke, but not both at the same time. You decide whether to change the fill or the stroke by selecting an object and then clicking the Fill (solid) or the Stroke (bordered) box. The box you click comes to the front; after that, every color change you make is applied to whichever one you chose . . . until you choose the other one.

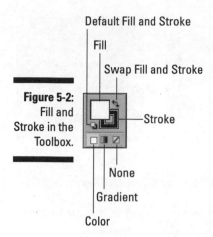

Default Fill and Stroke

Fill

Swap Fill and Stroke

Figure 5-2:
Fill and
Stroke in the
Toolbox.

Stroke

None

Gradient

Color

Some very useful features surround the Fill and Stroke boxes. Just to the upper right is a little curved line with arrows on both ends. Click this thingamajig to Swap Fill and Stroke colors.

To the lower left of the Fill and Stroke boxes are miniature white (Fill) and black bordered (Stroke) boxes. Click this Default Fill and Stroke button to set the Fill and Stroke boxes to their default colors: white for Fill and black for Stroke.

If you prefer fills and strokes in festive colors, here's the story: Beneath the Fill and Stroke boxes live three square buttons that handle colors. Click the first square (the Color button) to change the fill or stroke color to the last color that you used. Click the second square (the Gradient button) to change the color of the stroke or fill so that it matches the last-selected Gradient you used. Click the third square (the None button) to use no fill or stroke color at all.

Double-clicking the Stroke or the Fill box summons the Color Picker from which you can specify colors in a variety of ways. You can choose a color from a spectrum, using true color field and color slider, or define a color numerically. You can also select colors from the Color and the Swatches palettes, as we describe later in this chapter.

Filling and stroking paths with color

You can fill a path with one color and stroke it with another, as shown in Figure 5-3.

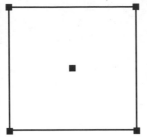 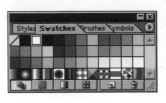 

Figure 5-3:
Filling and
stroking
a path
with two
different
colors.

To fill a path with one color and stroke it with another, just follow these steps:

1. **Using any of the Selection tools, select the path that you want to color.**

2. **In the Toolbox, click the Fill square (the solid one).**

   Doing so tells Illustrator to apply the next color you choose to the fill (but not the stroke) of selected paths.

3. **Choose Window➪Swatches.**

   The Swatches palette appears. The squares in this palette function in much the same way as do the three squares beneath the Fill and Stroke boxes in the Toolbox. Click any square in the palette to apply that swatch to the selected stroke or fill. (For more information, see "The Swatches Palette" later in this chapter.)

4. **Click any solid-color swatch.**

   (Well, okay, any swatch in the palette works. The ones that aren't solid colors are special colors, such as patterns and gradients — but sticking to solid colors is less confusing early on.)

5. **Click the Stroke box (the thick-bordered one) in the Toolbox.**

   Illustrator is ready for you to pick a stroke color.

6. **In the Swatches palette, choose a solid color, just as you did for the fill color in Step 4.**

 You can also drag and drop color onto your path. Simply drag a color swatch from the Swatches palette and drop it onto your path. Depending on whether the fill or stroke is selected in the Toolbox, either the fill or stroke will be colored anew.

Making a bold stroke

When you follow the steps to color a stroke and don't see any change, you probably have too narrow of a stroke. Stroke widths can range anywhere from 0 points (pts) to 1,000 points (18 inches, or about 46 centimeters). If the stroke is too narrow to be visible onscreen, you can change the stroke width by using the Stroke palette, as shown in Figure 5-4.

Figure 5-4:
The Stroke
palette.

To give the path a different stroke width:

1. **Select the path with any Selection tool.**
2. **Choose Window⇨Stroke.**

   The Stroke palette appears.
3. **Enter a new value or choose one from the Weight pop-up menu.**

Filling crossed and open paths

Sometimes a path crosses itself. For instance, a path in the shape of a figure eight crosses itself once. If you fill this path, the two round areas of the eight are full, as shown in Figure 5-5.

Figure 5-5:
A filled path
in a figure
eight shape.

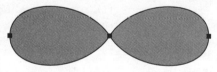

Open paths, which have separate starting and ending points, can be filled but the results are a little different from what you may expect. When you fill an open path, an *imaginary path* connects the first and last points of the original path. This imaginary path marks the limits of the fill area. If you apply a stroke to the figure, the stroke doesn't apply to the imaginary path. Figure 5-6 shows open paths with fills in them. We use a dotted line to show where Illustrator creates the imaginary path between two end points.

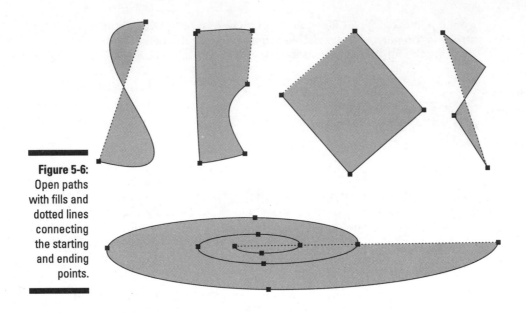

Figure 5-6:
Open paths
with fills and
dotted lines
connecting
the starting
and ending
points.

The Swatches Palette

Illustrator stores colors in the Swatches palette for quick and easy access —
and no matter how fast you grab a color, you never have to worry about
splattering paint. The Swatches palette comes with a whole set of colors that
are ready to use just by clicking them in the palette.

Additionally, Illustrator comes with many Swatch Libraries — sets of colors
created for special purposes — so if your first-grade crayon box never
seemed to have enough colors, you're in luck. You can even create your own
custom colors by using the Color palette (see the later section "The Color
Palette") and add them to the Swatches palette.

Using the Swatches palette (shown in Figure 5-7) is almost as easy as looking
at it. Select an object with any Selection tool, click the Stroke or Fill box in the
Toolbox, choose Window➪Swatches so that the Swatches palette appears,
and then click any square in the Swatches palette to choose that color. The
selected fill or stroke updates the instant you click the new color. No fuss, no
muss, no melted crayons.

All the colors in the rainbow and then some

The Swatches palette contains several different types of color swatches, each
with its own range of purposes and uses. Here's the lineup:

- **Process color:** This is your run-of-the-mill, straight-up color with no added bells or whistles. You can make a color for use onscreen or for print by mixing varying amounts of either red, green, and blue (RGB) or cyan, magenta, yellow, and black (CMYK). For more information on using RGB versus CMYK colors, see Chapter 1. These appear as solid color squares.

- **Spot colors:** (Nope, not for creating polka dots or Dalmatians.) Spot colors are used exclusively in printing. The four-color CMYK printing process can create only a limited range of colors from its four basic color ingredients. To compensate, the process can also use spot colors of specified inks that come in a particular color. Many companies make spot colors, but most countries have one dominant company that sets the standards for spot-color printing in that country. (In the U.S., it's Pantone; in Japan, it's TOYO.) The range of all colors that a company produces is its *library*. Illustrator includes swatch libraries from all the swatch-producing companies. Spot colors show up in the Swatches palette with little triangles in their lower right-hand corners; these triangles have a tiny spot in their centers.

- **Registration:** Registration is a special Illustrator color that uses 100 percent of all inks — but although it looks like black onscreen, it's not for artwork. Registration (as a color, at least) exists for a very specific technical purpose: creating the Registration marks used by commercial printers to get things in proper alignment on press. If you aren't a commercial printer or haven't been specifically told to do so by a commercial printer, you should never use Registration. Registration looks like a crosshair in the Swatches palette.

If you use Registration to color your artwork, you get an unprintable sticky mess that will probably stink (chemically, at least), waste ink, and never dry.

- **None:** This color choice differs from White (which tells a printer to *put no ink in a particular space,* on the assumption that the paper itself supplies the white color). None, on the other hand, is the *complete absence* of color. In a picture, a white object is opaque; it blocks your view of any objects behind it. (You can't see the electric outlet behind a white refrigerator.) An object with a color of None is transparent — invisible. If you want to use a stroke but also want other objects to show through the fill (or let the fill show through the objects), choose None for the specific onscreen area you want to see through. None appears in the Swatches palette as a white square with a diagonal red line through it.

- **Gradients:** Gradients combine two or more colors in a smooth transition that shades from one color into the other.

- **Patterns:** If you really love wallpaper, you can use one or more objects in a tiled pattern to fill other objects.

The icons at the bottom of your palette (see Figure 5-7) allow for different swatch viewing options.

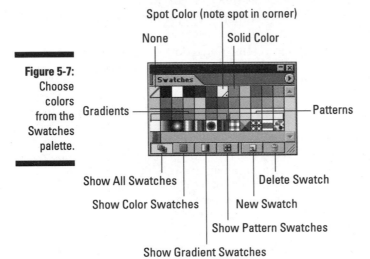

Spot Color (note spot in corner)

None   Solid Color

Figure 5-7:
Choose
colors
from the
Swatches
palette.

Gradients ——— Patterns

Show All Swatches   Delete Swatch

Show Color Swatches   New Swatch

Show Pattern Swatches

Show Gradient Swatches

Swatch Options for super colors

Swatches are a quick way to retrieve colors, but they do more. Double-click any swatch in the palette to open the Swatch Options dialog box, shown in all its useful glory in Figure 5-8.

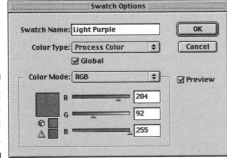

Figure 5-8:
The Swatch
Options
dialog box.

The Swatch Options dialog box keeps you busy with choices and gives you creative possibilities. Here's the list:

✔ **Swatch Name:** Here you can give the color a distinctive name (such as Maine Blueberry) or change its name.

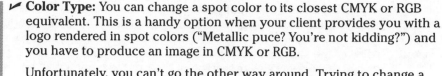

✔ **Color Type:** You can change a spot color to its closest CMYK or RGB equivalent. This is a handy option when your client provides you with a logo rendered in spot colors ("Metallic puce? You're not kidding?") and you have to produce an image in CMYK or RGB.

Unfortunately, you can't go the other way around. Trying to change a process color into a spot color doesn't give you the closest spot color equivalent from the Pantone, TOYO, or any other color library. (For more about color libraries, see the following section "Swatch libraries.")

✔ **Global:** After you select (check) this option, Illustrator remembers everything you color with a particular swatch. When you change the color of the swatch, everything with the old swatch's color updates to the new color. (Mercifully, Adobe didn't call this feature *The Old Swatcheroo.*) This feature's a great timesaver when you want to change a color scheme. You don't have to go back, reselect, and recolor everything — very handy, indeed.

✔ **Color Mode, gamut warnings, and color sliders:** These features are especially powerful when used with Global color. They all work just like the Color palette except that they apply your changes only to the currently selected swatch. See more on this palette in the section "The Color Palette" later in this chapter.

Swatch libraries

Illustrator comes loaded with color choices in the form of *swatch libraries* — sets of color swatches created for specific purposes. (Pantone, for example, has several libraries devoted just to spot colors.) The libraries you get with Illustrator draw from all the major spot-color sources in the world. A Web library provides tried-and-true colors that work best on the Internet. To peruse these libraries, click Window➪Swatch Libraries. If you turn up a color that you simply must have, add it to your Swatches palette: Open the specific library you need, find the color you want, and click it. Instantly the color shows up in your Swatches palette, ready for you to use.

Some libraries contain hundreds of swatches, which can make finding a particular color difficult. Fortunately, swatch libraries have a Find field at the very top of the window. For example, if a client wants a logo done on a report cover in Pantone 185, just open one of the Pantone libraries (by choosing Window➪Swatch Libraries➪Pantone Coated). When the swatch library appears, type **185** in its Find field (the empty white rectangle at the top of the palette) to highlight Pantone 185C (the C is for coated) automatically — you don't have to press any other key! Click Pantone 185C to add it to your Swatches palette and you're good to go.

If you need to choose spot colors for a project that will be offset printed, make sure to select your color from a printed swatch book manufactured by your chosen ink company. Never select the colors based on your onscreen view of the swatches in the library. Because of many variables, your screen can give you only its best match of the printed color. It will never be exact and frequently will be quite different.

The Color Palette

The Color palette is as close as Illustrator gets to a real-world artist's palette. You use it to create new colors by blending. Instead of mixing splotches of pigment and linseed oil with a brush (and getting half of it on your jeans), you move sliders to adjust how much of each component color goes into your new color.

Parts of the palette

The Color palette (see Figure 5-9) has several cool features, in addition to the color sliders, that make creating colors easier.

Out-of-gamut color warnings

Fill and Stroke boxes

Color sliders   Palette pop-up menu

Figure 5-9:
The Color
palette is
the closest
you can get
to a real
artist's
palette in
Illustrator.

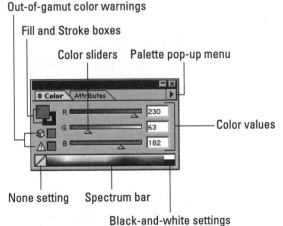

Color values

None setting   Spectrum bar

Black-and-white settings

Here's a list of Color palette features:

 ✔ **Fill** and **Stroke boxes:** These function identically to the Fill and Stroke boxes in the Toolbox. They're available here in the Color palette for your convenience.

✔ **Color sliders and color value boxes:** You can create a new color by dragging these sliders to the left or right. The color in the Fill or Stroke box (whichever is in front) updates to reflect the change, as does any selected artwork. To specify an exact amount of a particular color, type a number into the Color Value box to the right of each color slider.

✔ **None:** Click the None button to choose a Stroke or Fill value of None.

✔ **Black-and-white:** You guessed it! Click black to make the color black, and white to make it white. (Wait a minute. Was that a trick question?)

✔ **Spectrum bar:** In this little rectangle are all the colors that you can possibly create. Click anywhere on the Spectrum bar to choose a color. Well, okay, the spectrum is tiny; almost nobody picks exactly the right color on the first click. Use the spectrum to get a color that's in the right ballpark. Then use the sliders to make the color precisely what you want.

✔ **Out-of-gamut color warnings:** As you create colors, tiny color boxes appear, warning you whether the color is outside the color gamut for print or the Web. (The *gamut* is the total range of colors that a method can create without having to alter any of the colors.) For the Web, the gamut is 216 colors; for print, it's several thousand. If you choose a color outside this range, that color can shift to another color. The *Out-of-Web color warning* is a square of color with a little cube beside it; the *Out-of-gamut warning for print* is a square with an exclamation point inside a triangle beside it. Click the square to choose a color within the gamut that's closest to the color you chose. If you're creating for the Web, you can ignore the print gamut warning — and vice versa if you're creating for print.

To create a new color by using the Color palette, follow these steps:

1. **Choose Window⇨Color.**

   The Color palette appears.

2. **From the Color palette's pop-up menu, choose a color model.**

   See the upcoming section "Modes and Models" for more information.

3. **Click the Fill or Stroke box in the palette.**

4. **Move the sliders of each component color to the left or to the right until the color you want appears in the Stroke or Fill box.**

Of course, if you actually want to use the colors that you create in the Color palette (what a concept), you can do so in a couple of ways:

✔ **Use the color while you use the palette.** Anything already selected when you create a new Fill or Stroke color is filled or stroked with that color. (For example, you can fill a selected pterodactyl with pteal or pturquoise.)

✔ **Save the new color for later.** After you create the new color, you can save it to use again later. Here's how:

1. **Open the Swatches palette by choosing Window⇨Swatches.**

   The Swatches palette appears.

2. **Click the Fill or Stroke box (whichever you just created) in either the Toolbox or the Color palette.**

3. **Drag the Fill or Stroke box onto the Swatches palette**.

   Don't worry, you won't damage the Color palette when you drag away the Fill or Stroke box. Instead, you get a ghostly outline of the box while you drag it away. Release that outline on top of the Swatches palette to add the Fill or Stroke to the palette.

   After you release the mouse, the color shows up in the Swatches palette for you to use again and again! (Pteal pterodactyls ptravel in flocks? Who knew?)

With the new color in the Swatches palette, you can double-click it to open the Swatch Options dialog box. Here you can give it a name, make it a global color, or use any of the options we describe in the earlier section "Swatch Options for super colors."

Modes and models

Mode and *model* are the Illustrator terms to define color. *Color mode* is the language of color your document speaks — either CMYK or RGB. *Color model* is a way of describing how to form the colors in the mode (color-language) your document uses.

All the colors used in the document (except spot colors) exist in one particular color mode, no matter what color model you use to create them. When you open a new document, you must decide whether to work in RGB or CMYK color. (See Chapter 1 for the tale of two color modes.) Choose a color model by clicking the pop-up menu for the Color palette; see Figure 5-10 for a mug shot.

Figure 5-10:
Different
color
models
within the
Color
palette.

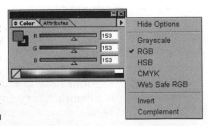

Suppose, for example, that you want a shade of gray while you're working in RGB mode. Shades of gray are hard to create in RGB because you have to drag all three red, green, and blue sliders to get the color you want. To dodge that complexity, switch the color model to Grayscale in the Color palette. Then you have just one slider to deal with and you can quickly create the exact shade of gray you want.

The Color palette is where you create the colors you need, using a variety of color models: Grayscale, RGB, HSB, CMYK, and Web Safe RGB. Each has a specific purpose, but really these different colors exist only to help you visualize the color that you're trying to create. The Color palette enables you to mix colors in any color model, but as soon as you apply them, they convert to the color mode you're using.

The following list describes these color models and the best ways to use each:

- **Grayscale:** Colors express everything as a shade of gray. This model is handy when you're creating a black-and-white printing or just want a quick way to specify a shade of gray. Grayscale is measured in terms of ink values, with black as 100 percent — the most ink possible.

- **RGB:** Colors are based on the three colors (red, green, and blue) used by your monitor to generate all the colors that you see onscreen. These colors are designed for onscreen use, such as graphics for the Web. The amounts that you see in the Color Values boxes range from 0 to 255. They correspond to the intensity of the light projected by your computer screen. Computer screens use tiny red, green, and blue phosphors that glow with different intensities to create the colors that you see. The higher the value, the brighter the glow. Specifying 255 for all colors gives you pure white; a 0 value for all colors gives you pitch black. These numbers, however, are less important than your practical results. Pay attention to your Fill or Stroke boxes when you drag the sliders and see the color that results.

- **HSB:** Colors are seen in terms of hue, saturation, and brightness. Think of an HSB color in terms of a crayon. Hue is the color of the crayon, such as red. Saturation is how red that crayon is, such as brick red versus cherry red. Brightness is equivalent to how hard you press down when you use that crayon. This way of thinking may seem weird, but many painters and traditional artists find it very intuitive.

- **CMYK:** Colors are based on the four colors (cyan, magenta, yellow, and black) used in process printing. (Cyan is a light, bright blue; magenta is a bright purple color that's almost pink. You're on your own for yellow and black.) CMYK colors are designed to specify colors for print. *Process printing* enables people to achieve a wide variety of colors (including photographic-looking images) using only those four colors. CMYK colors work the opposite of the way RGB colors work: The more of each individual color, the darker the total color becomes. For instance, 0 percent of cyan, magenta, yellow, and black results in white; 100 percent of cyan, magenta, yellow, and black results in black. But nobody who knows better would ever create black for print by using 100 percent of all four colors — that would put way too much ink on the paper, resulting in a sticky mess.

Well, okay, in theory you could create black by using 100 percent of cyan, magenta, and yellow — but printing inks (for the most part) are too cheaply made for that approach to work. To create a black that really looks black, you have to add black to cyan, magenta, and yellow (fortunately, black ink is cheaper than those colors). Try using 100 percent black for black, adding just a little of the other three colors to make it look really black. (Such complications of even a basic concept may have driven some folks to make graphics only for the Web.)

✔ **Web Safe RGB:** Most folks are probably used to working with the 16.7 million colors that most computer monitors can display these days. Of those colors, however, only 216 of them display consistently on Windows, Unix, and Macintosh computers. This reduced range of color is because of differences in operating systems, Web browsers, and color cards. Colors outside this range of 216 can dither when displayed on a system that can't really show them properly. *Dithering* is the computer's attempt to create the missing colors by using dots of two colors it can display, creating an optical illusion that the missing color is there. Dithering usually looks awful. (See Chapter 17 for more on dithering.)

Use Web Safe RGB when you need colors that look their best on as many different computers and browsers as possible. (A corporate logo is a classic example.)

✔ **Hide Options, Invert,** and **Complement:** The remaining choices aren't color models at all. Hide Options collapses the Color palette so that just the Spectrum, Black and White, and None show. Invert changes the selected color into its opposite, as if you had taken a color photograph of it and were looking at a negative. To understand Complement, think back to art class and the color wheel: *Complementary colors* are the colors on opposite sides of the color wheel. (Orange, for example, is the complementary color to blue. Roughly. Blue never looks more blue than when it's next to orange, and vice versa.) Put another way, choosing Complement chooses the one color that will contrast the most with the currently selected artwork.

Filling with Patterns and Textures

You can fill and stroke any path with a pattern. Patterns fill areas with repeating artwork.

Applying patterns to paths

To fill a path with a pattern, select the path, make sure the Fill box is active by clicking it in the Toolbox, and then click the pattern you want to use in the Swatches palette. The path fills with the pattern you selected. Figure 5-11 shows the same path filled with different patterns.

Figure 5-11:
The same
path with
several
different
pattern fills.

You can apply a pattern to a stroke as well as to a fill. Applying a pattern is exactly like applying a solid color. (See the section "The Swatches Palette" earlier in this chapter.) Click the object, click the Fill or Stroke box to put the pattern in the proper place, and then click the pattern swatch in the Swatches palette. When you apply a pattern to a stroke, you may need to make the stroke extra thick for the pattern to be visible. (See the section "Making a bold stroke" earlier in this chapter.)

Making patterns

You can easily turn most path-based artwork into a pattern (which hotly pursues the steps required to create a pattern out of paths).

To create a pattern out of paths, just follow these steps:

1. **Create the artwork that you want to use for a pattern.**

   For this example, a hammer.

2. **Select the artwork by using any of the Selection tools.**

3. **Drag the artwork from the document window onto the Swatches palette and release the mouse button.**

   A new swatch appears in the Swatches palette containing a very tiny version of your artwork. Give the new swatch a name to make it easier to identify later.)

4. **To name the new swatch, double-click it to open the Swatch Options dialog box.**

5. **In this dialog box, enter the name of the pattern.**

6. **Click OK.**

    The custom pattern appears in the Swatches dialog box.

7. **Apply your custom pattern to any path.**

    Our pattern inside the oval certainly hammers home the point (sorry about that). Check it out in Figure 5-12.

Occasionally, you may want to space out your pattern artwork so that the repeated pieces of artwork are farther away from each other. You can easily trick Illustrator into doing this by drawing an invisible rectangle (a rectangle with a fill and stroke of None) over your artwork. The bigger the rectangle, the farther apart the repeated pieces are. Select the artwork and the rectangle before you make your pattern. Illustrator isn't quite smart enough to realize that the rectangle is invisible. The program sees only the paths that make the rectangle and repeats the artwork based on those edges.

Using the Gradient Fill

Paths can be filled with colors that smoothly blend from one to another across a distance. These colors are *gradients*. Gradients can have any number of colors in them, with results that are nothing short of astonishing. Figure 5-13 shows several paths with gradient fills.

Figure 5-13: Path objects with gradient fills.

Filling a path with a gradient involves two steps: creating the gradient and then applying it to a path. However, you can do this in any order. Often, it's easier to create a gradient, apply it to a path, and then continue to tweak it by changing, adding, or removing colors or by modifying the position or angle of the gradient. You can see how the gradient looks on an object instead of just in a small box.

To fill a path with a gradient, select the path and then click a gradient in the Swatches palette. The object fills with a gradient that probably doesn't look a thing like what you want — but that's okay. By using the Gradient tool and the Gradient palette, you can tweak this gradient to your heart's content.

1.

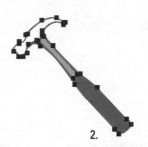

2.

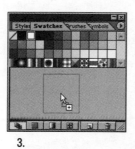

3.

4.

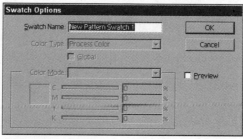

5.

6.

Figure 5-12:
Creating a
pattern from
vector art of
a hammer.

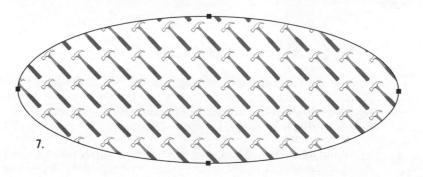

7.

The Gradient tool

 The Gradient tool (shown in the margin) doesn't actually create anything. Instead, it enables you to set the direction and the *duration* (the distance across which the gradient makes its transition from the beginning color to the ending color).

To use the Gradient tool, first use any Selection tool to select an object that's filled with a gradient. Then click and drag across the gradient with the Gradient tool and release the mouse button when you get to the other side. The direction that you drag sets the direction of the blend. The place where you click gets 100 percent of the start color; the place where you release gets 100 percent of the end color. The gradient happens as a smooth blend between those two points (as you can see in Figure 5-14).

Figure 5-14:
Left: The square shows a default gradient applied. Center: Clicking and dragging with the Gradient tool. Right: The result.

 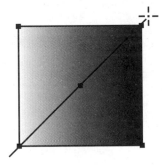 

The Gradient palette

If you don't like the colors of your gradient, you don't have to settle for the gradients that come in the Swatches palette. You can use the Gradient palette (by choosing Window⇨Gradient) to change colors, add colors, remove colors, and change the way the colors behave. (See Figure 5-15.)

 The Gradient palette looks simple compared with other palettes, but don't be deceived. In spite of its humble appearance, this palette lets you create just about any gradient you could ever want. The Gradient palette works with the Color palette and the Swatches palette, so keep both those palettes open whenever you edit a gradient.

Figure 5-15:
Control
color with
the Gradient
palette.

The *gradient sliders* slide left and right. You use them to change how gradually (or not-so-gradually) your colors blend with each other. If you want the colors to blend without much nuance over a short distance, drag the sliders closer together. If you want the colors to blend more gradually across a longer distance, move the sliders farther apart.

Gradient-mania: Color-tweaking made simple

When you change a gradient in the Gradient palette, selected objects that are filled with that gradient update to reflect that change. You can see what's going on with the gradient more easily if you make an object and fill it with the gradient before you start making changes in the palette.

To change gradient colors, here's the highly artistic approach (no smock needed):

1. **Click one of the gradient sliders beneath the gradient bar.**

   The color of the slider appears in the Color palette.

2. **Create a different color in the Color palette.**

   As long as the gradient slider is selected, the color updates in the Gradient palette automatically. Is that slick or what?

   As an alternative, you can click any solid color in the Swatches palette and drag it to the Gradient slider in the Gradient palette. You can also press the Alt key (Windows) or Option (Mac) and simply click on a solid color swatch in the Swatches palette. The gradient updates with the new color.

Adding colors to the gradient is a lot easier than going to the paint store. Just follow these steps:

1. **Click beneath the gradient bar where there isn't any gradient slider.**

   A new slider appears where you click.

2. **Change the color of the new slider in the Color palette or press the Alt key or Option (Mac) and click on a solid color in the Swatches palette.**

3. **Adjust the position of your gradient sliders if you desire.**

To remove a color, click the gradient slider and drag it off the Gradient palette. To save the gradient, drag the gradient swatch from the gradient palette (or from the fill box in the Toolbox) to the Swatches palette. You can also simply click the New Swatch button (a dog-eared page icon) in the Swatches palette.

Between every pair of gradient sliders (on top of the gradient bar) is the midpoint slider. This sets the point at which the two colors blend at 50 percent of each color. You can also move this point by dragging it to the left or to the right. Figure 5-16 gives you a look at different ways to change the gradient.

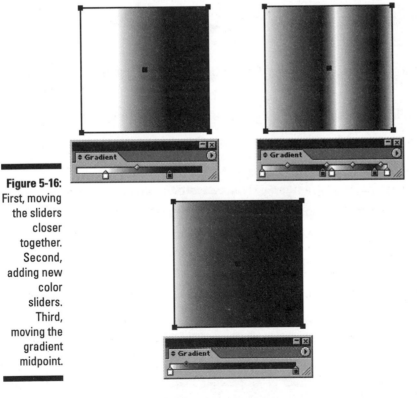

Figure 5-16: First, moving the sliders closer together. Second, adding new color sliders. Third, moving the gradient midpoint.

The secret Gradient

If you click the gradient swatches in the Swatches palette, you may notice that some gradients look like spheres or sunbursts. You may have tried to recreate one of these gradients, but no amount of clicking and dragging with the Gradient tool — and no amount of moving gradient sliders — enables you to do that.

The trick is in a hidden option in the Gradient palette. Click the little triangle in the upper-right corner of the Gradient palette. A menu with only one item (Show Options) appears. Choose this option to make several more options appear in the palette, as shown in Figure 5-17. The one you want is the Type option, which reveals two choices: Linear and Radial. Choose Radial. You edit radial gradients just as you do linear gradients. The only difference is that radial gradients radiate from the center. The beginning color is the center color. When you click and drag, the spot where you click sets the center of the gradient.

Figure 5-17:
Choose
Show
Options
from the
pop-up
menu to
work with
a radial
gradient.

 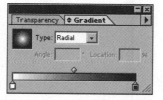

If you're creating a linear gradient, you can enter an angle or direction, from –180 to 180, for your gradient in the Angle option box. For both linear and radial gradients, you can enter a percentage, from 0% to 100%, in the Location option box. This moves the selected gradient slider to that location on the gradient bar.

Chapter 6

Selecting and Editing Paths

* *

In This Chapter

▶ Discovering different methods of selection

▶ Selecting objects, points, and groups

▶ Adding to and taking away from selections

▶ Using the new Magic Wand tool

▶ Selecting without tools

▶ Understanding the new Select menu

▶ Fine-tuning points

* *

*T*o change a path in Illustrator, you have to select it. In fact, 99 percent of the time you can't make any changes at all to a path unless it's selected. Some exceptions are when you change Document Color Mode (see Chapter 1) and when you use the Pen tool to continue on an existing path (see Chapter 7). Everything else requires that you make a selection.

When you make a selection in Illustrator, you're saying, "From this moment forward, I want to change this part of the artwork and nothing else." You're targeting a point, path, object, or objects for change. By using Illustrator's wide variety of Selection tools and commands, you can target everything from a single point to your entire document. And the changes you make — the size, rotation, fill or stroke colors, and so on — simultaneously affect everything that you select.

Selecting with Different Methods

Suppose you create a mondo-cool logo. With Illustrator, you can select

- The entire logo
- Any group of paths within the logo
- Any single path within the logo
- Any portion of any path or paths

All these possibilities make selecting in Illustrator seem a rather daunting task. As if that weren't enough, Illustrator gives you six different Selection tools, as shown in Figure 6-1. In the following sections, you find out about these tools and what happens when you use them.

Selection

Direct Selection

Group Selection

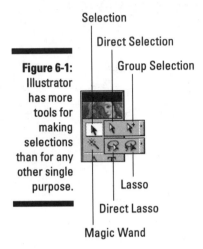

Figure 6-1:
Illustrator
has more
tools for
making
selections
than for any
other single
purpose.

Lasso

Direct Lasso

Magic Wand

Natural selection

Of the six Selection tools in Illustrator — Selection, Direct Selection, Group Selection, Lasso, Direct Select Lasso, and the new Magic Wand — the Selection tool is more-or-less the main Selection tool. It simply selects whatever you click. (The names of the other Selection tools aren't quite as accurate in describing their functions, but hey — *Selection tool* was already taken.) To keep the confusion to a minimum, we call the tools by their Adobe-given names — in part so you know what the cute label refers to when you pause the cursor over a tool and see the name in the ToolTip.

You use the Selection tool to select objects or groups of objects. When you click a path, you select the entire path. If the path is part of a group, you select that group as well. A *group* is two or more separate objects that are joined together by choosing Object➪Group. You join objects into a group to get the advantage of selecting all of them at once when you use the Selection tool to select them — which saves all that tedious clicking. (The Object➪ Group command is just one of the fiendishly clever ways you can organize things in Illustrator — explore 'em all in Chapter 14.)

You can select onscreen items with the Selection tool in two ways:

- **Click the object that you want to select.** The object and any other object that's grouped with it are selected.

- **Click and drag with the Selection tool.** As you do, a dotted rectangle called a *marquee* appears. Anything inside or touching the marquee is selected, enabling you to select more than one object or group at a time, as shown in Figure 6-2.

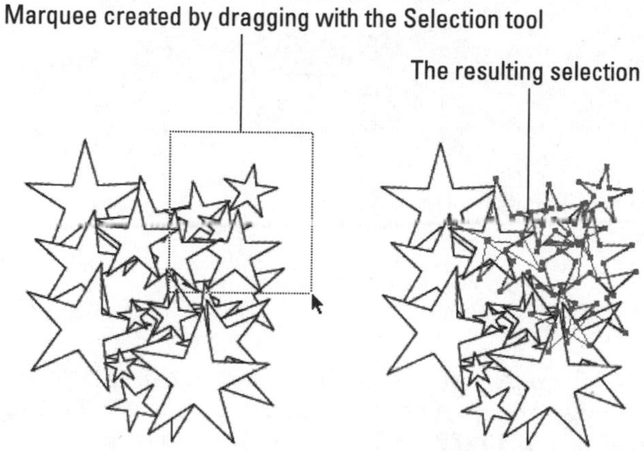

Marquee created by dragging with the Selection tool

The resulting selection

Figure 6-2:
The Selection tool selects objects that are within (or touched by) the marquee.

If you click another path when one path is already selected, the path that you click is selected — and the previously selected path is deselected. If you click an empty area, *everything* is deselected.

Also, if you click inside a path that's filled with None, you can't select that path. To select a path that has no fill, click the path itself. Similarly, when you're in Outline view mode (a way of looking at your paths with all fill and stroke colors hidden, accessed by selecting View⇔Outline), you click your paths to select them. (See Chapter 5 for more info on fills and strokes.)

Direct selection

Use the Direct Selection tool to select individual points, path segments, type objects, and placed images by clicking them one at a time. If you drag a marquee with the Direct Selection tool, everything that the marquee encloses gets selected — all placed images, type objects, and portions of paths. Figure 6-3 shows what's selected when you drag the Direct Selection marquee around several objects. (Note especially the star in the very center of the selected objects at the right of the figure: Some of its points are included in the selection; others aren't.)

Marquee created by dragging with the Direct Selection tool

The resulting selection (note that only what was inside the marquee is selected)

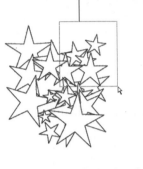

Figure 6-3:
A selection in progress with the Direct Selection tool.

Anchor point of unselected object
(or part of object) that was outside marquee

Anchor point of a selected object

With the Direct Selection tool, if you select the interior of a path (if it's filled) rather than the edge or actual line of the path, you select the entire path rather than just the individual anchor point and path segments.

Group selection

Illustrator provides a special tool (Group Selection) for selecting — surprise! — groups. But the tool selects groups in a way different from the plain old Selection tool (which selects everything that's grouped to the object that you select). The Group Selection tool selects only one subgroup at a time.

A *subgroup* is a group within a group. Remember Statistics 101? (Don't make that face. What if it froze like that?) Suppose you want to create a graphic of a pencil. You start with the easy part — the lead. Then you go on to create something harder: that conical bit of wood that flares out around the lead and eventually becomes the rest of the pencil. After you get those two pieces positioned together the way you like, you want to keep them that way — so you group them together. (That way, you have to click only one of them with the Selection tool, and they move together.) Next, you create the rest of the pencil separately. After you bring all the pieces together, you want to keep them that way — so you group the lead and the cone with the rest of the pencil. All three objects are now a group. The lead and the cone are a subgroup of that group. You can continue grouping things, having as many subgroups as you want. Illustrator remembers the order in which you group things from the first subgroup to the last big group. So when you click multiple times with the Group

Selection tool, the first click selects the pencil lead, the second selects both the lead and the wood, the third click selects the lead, the wood, and the rest of the pencil.

The Group Selection tool selects only one subgroup at a time, such as an object within a group, a single group within multiple groups, or a set of groups within the artwork. To find out how the Group Selection tool works, follow these steps:

1. **Select the Group Selection tool from the Toolbox.**

2. **Click a path that's part of a group.**

   The path is selected entirely (all the points are solid; none are hollow), but the other objects in the group are not selected. (This result is an oddity of the tool. It first selects a single object, even though an object isn't really a group.)

3. **Click the same path again.**

   The next higher level of grouped objects is selected, as well as anything that has already been selected. Each time you click, you select the next higher level of grouping, until finally the all-encompassing group-of-all-groups is selected.

If you continue this crazed clicking, you wind up with groups of groups. For example, if you make several onscreen drawings of pencils, you can group them so that you can move them all at once, draw a pencil box, and then group the pencils with the box. The Group Selection tool lets you select "up" from a single object to the group that the object belongs to, and so on. Figure 6-4 applies this principle to the objects that form a pencil when grouped together.

Two oddities of selecting in Illustrator

When selecting in Illustrator, you may find a couple of oddities. For example, if you select just a point on a path, the point is all that you've selected. It shows up solid, but the rest of the points on the path remain unselected and show up as hollow. Then things get weird. Even though only one point is selected, any change that you make to the fill or stroke affects the entire path. (For more information on fills and strokes, see Chapter 5.)

Another odd thing is that you can select a line segment, but Illustrator never shows you that the line segment is selected. If you click a segment, all the points on its path show as unselected (hollow). Nothing appears onscreen to indicate that only the segment is selected — but once again, changing the fill or stroke affects the entire path.

Figure 6-4:
Group
Selection
tool selects
first the
path, then
the group
that the path
is in, and
then the
group that
the first
group is in.

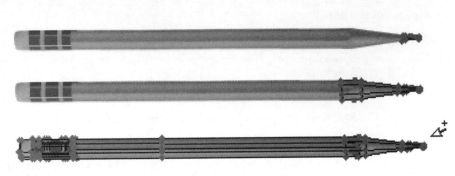

Selecting more or less of what you have

Suppose you want to select a path on the left side of your document, and you also want to select a placed image on the right side of your document, but lots of paths are in between. You can't drag a marquee because you get all those unwanted paths in the middle. So you select the path on the left and then click the object on the right — and the path on the left becomes deselected. Drat!

Use the Shift key to select more than one item at a time. If you hold down the Shift key and click a path with the Selection tool, you add that path to whatever is currently selected. If two paths are selected, pressing the Shift key and clicking another path results in all three paths being selected. You can also use the Shift key in conjunction with a selection marquee. The process is called *Shift-clicking,* and you can also use it to select fewer paths. For example, if you Shift-click one of the three selected paths shown in Figure 6-5, you deselect that path, leaving only two selected paths.

Shift-clicking also works with the Direct Selection tool, except this action adds or subtracts single points instead of complete paths, unless you click the interior of a filled path, in which case you add or subtract complete paths.

Freeform selections

The Lasso tool and the Direct Select Lasso tool act similarly to dragging out a selection marquee, except this marquee can be any shape, not just rectangular. To use either tool, click and drag around the area that you want to select. When you release the mouse button, all objects or groups touching that selection are selected. (If you're using the Direct Select Lasso tool, all points in that area are selected.)

Figure 6-5:
On the left are three selected paths. Shift-clicking the middle path leaves only two paths selected, as shown on the right.

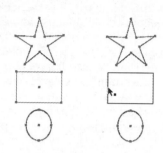

Selecting Magically with the Magic Wand

 No longer reserved solely for Photoshoppers, the much beloved Magic Wand tool (in the margin) makes its debut in this version of Illustrator. Offering a wide array of selection criteria, this tool can make your selection woes a thing of the past.

Working wizardry with the Wand

Use the Magic Wand tool to make selections based on similarities in various object attributes — exactly the same or based on a range of settings.

To use the new tool, click on the object, which can be either an open or closed path (for example, a square or a line). Illustrator then goes out and selects all objects that are similar to the object you clicked. How similar do the objects have to be? Excellent question! Read on to get the scoop.

Magic Wand options

Choose Window⇨Magic Wand or simply double-click the Magic Wand tool to bring up the Magic Wand palette, as shown in Figure 6-6. Here you find settings for Fill, Stroke, Stroke Weight, Opacity, and Blending Mode attributes. Checking one or more of these attributes selects objects based on that particular attribute or attributes. The tolerance setting establishes the range within which the attribute must fall to be selected. For example, if you select stroke weight with a tolerance of 2 points (pt) and click an object with a stroke weight of 5 pt, all objects with a stroke weight between 3 and 7 pt will be selected (5pt minus 2pt, and 5pt plus 2pt). Similarly, if you check Opacity and set your tolerance to 10%, all objects with an opacity between 40% and 60% are selected when you click an object with an opacity of 50%. The Tolerance settings for Fill and Stroke ranges from 0 to 255, which equates to the number of brightness levels. Rather than go into the techno-geek definition of brightness levels, a lower Tolerance number selects only colors that are very similar to the object you click, whereas a higher Tolerance number selects a wider range of colors. The only attribute that must be exactly the same is Blending Mode. (For more on blending modes, see Chapter 10.)

Figure 6-6:
The Magic Wand palette offers tolerance settings for various object attributes.

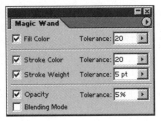

Selecting without Tools: The New Select Menu

Sometimes selecting objects in Illustrator without using tools is easier or more convenient than selecting with tools. Although Illustrator 9 has a few selection options under the Edit menu, Illustrator 10 provides a new menu entirely devoted to selection commands.

A giant vat of really sticky stuff

By far, the most common selection method in Illustrator is a keyboard command. By pressing Ctrl+A (⌘+A on the Mac), you select all the objects in the document. You can also choose Select⇨All, but the keyboard command is so useful that you'll probably memorize it in no time at all.

The opposite of All is Deselect, which deselects anything selected in the document (but you knew that). You don't have to select everything to use the command. If you have just one thing selected out of a hundred objects, Deselect deselects it. The keyboard command is easy to remember: Ctrl+A (⌘+A on the Mac).

The new Reselect command is a handy addition to the selecting repertoire. This command reselects whatever was last selected using the Selection menu. The keyboard command is Ctrl+6 (⌘+6 on the Mac).

The Inverse command selects the art opposite of what's currently selected. In other words, everything that's currently selected becomes unselected, and everything else becomes selected. For example, if you select one of four squares, using the Inverse command selects the remaining three squares. Inverse works only with entire paths. (The same goes for Reselect.) Using the same example, if you have only a single anchor point selected on the first square, Illustrator still selects the other three squares and ignores the unselected three anchor points on the other three squares.

Two new commands — Next Object Above and Next Object Below — select objects based on their stacking order. For example, say you draw a square, a circle, and then a polygon. If you then select the square and choose Select⇨Next Object Below, Illustrator selects the circle. If you choose the command again, Illustrator selects the polygon, and so forth.

The Save Selection command allows you to save selections. Select an object (or objects) and choose Select⇨Save Selection. In the Save Selection dialog box, name the selection and click OK. The saved selection now appears at the bottom of the Select menu, just begging to be chosen. You can delete the saved selection or modify its name by choosing Select⇨Edit Selection and making the necessary changes in the Edit Selection dialog box.

The Select⇨Layer⇨All command selects everything that resides on the layer, selecting only the text on a layer. This is especially handy if you have several blocks of text.

Specialized selection functions for important occasions

The Select menu contains a lot of other selection functions besides those mentioned in the earlier section "A giant vat of really sticky stuff." Located under the Same and Object submenus, these functions are designed to select objects that are similar in some way (such as style or fill color) to the object(s) already selected. Figure 6-7 shows the Select menu.

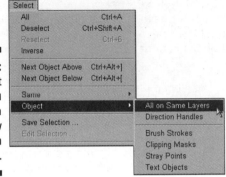

Figure 6-7:
The Select
menu
provides a
whole slew
of selection
goodies.

The four options that fall under the Object submenu are a bit less obvious:

- ✔ **Brush Strokes:** Selects all paths in the document that have brush strokes assigned to them.

- ✔ **Clipping Masks:** Selects paths used as masks in the document.

- ✔ **Direction Handles:** Selects the direction handles of the Bézier curves of selected objects. (For more on direction handles, see the next section "Editing and Adjusting Points.")

- ✔ **Stray Points:** Selects paths in your document that contain only a single point.

All these commands can be vastly helpful in streamlining the editing process. For instance, if your client loves everything about the image except for that certain shade of blue, you can select one object that has that blue color in it, and then choose Select ⇨Same⇨Stroke Color or Fill Color. With everything in that color selected, you can edit them all at once! If you're having trouble printing lines of a certain stroke weight, choose Select⇨Same⇨Stroke Weight and increase the stroke weight of all the lines. (See Chapter 5 for more information on fills and strokes.) Other commands select items that have a history of problems printing on certain printers, such as stray points, brushstrokes, and masks. Selecting such items lets you modify them before printing. (See Chapter 16 for more about printing.)

Editing and Adjusting Points

After you go through the trouble of selecting specific points, what will you do with them? Well, you can move them and change the kinds of points they are. You can also adjust their handles to change the shape of a curve.

A relocation bonus for points

You can move any selected point to any location. Because points (and not entire paths) are what you're moving, use the Direct Selection tool. Click any point with the Direct Selection tool and then drag the point to move it. You can do this in one step (click and drag at once) or in two separate steps (click and release and then drag the point). Figure 6-8 shows a path with a point in its original location after it was moved with the Direct Selection tool.

Figure 6-8:
Left: The original path. Right: The path after you move the selected point with Direct Selection.

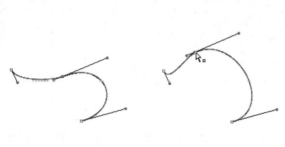

To move points just a tiny little bit at a time — but with precision — use the arrow keys to "nudge" selected points in the direction of the arrow. One keystroke moves the point by an exact, smidgen-sized unit of measurement ($\frac{1}{72}$ of an inch, or .3528 millimeters) — a unit of measure known in the design and publishing trades as a *point*.

Fine-tuning curves with direction points

If a point has *direction points* (those little gearshift-like line segments) sticking out of it, you can use the Direct Selection tool to adjust the direction points, which adjusts the curves that shoot out from the points where the direction points connect to the curves.

Incidentally, the line that joins the direction point to the curve is called the *direction line*. Don't worry, only you can see the direction lines. They don't print or show up in the graphic when it's on the Web. Their only purpose is to show which anchor point is currently under the control of the direction point. The combination of the direction line and direction point is also commonly referred to as *direction handles* or just plain *handles*.

You probably noticed already that sometimes you see those gearshift-like direction lines and direction points sticking out of points and sometimes you don't. When you click a point or a segment with the Direct Selection tool, you see the handles associated with that point or segment. However, if you Shift+click additional points, you lose those handles. Figure 6-9 shows what happens when you use the Direct Selection tool to click (or enclose in a marquee) a variety of different areas.

Figure 6-9:
A selected curve reveals its direction points and direction lines.

When you can see the handles that you want to move, click and drag them. Note that missing a handle is very easy if you aren't really careful. (And making crude remarks when you do miss them is still considered bad form, even if no one else is around.) Figure 6-10 (in the following section) shows the path from Figure 6-9 with the direction points moved to different positions.

Converting anchor points

Illustrator has three types of anchor points: corner points, smooth points, and direction-changing points. *Corner points* are in the corners of squares or triangles. Two path segments join in a corner point when neither of the connecting ends has a direction point associated with it. *Smooth points* are used when two path segments continue smoothly, as in a circle or in a curving path. Both path segments have direction points linked together so that when you move one point, the other point moves in an equal and opposite direction, preserving the smooth curve. A *direction-changing point* has two direction points that move in different directions, enabling you to impose abrupt changes in direction. (For more on anchor point types, see Chapter 7.)

Figure 6-10:
The curve
from Figure
6-9 after the
direction
points are
moved.

You can use Illustrator's Convert Anchor Point tool (which looks like an acute angle located in the same slot as the Pen tool) to change a point from one type into another. (For more about the types of anchor points and their usual behaviors, see Chapters 2 and 7.) To use the Convert Anchor Point tool, put it on a point and click. What you do next determines the resulting point type:

✔ **To get a corner point:** Click an anchor point and release to change it into a straight corner point with no direction points.

  This is a *quick-retract* method of point conversion.

✔ **To get a smooth point:** Click an anchor point and drag it to change it into a smooth point with two linked direction points.

✔ **To get a direction-changing point:** Click a direction point and drag. It moves independently of the opposite direction point.

Adding and subtracting points (path math)

Illustrator has two tools that are used specifically for adding points to a path or for removing them. The Add Anchor Point tool adds points, and the Delete Anchor Point tool removes points. Both tools are located in the same slot as the Pen tool.

When you add an anchor point (or even several anchor points) with the Add Anchor Point tool, the path doesn't change shape (as shown in Figure 6-11), but you can move the point or points with the Direct Selection tool or convert them to other types of points by using the Convert Anchor Point tool.

Figure 6-11:
Left: Original
path. Right:
Unchanged
shape with
new anchor
points
added to
three of the
star's arms.

When you remove a point with the Delete Anchor Point tool, the path can change shape — either slightly or dramatically, depending on the shape. Figure 6-12 shows what happens in two different circumstances.

Figure 6-12:
Left: Original
path. Right:
Removing
two anchor
points to
create two
different
shapes.

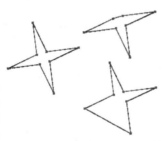

Okay, have a squint at Figure 6-12 for a moment. (Ow, that's gotta hurt. Not that hard.) You can probably tell immediately which anchor points were zapped with the Delete Anchor Point tool to change the image on the left into the upper- and lower-right images. In each case, only one point was removed. Powerful creatures, those anchor points.

Chapter 7

Wielding the Mighty Pen Tool

In This Chapter

▶ Using the Pen tool to create four different anchor points

▶ Drawing straight lines with the Pen tool

▶ Exploring the differences between open and closed paths

▶ Drawing smooth-curved lines with the Pen tool

▶ Making a seamless transition between curved and straight lines

▶ Drawing basic shapes with the Pen tool

$\mathcal{B}$ack in medieval times, circa 1982, straight and smooth-curved lines were drawn with elegant handheld implements — such as a Rapidograph pen (an unwieldy tool), a ruler, and a French Curve. If you never had to use these torturous instruments, consider yourself lucky. With a Rapidograph pen, you got bumpy globs of ink and huge splotches that goosh onto the page each time you paused or changed direction.

 Today, if you need a straight line or a curved one — or even if you *want* the appearance of bumpy globs of ink — you want to use the Illustrator Pen tool. This tool is a bit intimidating at first, but after you grasp a few concepts, you'll be drawing floor plans, customizing logos, and feeling really sorry for people who don't have Illustrator.

Unlike its handheld, inky counterpart, the Pen tool is not intuitive. You can't just pick it up and doodle; its functionality is far from obvious. This tool is unlike any drawing instrument in the world. But locked within the Pen tool are secrets and powers beyond those of mere physical ink. The Pen tool is a metaphysical doorway to the heavens of artistic exaltation; after you master the path of the Pen, all the riches of Illustrator can be yours. (You may even be unfazed by such hokey metaphors.)

Performing with the Pen, the Path, and the Anchor Points

No, this section isn't a retro look at obscure rock bands; it's about telling Illustrator where to go — by creating the paths Illustrator relies on to create shapes and objects. *Paths* are instructions that tell your computer how to arrange straight- and curved-line segments onscreen. Each path is made up of *anchor points* (dots that appear onscreen). Between every two anchor points is the portion of the path called a *line segment*.

The Pen tool is probably as close as you ever get to calling up paths with the PostScript language — unless you're an Adobe programming geek (in which case, the thought that you might need this book is frightening). For sanity's sake, we assume otherwise and get right to the point. Make that *points*. Understanding the anchor points that make up paths is critical to using the Pen tool. Anchor points have the following traits:

- At least two anchor points are required for every path. ("One point maketh not a path," sayeth the sage.)

- Any number of anchor points can appear on a path — dozens, even hundreds, as long as that number is *not* one or zero. ("Zero points make not a path, either, O wiseacre," grouseth the sage.)

- If an anchor point has a *direction point* (a black box you can grab and move with the mouse), the line segment extending from the anchor point is curved.

  Direction point is the official Adobe term for this handy little black box. You may also hear Illustrator veterans talk about *handles* or *control handles* — same thing.

- If an anchor point has no direction point, the line segment extending from the anchor point is straight.

- You can use the Pen tool to create four types of anchor points (smooth, straight corner, curved corner, and combination corner) to tell the computer how to get from one line segment to another. Care for a closer look? Coming right up.

Smooth anchor points

Smooth anchor points create a smoothly curved transition from one line segment to another. When you want a line that reminds you of the letter *S* (or some S-words, such as *sinuous* and *snaky*), use smooth anchor points. Figure 7-1 shows two direction points creating a smooth anchor point on a path. The curve bends to follow the two direction points.

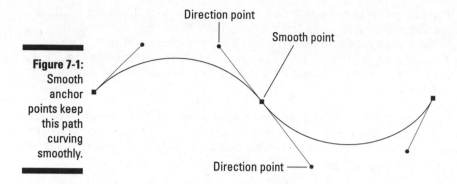

Direction point

Smooth point

Direction point

Figure 7-1:
Smooth
anchor
points keep
this path
curving
smoothly.

If you want to create circles or freeform shapes — such as puddles or shapes like those nonslip flower stickers for your bathtub floor — smooth anchor points are the way to go. Use the Pen tool to create a smooth anchor point by clicking and dragging with the mouse. As you drag, direction points, connected to the anchor point by direction lines, appear on either side of the anchor point (one at the tip of the Pen, the other on the opposite side of the anchor point). Think of those wacky direction points as magnets pulling the line segment towards them. The line segment bends to follow the direction point — just that easy, just that simple. (So far.)

Straight-corner anchor points

Straight-corner anchor points function as their name suggests and can have one of the following characteristics:

- ✔ One or two straight lines sticking out of them. In Figure 7-2, for example, the anchor point is where you find the hub if the two line segments were the hands of a clock.

- ✔ No direction points sticking out of them. (Remember, direction points make curves).

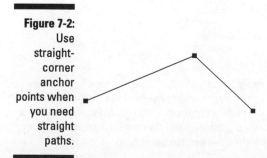

Figure 7-2:
Use
straight-
corner
anchor
points when
you need
straight
paths.

Think of these anchor points as the corner of an angle that you draw with a pencil and a protractor — except that you draw them on your computer (nobody bumps your arm so your nice sharp lead breaks off and . . . uh, never mind). To create straight-corner anchor points with the Pen tool, click and release; *do not drag*. Promptly release the mouse button the second you hear it click.

Use straight-corner anchor points to draw objects with hard angles — rectangles, triangles (note the whole "angle" theme here) — anything that consists entirely of straight lines and *no* curves. Snakes, clouds, and country roads are entirely out of the question.

Curved-corner anchor points

This book starts to take a few corners of its own here, so hold on tight. Nice grip.

Think of the *curved-corner* anchor point (also referred to as a *cusp point*) as the *m-curve* anchor point, or the point where the two bumps on a lowercase *m* are joined. If you look at this nice lowercase *m* through a magnifying glass, you can see a corner between the two bumps — with curves coming out of it. The curved-corner anchor point may also remind you of a double fishhook turned upside down. You need these points to create not just lowercase *m*'s, but also hearts (the Valentine variety, as in Figure 7-3).

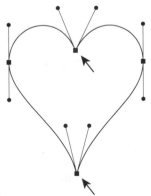

Figure 7-3: This heart, though not anatomically correct, shows two curved-corner anchor points.

Consider the possibilities — clovers, moons (old-fashioned crescents-with-little-noses), and other shapes you may see in a cereal bowl (except for blue diamonds — those you draw with straight-corner anchor points). But beware that curved-corner anchor points are a little weird. To create one, you have to modify an existing anchor point by following these steps:

1. **Create a smooth-anchor point while you're creating a path.**

   This works best after you draw at least one line segment.

2. **Press Alt (Option on a Mac) and then click-and-drag the smooth anchor point.**

   A direction point appears — totally independent of the anchor point — on the opposite side of the point. This new handle controls where the double-fishhook corner goes. You can drag the new handle nearer to the first direction point (the one for the original smooth anchor point) — or anywhere else — without affecting that first direction point.

You can also change a smooth-anchor point into a curved-corner anchor point by pressing the Alt key (Option on a Mac) as you drag the smooth anchor point.

Combination-corner anchor points

If you want to use the Pen tool to draw rounded-corner rectangles — such as classic TV screens, archways, and cylinders — you need *combination-corner* anchor points. The combination that identifies this type of anchor point is a blending of two other types: smooth- and straight-corner anchor points. You can identify a combination-corner anchor point by what you find sticking out of it: two line segments and only one direction point. This handle curves one of the line segments and leaves the other segment straight. Keep in mind that the handle is controlling the curved segment, not the straight segment, and these points are much easier to use.

As with curved-corner anchor points (mutant versions of their straight-corner cousins), you can't just say, "I want one of *those*" and *poof!* have one appear onscreen. To create the exotic combination-corner anchor point, you must modify an existing smooth- or straight-corner anchor point. Which type you modify depends on where you want the curve to go:

- If you want the curve *before* the anchor point (the existing line segment is curved), you modify a smooth-anchor point.

- If you want the curve *after* the anchor point (the existing line segment is straight), you modify a straight-corner anchor point.

Figure 7-4 shows how to create a combination-corner anchor point in either situation.

Starting with a Smooth Path   Starting with a Straight Path

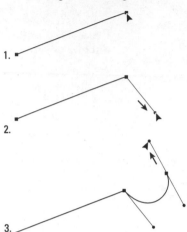

Figure 7-4:
Two ways to
create
combination-
corner
anchor
points:
starting
smooth (left)
or straight
(right).

Starting with a smooth path

To create a combination-corner anchor point from a smooth one (so that the curve precedes the anchor point), follow these steps:

1. **Click and drag the Pen tool; then, at another location, click and drag again to create a curved line.**

   To get an image that resembles Figure 7-4, start in the upper-left quarter of a blank Illustrator document, click and drag up and to the right for the first drag in Step 1. Start your second drag at a place roughly parallel to your original starting point and about an inch to the right, dragging down and to the right.

   To see what you're doing, you have to draw at least one line segment before you change the anchor point. That's the rule!

   When you complete the two drags in Step1, the most recent line segment ends in a smooth anchor point.

2. **Click the smooth-anchor point that appeared after you clicked and dragged the second time in Step 1.**

   The direction point (handle) that extended out from the anchor point disappears.

3. **Move the mouse pointer to a place about an inch to the right of the most recent anchor point and click.**

A straight path segment (straight because it's free from the influence of the direction point) appears. After you click, the two direction points (handles) disappear from the curved line that you drew in Step 1. The anchor point from which you drew your new straight segment is a combination-corner anchor point.

Starting with a straight path

To create a combination-corner anchor point from a straight-corner anchor point (so the curve comes after the anchor point), follow these steps:

1. **Using the Pen tool, click once and (without dragging) click again in a nearby location in the document.**

   To get an image that resembles the one in Figure 7-4, start in the upper-right quarter of a blank Illustrator document, click once, and then — after moving the mouse pointer to the right and slightly higher — click again.

   A straight path segment appears. You need this line segment so that you can see the difference in the path as you change the straight-corner anchor point to a combination-corner anchor point.

2. **Click the straight-corner anchor point you just created; hold down the mouse button and drag.**

   To get an image that resembles the one in Figure 7-4, drag down and slightly to the right.

   A new, single direction point (handle) extends from the anchor point.

3. **Click in another location and drag away from the anchor point.**

   To get an image that resembles the one in Figure 7-4, click a spot in line with the previous anchor point, and then drag up and slightly to the left.

   A curved path segment appears. The anchor point between the straight and curved line segments is now a combination-corner anchor point.

Creating Straight Lines with the Pen Tool

Using logic as valid as any followed by Holmes and Watson (not to mention Spock), you can deduce that you use straight-corner anchor points to draw straight lines with the Pen tool. Elementary. . . .

Harrumph. Elementary or not, you should jolly well see this marvel in action. To draw a triangle with the Pen tool (see Figure 7-5), just follow these steps:

Figure 7-5:
Drawing a triangle with the Pen tool, using straight-corner anchor points.

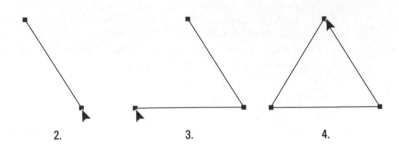

1.   2.   3.   4.

1. **With the Pen tool, click (do not drag) in the document window.**

   An anchor point appears after you release the mouse button. (Cute, isn't it? But lonely; it needs friends.)

2. **Click (don't drag) somewhere below and a little to the right of the first anchor point.**

   After you release the mouse button, a line appears between the first and second anchor points. They're joined, open, and ready to rock. You've created a fine-looking path.

3. **Click (don't drag!) somewhere a bit to the left of the second anchor point.**

   A stunning-looking angle appears. Maybe it's a skateboard ramp. Maybe it's a less-than sign flopped over, worn out from all those equations.

4. **Put your cursor on the first anchor point and click that puppy.**

   You created a triangle! Congratulations! Euclid would be proud.

If you make a mistake — such as (ahem) dragging instead of just clicking — you can always undo the last step by choosing Edit⇨Undo. Or do what all the pros do — press Ctrl+Z on the PC or ⌘+Z if you're bossing a Mac. For that extra-authentic pro sound, you can mutter something nasty about computers if you goof up.

Well, okay, you've heard this tune before, but once more with feeling: *Do not drag* if you want straight lines. If you drag, you're going to get curves. In fact, *not* dragging to get straight lines is probably harder than dragging to get curves. (If you want to take a break and go drag something, be our guest; you've earned it.)

You can create right angles and 45° angles with the Pen tool by holding down the Shift key while you draw.

Open and Closed Paths

Paths in Illustrator are either open or closed, one or the other, with nothing in between. Open and closed paths differ in the following ways:

- An *open path* has endpoints. It starts in one place and ends in another place — clearly a line segment, and not a polygon.

- A *closed path* has no starting point and no endpoint. Like that psychotic bunny in the battery commercial, it just keeps going and going in the same place — clearly the boundary of a solid shape. (Think of complete circles, Möbius strips, and so forth.)

As you draw with the Pen tool, you're creating an open path. If you click the point where you started drawing the path, you close the path. Look for the small circle icon that appears next to the cursor as you approach your starting point. It's a sure-fire sign that you're about to close the path.

Creating artwork with the Pen tool is much easier if you set your fill color to None, regardless of the final color you're going to fill your artwork with. When you use the Pen tool with a fill color selected, Illustrator treats every line you make as though it were a completed object by drawing a temporary, invisible line straight from the first anchor point in the path to the last anchor point, and then fills the enclosed area with the selected fill color. This is confusing at best because it hides parts of the path that you are creating and creates an object that appears to change shape completely with every click of the mouse. To avoid this mess, set your fill color to None while you create your path and change the fill color when the path is complete.

Creating Super-Precise Curves with the Pen Tool

Illustrator's Pen tool is a model of precision and accuracy. With it, you can draw virtually anything (or draw anything virtually). That is, of course, after you master drawing curves.

The Pen isn't designed to be maddening (as far as we know), but using it to draw successful curves *does* seem to require a psychological breakthrough. Illustrator users who struggle to figure out the Pen tool by themselves, without the handy guide you hold in your hands, may slog through months (or even years) of frustration before the breakthrough occurs. They happen upon shapes and curves that work for them — and then they finally "get it."

Therefore, we vow to spare you the pain of all that trial and error. The following sections begin this noble quest, in which we find the knight. . . .

Taming the draggin'

(Sorry about the bad pun.) Where do you want your curve to go? Just drag in that direction. We know, we know, we told you *not* to drag. But in that situation, you were making straight lines. What's even less helpful, dragging is perhaps the most anti-intuitive action imaginable for creating curves. Regardless, we charge into the fray.

If you click and drag with the intent to create a curve, you get what looks like a straight line, as shown in Figure 7-6. (Weird, isn't it?) Oddly enough, the "line" you get is twice as long as the distance you drag, extending in two directions from the spot where you initially click. After you release the mouse button, this "line" is *still* a straight line and still no curve in sight.

Figure 7-6: When creating a curve, drag out a straight line; the arrow shows the direction of the drag.

At this stage, what do you suppose is the most natural thing in the world to do? Sure — it's to drag in another direction (typically at a 90° angle) from where you last released the mouse. And what are the most natural results? An ugly, curvy bump; a new "straight" line extending in both directions from the second anchor point; and a sudden yearning to direct a few choice expletives at Illustrator.

The problem is the second anchor point. Instead of clicking and dragging at a spot near where you first released the mouse button (a *big* no-no), you always click and drag (you don't *have* to drag, but we get to that later) *away* from where you released the mouse button as shown in Figure 7-7. You understood correctly — *away.* Weird, isn't it?

To create a lovely, flowing curve for your own purposes, just follow these steps:

1. **Click and drag with the Pen tool.**

   A line extends from the anchor point where you clicked. That's okay; it's supposed to happen that way.

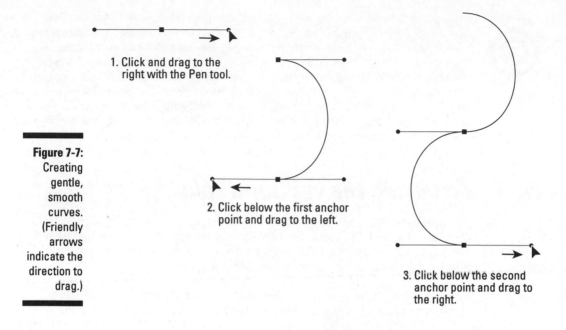

1. Click and drag to the
   right with the Pen tool.

2. Click below the first anchor
   point and drag to the left.

3. Click below the second
   anchor point and drag to
   the right.

Figure 7-7:
Creating
gentle,
smooth
curves.
(Friendly
arrows
indicate the
direction to
drag.)

The line you see is actually a set of *two direction points* (connected to
the curve by direction lines), cleverly disguised as lines with little
control-handle boxes at each end. Whether you call them direction
points or control handles, lines or boxes, they don't print out. They're
just tools for *controlling* the direction of the line segment that you're
drawing.

2. **Without clicking, place your cursor *away* from both the anchor point
   and the direction points. Then click and drag in the direction *opposite* the direction you dragged to create the first anchor point.**

   At this stage, the best approach is to place that second click perpendicu-
   lar to the direction lines. Note that as you drag, you can actually see the
   curve between the two anchor points take shape and change. If you drag
   the same distance that you dragged for the first anchor point, you create
   an even-looking curve.

3. **Finally, place your cursor away from the second point, still moving
   away from the first anchor point, and click and drag back in the same
   direction you dragged for the first anchor point.**

   After you release the mouse button, you see an *S* shape (or a backward
   S, depending on which way you first dragged). Rejoice! If you don't see
   the *S* or reverse-*S* shape, breathe deeply, count to 10, and try again, exer-
   cising superhuman patience and care. Think Clark Kent.

TIP

Remember that whole song and dance about pressing the Shift key so that new anchor points appear angled at 45° relative to the last anchor point? Well, you can also use the Shift key to *constrain* the angle of control-handle lines to 45°, if you prefer. This action lets you make much more accurate curves than by drawing freestyle. Just don't press and hold the Shift key until *after* you begin dragging with the Pen tool. If you press the Shift key before you drag — and release the key while you're dragging — you get the 45° anchor point. If you continue to hold down the Shift key, you get the whole shebang: 45° control-handle lines as well as the anchor point.

Following the one-third rule

The optimal distance to drag a direction point from an anchor point is about one-third the distance you expect that line segment to be. So, for instance, if you plan to draw a curve that's about three inches long, drag the direction point out about one inch from the anchor point.

The one-third rule is perfect for creating the most natural, organic-looking curves possible. Breaking the rule can have the following dismal results:

- If you drag too little, you get curves that are too shallow around the middle of the line segment and too sharp at the anchor points.

- If you drag too much, you get curves that are quite sharp (like Dead Man's Curve) around the middle of the line segment and too straight around the anchor points (like that curve on the right in Figure 7-8).

Fortunately, on the left, Figure 7-8 shows a "perfect" curve created with the proper use of direction point lines set to one-third the length of the path. Because you can use the Direct Selection tool (the hollow arrow) to adjust the position of the direction points after they're drawn, try to follow the one-third rule whenever possible. Doing so may keep you out of trouble and your vocabulary fit for sensitive listeners.

Figure 7-8:
Left: Anchor points with direction-point lines one-third the distance along the path. Right: Dragging too much.

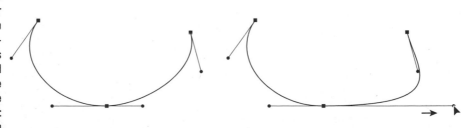

Following rules for the other two-thirds

The one-third rule is the most important rule when you're using the Pen tool to draw curves. Of course, you still have to deal with the *other* two-thirds of the line segment; that's where a few humble rules can serve you well. Even if you don't plan to follow them right away — because you're still at that awkward, rebellious age — you at least want to be familiar with these rules:

- ✔ **Drag in the direction of the path.** Dragging back toward the line segment you just drew results in hard-to-control curves and awkward-appearing line segments between the previous anchor point and the anchor point you're working with. If you need to go back toward the line segment, place an anchor point closer to the previous anchor point you created.

- ✔ **Focus on the upcoming segment as well as the current one.** You may notice that the line segment between the prior anchor point and the current anchor point can distract you because it changes as you drag. If you concentrate only on this line segment, the direction point you're dragging out for the *next* line segment probably won't be the right length or angle. You must master the past, present, and future when you use the Pen tool. (Aside from that, it isn't hard at all.)

- ✔ **Don't overcompensate for a misdrawn curve.** If you mess up on that last outgoing direction point, don't try to "fix" the line segment with the anchor point you're currently dragging. Instead, focus on the *next* segment; try to ignore the goof-up for now. You can always use the Direct Selection tool to fix the poor thing *after* you finish the path. Chapter 6 has the lowdown on how you can adjust your path after you draw it.

- ✔ **Use different lengths for each direction point, as necessary.** This rule is the exception to the previous two rules. (You knew there had to be an exception.) If you click and drag and get a segment just right — only to realize that the next segment requires a longer or shorter control-handle line but the same angle — *release the mouse button when the segment is just right*. Then click the same anchor point again (*not* the direction point) and drag in the same direction as you previously dragged. Note that as you change the angle of the direction point on the "other" side (where the previous segment is), you aren't changing the length of that direction point line. And you can match the angle pretty easily because you can see both "before" and "after" versions of the previous line segment.

- ✔ **Place anchor points at curve transitions.** A *curve transition* is a place where the curve changes. Maybe it changes direction (going from clockwise to counterclockwise or vice versa). Maybe the curve gets smaller or larger. Although you can cheat to achieve similar effects, the results aren't as good — and editing those curve changes can be a nightmare. Figure 7-9 shows a nice curvy path with anchor points placed properly at the transitions.

✔ **Be environmentally conscious in your anchor-point usage.** Don't place anchor points where they're not needed. This rule goes for all types of anchor points. The fewer you have makes editing sections of the path easier (keeping in mind the previous rule, of course). Fewer anchor points also allows for quicker and trouble-free printing.

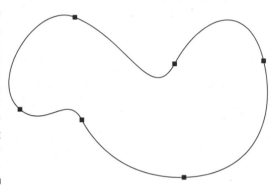

Figure 7-9:
This path
has points
placed
at the
"correct"
locations for
the best
possible
curve.

Holding down the Ctrl key (⌘ on the Mac) changes the currently selected tool into whatever Selection tool you used last. This is very handy when you're drawing with the Pen tool because it enables you to move points while keeping the Pen tool selected. Click the Direct Selection tool *before* you choose the Pen tool. If you click, start to drag, and then realize that you clicked in a spot that just isn't going to work, you don't have to stop, undo, and try again. Just press the Ctrl key (⌘ on the Mac). This temporarily changes the Pen tool into the Direct Selection tool. Move your anchor point to a new location. Release the Ctrl key (⌘ on the Mac) and your anchor point moves to the new location, just like that!

Drawing the tricky anchor points with the Pen tool

A bit of practice with curves and smooth anchor points may get you used to smooth transitions from one line segment to another. Those anchor points are fairly easy to create — just click and drag a new point, and *whammo!* you have a smooth anchor point. But both the curved-corner anchor point and the combination-corner anchor point are a little trickier — they always require two steps. Still, they can't scare a veteran of the draggin' wars. Not a bit.

Curved-corner anchor points revisited

Because curved-corner anchor points have two curves sticking out of them (one on each side), they need two direction points (one for each curve). But because these points are anchoring independent curves, you have to make those direction points independent of each other. Here's the move: As you're dragging out a smooth anchor point, you can quickly change it into a curved-corner anchor point by pressing and releasing the Alt key (Option on the Mac). Doing so "breaks" the control-handle lines into independent lines.

Be sure to make your original line segment the proper length and angle before you press the Alt key (Option on a Mac). After you press the key, the only way to edit the line is to stop drawing and modify it with the Direct Selection tool. See Chapter 6 for all sorts of great tips on how to get the most out of point adjustment by using the Direct Selection tool.

Combination-corner anchor points revisited

Using a similar fancy move, you can create combination-corner points from smooth or straight-corner anchor points — while you're drawing. Here's how:

- ✔ **To go from a straight line into a curved line,** as you're drawing a smooth anchor point, press the Alt key (Option on a Mac) after you click but before you release the mouse button. This action lets you drag the direction point for the next line segment without affecting the previous segment as Illustrator normally does. To create the curve, drag the direction point to wherever you need it.

- ✔ **To go from one curved line into another** (with a curved-corner point instead of a smooth point), click and drag as though you were creating a smooth point. After you have the first curve the way you want it, but before you release the mouse button, press the Alt key (Option on a Mac). As soon as you press Alt (Option on a Mac), the second direction point moves independently of the first. Use this Alt (Option on a Mac) technique to move the direction point to wherever you need it.

These two techniques take a little practice because so much depends on the timing of when you press Alt (Option on a Mac). Don't worry, though. If you don't get it right the first time, you always have the Convert Anchor Point tool to fall back on.

Drawing Shapes with the Pen Tool

This section walks you through drawing some other basic shapes — because knowing the best ways to do that can make the more complex shapes much easier to draw. Take, for example, a garden-variety circle — shapes don't get any simpler than that. . . or do they? When you draw one in Illustrator, you can get widely differing results with the Pen tool.

Drawing a sad, lumpy circle with the Pen tool

You're probably saying to yourself, "Why would anyone be foolish enough to draw a circle by using the Pen tool when you can draw a perfect circle in a single step by using the Ellipse tool?" (which we cover in Chapter 4). A couple of reasons are

- ✔ **Practice makes perfect.** A circle is an object made entirely of smooth anchor points. Master the circle and you're the master of smooth curves!

- ✔ **The Ellipse tool makes perfect circles *every time*.** Sometimes you may want to be a little more creative than that, and drawing the imperfect circle you want with the Pen tool can be a lot faster than modifying a perfect circle created with the Ellipse tool.

So, without further ado, follow these steps, as shown in Figure 7-10:

1. **Hold down the Shift key and click and drag to the right with the Pen tool; extend the direction point line about ¼ inch.**

2. **Keep pressing the Shift key, click about ½ inch above and to the right of the first anchor point, and drag up about ¼ inch.**

   You've drawn an eye-pleasing arc — kind of a skateboard-ramp sorta thing.

3. **Keep pressing the Shift key, click about ½ inch above the second anchor point (directly above the first anchor point), and drag left about ¼ inch.**

   You've drawn a lovely half circle. You're actually more than halfway there.

4. **With your left hand developing a cramp from holding down the Shift key, click about ½ inch to the left of the first anchor point and directly opposite the second anchor point, and then drag down about ¼ inch.**

   (You can probably guess where we're going with this last click. . . .)

5. **Click the first anchor point, drag to the right about ¼ inch, and then (finally) release the Shift key.**

   Your creation is a perfectly *lumpy* circle! If your circle isn't as round as you want, select the Direct Selection tool (the hollow arrow) and tweak the points and direction points until the circle looks less lumpy.

Congratulations — you just drew a circle! Try drawing a second circle using the same steps. And another. You'll find that not only does each circle get easier and better, but you'll have much more control whenever you create a smooth curve anywhere.

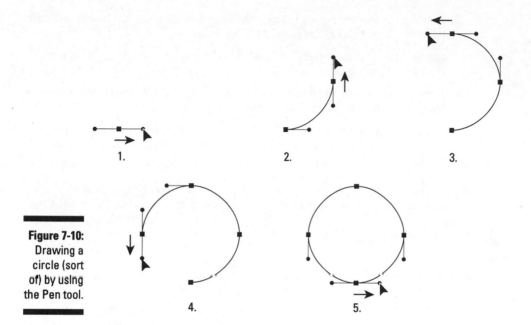

1.

2.

3.

Figure 7-10:
Drawing a circle (sort of) by using the Pen tool.

4.

5.

Drawing a heart

Ah, a *real* challenge. None of this "circle" stuff for you! Still, similarities to our circle friend abound. You do need four anchor points — two of them smooth points. And most of the anchor points need to be in similar positions to the anchor points you drew for the circle. Hmmm. Figure 7-11 shows the procedure in all its glory. Just complete the following steps:

1. **Click and drag up about ¼ inch; use the Shift key to constrain the angle of the direction point line to a perfectly vertical line.**

2. **Move your cursor about ¾ inch above and ½ inch to the right of the first anchor point and click and drag up about ¼ inch. Use the Shift key to constrain the angle of the direction point.**

3. **Move your cursor about ½ inch to the left (above the first anchor point), and then click and drag down about ¼ inch.**

   This procedure is almost too easy, isn't it? Well, take heart (so to speak). The next step tests your mettle.

4. **Press the Alt key (Option on a Mac), click the anchor point you just created, and drag *up* about ¼ inch.**

   This action breaks the two control-handle lines and sets you up for a nice, curved-corner point at the top of the heart.

5. **Move your cursor about ½ inch to the left of the last anchor point and then click and drag down about ¼ inch.**

Again, you can press the Shift key to make sure you're dragging a perfectly vertical line.

6. **Move your cursor onto the first point, press the Alt key (Option on a Mac) and click and drag down about ¼ inch.**

This completes the heart. With all the practice you have, this shape probably looks a lot better than that circle you drew in the previous exercise.

That was the toughie. After you draw a heart, you can try your drawing prowess on pretty much anything anyone throws at you. If you have the time, you can recreate the ceiling of the Sistine Chapel to scale within Illustrator. That is, if you have the time and the inclination.

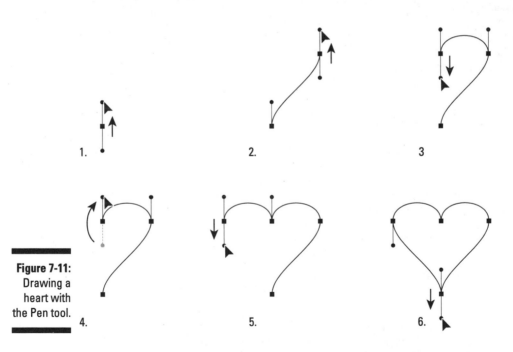

Figure 7-11:
Drawing a
heart with
the Pen tool.

Chapter 8

Wielding the Versatile Pencil, Line Segment, and Arc Tools

- -

In This Chapter

▶ Discovering why the world loves to draw with the Pencil tool

▶ Generating paths with the Pencil tool

▶ Editing existing paths

▶ Using the Pencil Tool Preferences settings

▶ Smoothing out bumpy paths easily

▶ Deciding when to use the Pen or Pencil tool

▶ Using the new Line Segment tool

▶ Creating and editing an arc

- -

*I*n the beginning, there was the Pen tool. And users said that the Pen was good. But the users also said that the Pen was too hard. And too frustrating. And inefficient for quickly creating paths. And the users griped. And behold! Adobe gave them the Pencil tool — the wondrous, magical Pencil tool that makes creating paths as easy as drawing with a, well, *pencil*. And there was great rejoicing. But Adobe wasn't content to stop there. In this latest version of Illustrator, you're also blessed with two new tools — the Line Segment and Arc tools.

In this chapter, you find out all about the Pencil tool and its new buddies, the Line Segment and Arc tools. You discover how to create and modify paths, and customize these tools to match your personal drawing style. And then you can join in the rejoicing!

Using the Pencil Tool as a Pencil

 Computer mice (mouses?) have never been good drawing tools; often you need a steady hand and more patience than the guy at the mall in the Santa suit needs. That was then. These days, the Illustrator Pencil tool makes even the most hopped-up-on-caffeine, impatient Picasso-wannabe into a computer artist. (Just looking at it makes you feel better about drawing, doesn't it?)

Minimal effort and hefty stress reduction

The whole idea behind the Pencil tool is to let you draw exactly what you want — as quickly or slowly as you want. Regardless of the speed at which you draw, the resulting path appears the same (a nice thought for those of us on a deadline).

The Pencil tool creates smooth lines even when you're jittering around. (Unless you don't want it to — in which case it makes jittery lines.) The Pencil tool is also intuitive. It looks like a pencil, and when you click and drag with it, it creates a line that more or less follows where you dragged, pretty much as a real pencil would do. (For contrast, look at the Pen tool. It looks like a pen, and yet it does nothing even remotely penlike!) And it allows you to fix your mistakes without ever having to push or pull a point or a handle.

The following steps (deftly illustrated in Figure 8-1) show you how to use the Pencil tool:

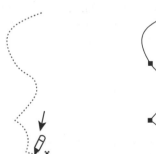

Figure 8-1:
Drawing
with the
Pencil tool.

1. **Choose the Pencil tool from its slot in the Toolbox.**

   Your cursor changes into (surprise!) a pencil.

2. **Click and drag in the document window. As you drag, a dotted line appears.**

   Think of these dots as breadcrumbs that show you where you've been.

3. **Release the mouse button after you amass a nice little trail of bread-crumbs (dots).**

   A path forms where the breadcrumbs were. (If Hansel and Gretel had used the Pencil tool, that poor witch would be alive today.)

If you stop drawing with the Pencil tool, you can just start up where you left off — simply by clicking at the end of the path and continuing. Be careful, though. If you don't click close enough to the end of the path, you start a whole new path. Fortunately, the Pencil tool tells you when you're in the right place. When you're creating a new path, a little X appears to the right of the tip of the Pencil. When you're close enough to a selected path to add to it, the X disappears.

A few unexpected exceptions to all this bliss

You're right. Using the Pencil tool *does* sound too easy. Although the Pencil tool is undeniably wonderful, it can cause frustration (or at least uncertainty) in the unwary. Here are instances to watch out for (and avoid if possible):

- ✔ **You can't continue your path.** You need to select a path in order to add to it. For example, if you stop drawing, do something that deselects the path, and then return to drawing your path, you create a *second* path instead of extending the first one. To continue the path you were origi-nally working on, you must select it *before* you start drawing again with the Pencil tool. Just hold down the Ctrl key (⌘ on a Mac) to temporarily change the Pencil into the Selection tool. Click the path, let go of the Ctrl key (⌘ on a Mac), and start drawing, starting at either end of the newly selected path.

  To get to the selection cursor right away, hold down the Ctrl key (⌘ on a Mac).

- ✔ **You accidentally edit an existing path.** If you start a new Pencil path near a *selected* path, you can edit the selected path instead of creating a new one. In fact, you can do so with *any* path that was created with the Pen, Pencil, Line Segment, Arc, Star, or any other tool in Illustrator. You can edit any of them with the Pencil tool. (So is the Pencil versatile or overzealous? Your call.)

- ✔ **You create a path that's too lumpy or too smooth.** You can set up the Pencil tool to be very smooth *or* very accurate. (In this case, *accurate* really means that it follows all the skittles and bumps you make as you draw). If someone you love changes the Pencil tool preferences (which you can access by double-clicking the Pencil tool), the Pencil retains those settings. Pencil tool preferences are loyal to the most recent user; they never return to their original settings.

✔ **You get a wacky fill or stroke as you draw.** This situation really isn't the Pencil tool's fault, but it's not exactly unknown to habitual Pencil tool users. If, before you start to draw, a nameless *somebody* sets the fill or stroke to something a little odd, *boom!* you get a mess. Fortunately, you can change the fill or stroke back to the default settings by pressing D. Before you know it, you're back to normal. (Well, at least the *path* is. . . .)

✔ **You can't close a path.** Often when you use the Pencil tool in an attempt to create a closed path (by ending the path where you started), you wind up with two points that are very close to one another without actually being joined. For some reason, the Pencil tool has a hard time making a closed path if you draw the entire path with one continuous stroke. When you near the end of the path, hold down the Alt key (Option on a Mac) and release the mouse with Alt (Option on a Mac) still pressed when the end of the line that you are drawing is near the beginning. The two ends of your path will be joined together.

✔ **You can't draw a straight line.** In Illustrator, pressing the Shift key doesn't keep the Pencil tool on a horizontal or vertical plane. Just about every other tool in Illustrator draws or moves in straight lines at 45° angles. In fact, just about every other tool in every Adobe product moves or draws in straight lines when you hold the Shift key down! But the Pencil tool can't even *think* straight! Fortunately, you can switch over to the Pen tool to draw straight lines and then switch back to the Pencil tool to create the rest of the drawing.

Cherishing the Multipurpose Pencil Tool

If you ever had one of those pocketknives with enough blades to do or fix anything, you can appreciate how much more the Pencil tool does than a mere pencil! Use the amazing Pencil tool to edit existing paths, create new paths, append one path to another, and close existing paths.

But wait, there's more! You can set the Pencil tool to work in a variety of ways so that it accurately reflects the way you want to draw, by setting its preferences. You can also use variations on the Pencil tool: the Smooth tool and the Eraser tool. The Pencil tool slot contains these two other Pencil-like tools. Use the Smooth tool (looks like an iron) to make paths less bumpy, with nary a smear. Use the Eraser tool (looks likc an art gum eraser) to zap away portions of paths, leaving no rubber crumbs to get into your keyboard.

Making the Pencil tool work just for you

You can set preferences for the Pencil tool by double-clicking the Pencil tool in the Toolbox. Figure 8-2 shows the Pencil Tool Preferences dialog box. Straight out of the box, the Pencil tool works pretty well. But to be honest, it's really set up to work reasonably well for everyone and not set up to work as well as it possibly can for *you*. Use the Pencil tool preferences to make the tool work *just* for you, and don't settle for less than the best!

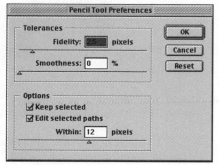

Figure 8-2:
Using the Pencil Tool Preferences dialog box, you can change the attributes of the Pencil tool.

Hi-fi and lo-fi paths

The first slider under Tolerances (at the top of the dialog box; refer to Figure 8-2) is labeled *Fidelity*. Nope, nothing to do with divorce courts — this kind of fidelity affects how closely the path follows where you drag the Pencil tool. A high setting (toward the left of the dialog box) means that the path matches precisely what you drew with the Pencil, adding as many points and corners as necessary. A low setting (toward the right of the dialog box) means that the path loosely follows what you drew, making a smoother line with fewer points. Paths created with the Fidelity slider all the way to the left appear more natural and bumpy; paths drawn with the slider all the way to the right appear smoother and more computer-like. Compare the images shown in Figure 8-3. This Fidelity setting isn't just an arbitrary special effect; it's a way to make the Pencil tool match your personal drawing style.

Fidelity is measured in pixels. A pixel can mean many things as a unit of measurement. In this case, a *pixel* refers to a distance on your screen. (For more information, see the sidebar "Just how big IS a pixel?")

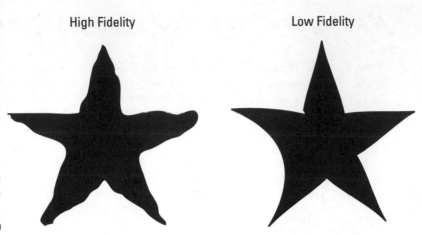

High Fidelity

Low Fidelity

Figure 8-3:
The path on
the left was
drawn with
a Fidelity
setting of .5
pixels; the
path on the
right was
drawn with
a Fidelity
setting of 20
pixels.

Drawing with the mouse is about as easy as drawing with a brick; the lines that you make tend to be pretty shaky. The Fidelity slider determines how shaky your hand can be and still produce a smooth line. As you use the Pencil tool, create a breadcrumb trail (a dotted line). After you release the mouse button, your computer pauses for a split second to create an imaginary line that's the average of all the movement you just made with the mouse. Then Illustrator compares that imaginary line with your breadcrumb trail and creates the actual path based on the Fidelity slider's setting.

Suppose that your Fidelity setting is 20 pixels — the lowest Fidelity setting possible. As you draw your naturally shaky line, you move away from the imaginary average line. With a setting of 20 pixels, Illustrator assumes that everything less than 20 pixels away from that imaginary line is unintentional shaking, induced by the unwieldy nature of the mouse (or by too much caffeine), so Illustrator just ignores that stuff when it creates the path. Everything more than 20 pixels away is considered intentional, which prompts Illustrator to put in a curve or a corner point.

All this is just an extended way of saying that if you're at one with yourself and the Universe and are a Zen master of mouse movement, you want to keep your Fidelity settings high. That way, you only move the mouse to exactly where you want the path, and you don't have Illustrator second-guessing what you *really* intended. However, if you have really shaky hands (as most of us do when we get too much caffeine and not enough sleep), you probably want to use a low-Fidelity setting. More than likely, you fall somewhere between these two extremes. So just double-click the Pencil tool and set the Fidelity slider to match your style!

Just how big IS a pixel?

That question has no easy answer, my friend. In the olden days, a pixel was ¹⁄₇₂ of an inch because computer screens used a fixed grid of 72 pixels x 72 pixels for every inch of screen. Nowadays, we use multisync monitors that let us change the number of pixels on the screen.

How big is a pixel? Take the current resolution of your monitor, divide by its size, and then. . . . Better yet, forget all that and just pay attention to how the Pencil tool works with different Fidelity settings. Choose the one that works best for you, and don't worry about the numbers!

Now, that is smooth!

The second slider (refer to Figure 8-2) is a little harder for most people to figure out. The slider reads *Smoothness* — but didn't the first slider smooth out the image? Drawing with the mouse can be pretty shaky, so this setting helps compensate for the shakiness in a slightly different way from the Fidelity setting. The Fidelity setting helps Illustrator determine whether you drew the path because you meant to — or if it was just because of the shaky mouse. The Smoothness setting helps Illustrator figure out what kind of corner you meant to create when you deliberately changed the direction of the path. When you change the direction of a path, you can do it with a sharp corner point or with a smooth, curving point. When Illustrator converts your breadcrumb trail into a path, it must determine which of these points you truly intended to use. A Smoothness of 0% makes the Pencil tool use a corner point almost everywhere that the path changes direction. A Smoothness of 100% makes the Pencil tool use a smooth point in all but the most extreme path direction changes.

Again, the setting that works best for you is a matter of your personal style. If your lines are as shaky as a balloon vendor at a porcupine convention, set your Smoothness to 100%. If your hands are as steady as a gunslinger in a Western movie, leave it set to 0%. Otherwise, experiment until you find the right setting for you. Figure 8-4 shows the same image created with different Smoothness settings. Note how the settings change the way the drawings look.

At first glance, the differences between the drawings on the right in Figures 8-3 (low Fidelity) and 8-4 (high Smoothness) appear minimal. However, looks can be deceiving. The Smoothness and Fidelity settings are actually two distinct approaches to making a path: A low Fidelity setting creates a simplified curve by following the path you draw more loosely and using fewer points; a high Smoothness setting creates a smoother curve by using *different types* of points (smooth points as opposed to corner points) to create the path. Which is better? It really depends on your drawing style — and some experimenting!

Low Smoothness   High Smoothness

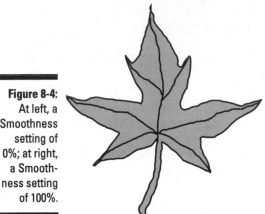 

Figure 8-4:
At left, a Smoothness setting of 0%; at right, a Smoothness setting of 100%.

Tweaking the Pencil tool: It's your option

Under Options in the Pencil Tool Preferences dialog box, you find two options: Keep Selected and Edit Selected Paths. These settings determine what happens to the path after you draw it and how the Pencil tool interacts with that path (or with other selected paths).

- ✔ **With Keep Selected checked:** The path you just created with the Pencil tool stays selected after you finish drawing and release the mouse button.

- ✔ **With Keep Selected unchecked:** The path you just created doesn't stay selected. (But you knew that.)

The Keep Selected option also determines how the Pencil tool affects selected paths, as follows:

- ✔ **Edit Selected Paths:** When you use the Pencil tool near any selected path (with the Keep Selected option checked), the path you just drew with the Pencil tool replaces the previous path. You can even adjust how close you need to be to that path to edit it; just tweak the Within setting, located just beneath the Edit Selected Paths option.

When the Edit Selected Paths option is not checked, the Pencil tool works the same regardless of whether Keep Selected is checked or unchecked. When the Edit Selected Paths option is checked, it changes the way the Pencil tool works. Instead of moving on to create a new path when you draw near a selected path, you linger over the old one to modify it.

✔ **With Keep Selected checked:** You can start drawing a path, stop, and then continue where you left off. If you decide to replace the path, you can place the Pencil tool near the path you just drew and start drawing a new one. (*Poof.* The old one disappears.) But beware: You have forbidden the Pencil tool to draw multiple paths that are close together.

✔ **With Keep Selected *and* Edit Selected Paths checked:** Every stroke you make that's close to another selected stroke replaces the old stroke with the new stroke.

✔ **With Keep Selected unchecked:** The Pencil tool can change only the paths you tell it to change (by first using a Selection tool). By removing the check mark from Keep Selected, you enable the Pencil to draw hair or grass (for instance) with utter abandon. With Keep Selected unchecked you can also *edit* hair or grass, but don't forget to select the part you want to edit (by first using a Selection tool).

Changing the path not penciled

A really amazing attribute of the Pencil tool is that you can use it to edit any path, and not just the paths created with it. For example, you can edit a circle, star, or path drawn with the Pen tool. You can replace any portion of any path with the Pencil tool, provided that the path is selected and the Edit Selected Path option is checked in the Pencil Tool Preferences dialog box. (See "Making the Pencil tool work just for you" earlier in this chapter.) Just make sure that the path is selected — and then click and drag near the path to reshape it. The following steps walk you through the process of editing an existing path:

1. **Using any Selection tool, select the path you want to modify.**

   The path need not have been created with the Pencil tool.

2. **Select the Pencil tool.**

3. **Click near the part of the path you want to modify.**

   When the little X at the bottom right of the Pencil tool disappears, you know that you're close enough to click.

4. **Click and drag a new shape for the part of the path.**

   You can create any shape you want, but it must start and end near the existing path; otherwise, the new path won't reconnect with the old path.

5. **Release the mouse button.**

   The path reshapes itself into the new path you just drew.

Working with the all-natural "Smoothie" tool

Use the Illustrator Smooth tool to make your paths, well, *smoother*. (Not that you need us to tell you that, huh?) The Smooth tool lets you change the way a path looks *after* it's drawn, in the same way that the Pencil tool lets you change the way a path looks as it's being drawn.

Drag the Smooth tool over any selected path to "smooth" it. You aren't limited to smoothing paths drawn with the Pencil tool; you can smooth any path in Illustrator. Your results, however, depend on the path that you're smoothing (if you try smoothing a path that's already smooth, you aren't going to see much difference) and on the Smooth Tool Preferences.

You access the Smooth Tool Preferences by double-clicking the Smooth tool. The only two settings (which should seem hauntingly familiar from the discussion of the Pencil tool) are Fidelity and Smoothness. These settings function identically to the settings in the Pencil Tool Preferences dialog box. (See the section "Making the Pencil tool work just for you" earlier in this chapter.) The only difference is that you apply them to lines that have already been drawn. Just sweep over them with the Smooth tool, and the result is as if you drew those paths by using different Pencil Tool Preferences settings.

As you may expect, using the Smooth tool is pretty smooth. Here's the drill (or is it a sander?), as shown in Figure 8-5:

1. **Using any Selection tool, select the path that you want to smooth.**

2. **Drag the Smooth tool on or near the path that you want to smooth.**

    Et voilá! The path is smooth.

The Eraser tool is so basic that it doesn't even warrant its own section. To use the tool, simply click and drag the tool over the portion of the path you want to remove. It may take a couple of swipes to eliminate what you want, so be patient. The Eraser tool also works with any path — not just those created with the Pencil tool. Also, with the Eraser tool, you don't have to set preferences.

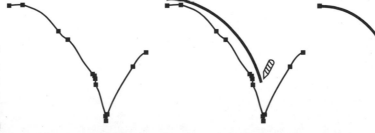

Figure 8-5:
The Smooth tool in action.

Using the Pen with the Pencil

The Pen and Pencil tools are the primary tools for drawing in Illustrator, and they work really well together. As you gain a knack for knowing which tool to use when, your work flows more smoothly — and your illustrations look more and more the way you want them to.

Swapping one tool for another

A common technique that's useful for combining the Pen and Pencil tools is to switch between them while drawing. You *can* click each tool whenever you decide to change from one to the other, but the really zippy way to do this is to press the key that corresponds to each tool. Press the P key (on your keyboard) to switch to the Pen tool and press the N key to switch to the Pencil tool.

As your drawing changes from free-flowing curves to precise straight lines and back, you want to change between the two tools: Just click the endpoint of the path you were previously drawing with the other tool and then continue drawing.

Watch those icons! Working with the Pen and Pencil tools together is much easier if you pay attention to what the icons are doing. When the Pen tool is over an endpoint, a little slash (/) appears to the lower right of the pen icon. When you're about to close a path, a hollow circle appears beside the tool. When you have the Pencil tool in position to edit a path, its icon doesn't have anything beside it. Both tools, however, get Xs beside them when they're about to create a new path.

Precision versus speed: You make the call

Keep in mind the types of shapes and paths that are best drawn with each tool. Here's a breakdown of the shapes and paths each tool draws best.

Shapes and paths best drawn with the Pen tool

To draw anything with straight lines, choose the Pen tool because the Pencil tool really can't draw a straight line. To create a path or shape that has a smooth curve, you choose the Pen tool because the line the Pencil tool creates is just an average of the total strokes you make, which means absolute precision is impossible. Finally, to trace a logo or other scanned art that requires precision and accuracy, you're better off choosing the Pen tool because it offers you precision down to the thousandth of a millimeter.

Shapes and paths best drawn with the Pencil tool

When speed is more important than accuracy in your drawing, for example, when you need to put a lot of hairs onto your lovely kiwi-fruit illustration, and the precise length and position of each and every hair doesn't matter, choose the Pencil tool. For quick sketching, such as doodling an insulting picture of your favorite co-worker, choose the Pencil tool because you don't have to worry about each and every point and handle the way you do with the Pen tool. The Pencil tool lets you focus on creating the lines where they should be — and lets Illustrator do the rest of the work for you. (Ah, progress.)

Lines Made Quick and Easy

You know you can't draw a straight line with the Pencil tool, and you've seen how tedious the pen can be. So, you're probably thinking that drawing a line would be easier with that gloppy rapidograph pen and a metal ruler. Don't fret! The powers at Adobe have bestowed yet another tool for pen-phobic users: the Line Segment tool. With the Line Segment tool, you can make lines quickly and easily.

Working with the Line Segment tool

To create a line with the Line Segment tool, simply click at your desired starting point, drag, and release at your desired ending point. You can also click on your Artboard, enter a desired angle and length in the dialog box (explained in "Setting the tool options" section), and click OK. Like most things that are super easy, the Line Segment tool has its drawbacks. For example, you're limited to creating a single line, as shown in Figure 8-6. You can't create connecting lines like you can with the Pen or Pencil tools. You can, however, create lines that are perfectly vertical, horizontal, or at 45° angles. Just press the Shift key as you draw. You'll discover that as you drag your cursor, your line constrains to a 45° angle. After you create your line, you can edit it by selecting and moving either endpoint with the Direct Selection tool.

Setting the tool options

Double-clicking the Line Segment tool in the Tool palette brings up the Line Segment Tool Options dialog box, in which you find only a few options: Length, Angle, Fill Line. By unchecking the Fill Line option, the line appears with only a stroke, regardless of whether you have a fill selected in the Toolbox or Color palette. After you complete the drawing of your line, the Fill swatch in both the Toolbox and Color palette automatically reverts to None.

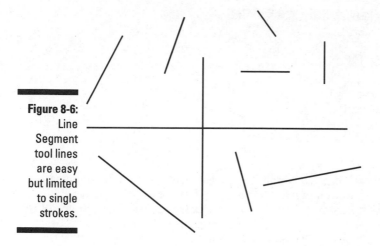

Figure 8-6:
Line
Segment
tool lines
are easy
but limited
to single
strokes.

Getting Curvy with the New Arc Tool

Boy, the folks at Adobe just don't stop making our lives easier. (Maybe the screams of agony they've been hearing from users trying to create Bézier curves is getting unbearable.) Either way, the result is the fantastic new Arc tool. Read on to find out the scoop on this new curve-making tool.

One-step Bézier curves

In Chapter 7, we tell you how to create a curve with the Pen tool — a sometimes painful two-step click-and-drag process. With the Arc tool, however, all you do is just click and drag. The longer you drag, the larger the arc. The angle you drag affects the angle of the arc. That's it. If only everything in life were so simple. To edit your arc, treat it is as you would any other curve. Use the Direct Selection tool to select and move either of the anchor points or direction points on the curve. See Chapter 6 for the complete editing lowdown.

Getting the arc you want

Maybe you're the finicky type and not completely satisfied with the arc created by using the default settings. Fortunately, the options in the Arc Segment Tool Options dialog box are numerous. Double-click the Arc tool to bring up the dialog box shown in Figure 8-7. The best thing about this dialog box is that it gives you a preview of the settings as you adjust them.

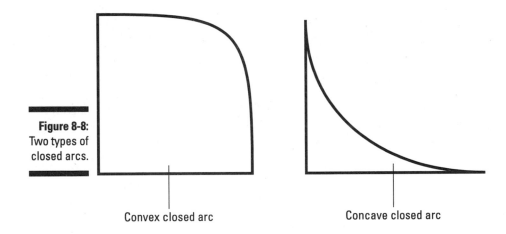

Figure 8-7:
Design your
arc here.

For the slightly mathematically challenged, the preview thumbnail gives a nice visual representation of what happens to the arc as you change the lengths of the X (horizontal) and Y (vertical) axes. You have the choice of the type of arc — open or closed (think a slice of pizza). You can also choose where the base of your arc is anchored — either the X or Y axis. The slope slider allows you to adjust how concave (pushed in) or convex (pushed out) your curve appears. Figure 8-8 shows examples of both concave and convex closed arcs. Uncheck Fill Arc to create arcs with no fill, regardless of whether a fill is selected or not. The small square to the left of the OK button is a proxy box, which allows you to specify the point of origin for the arc.

Figure 8-8:
Two types of
closed arcs.

Convex closed arc   Concave closed arc

When you select the Arc tool and click on your Artboard, the Arc Segment Tool options dialog box appears. When you click OK, an arc is drawn with the settings established in the dialog box.

Chapter 9

Creating Magnificent Brushstrokes

· ·

In This Chapter

▶ Understanding why the Paintbrush is unlike the Pen and Pencil tools

▶ Creating brushes from Illustrator artwork

▶ Looking at the four brush types

· ·

Hardcore users of Illustrator would never call it a *painting* program. So what if you can mix colors and use a paintbrush tool: To hardcore users, all painting programs are pixel-based and only drawing programs are vector-based. Regardless of what the hardcore users think, Illustrator is a painting program, with some of the most powerful painting capabilities of any graphics program, vector- or pixel-based.

 What, for example, would you call this tool in the margin? In Illustrator, its name is the Paintbrush tool, but it's also at least one-third magic wand (the kind magicians use, not the Magic Wand tool). In this chapter, you discover the magic of the Paintbrush tool and the wonders of vector-based brush strokes. You get to push the definitions of "brush" by creating brushstrokes of every conceivable size and shape, from brushes that make simple calligraphic strokes to brushes that make strokes using other Illustrator artwork.

Brushing Where No Stroke Has Gone Before

Brushes are wildly creative strokes that you can apply to paths. If you think of them this way, brushes become much easier to get a handle on (especially if they make you bristle with frustration).

Brushes, as shown in Figure 9-1, can be any of four different types: Art brushes, Scatter brushes, Calligraphic brushes, and Pattern brushes.

- **Art brushes:** Stretch a single piece of artwork along an entire path.
- **Scatter brushes:** Scatter artwork around a path. The artwork is repeated, scaled, and rotated randomly.
- **Calligraphic brushes:** Emulate drawing or writing with a calligraphy pen.
- **Pattern brushes:** Repeat artwork along a path that you draw with the Paintbrush tool. Unlike the random Scatter brush, the Pattern brush repeats the artwork in a precise pattern.

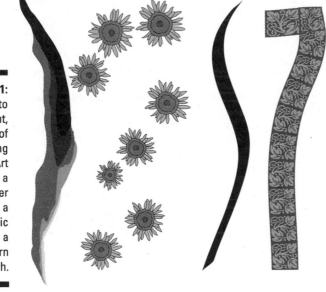

Figure 9-1:
From left to right, examples of painting with an Art brush, a Scatter brush, a Calligraphic brush, and a Pattern brush.

The Illustrator Brushes palette, shown in Figure 9-2, contains samples of each of the four brush types. (Choose Window⇨Brushes to display the Brushes palette.) In addition, see the "Creating a New Brush" section later in this chapter for help on taking virtually anything that you create in Illustrator and turning it into a brush.

Calligraphic brushes

Scatter brushes

Art brushes

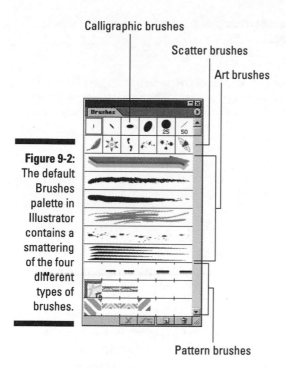

Figure 9-2:
The default
Brushes
palette in
Illustrator
contains a
smattering
of the four
different
types of
brushes.

Pattern brushes

Embracing your inner artist

Regardless of your artistic background or intentions, you can make astounding artwork by using the Paintbrush tool in combination with the different types of brushes. Of course, someone with an utter vacuum of talent (or more than the legally allowed measure of bad taste) may have an uphill battle to create something that looks good. Even so, you may be surprised at how quickly you can tool up some snazzy images, as shown in Figure 9-3, by using the Paintbrush — even if you're new to computer graphics. (Your secret is safe with us.) Just follow these steps:

1. **Choose the Paintbrush tool from the Toolbox.**

   Your cursor changes into a little paintbrush.

2. **Choose Window⇨Libraries⇨Artistic Sample.**

   After you release the mouse button, the Artistic Sample brush palette appears quicker than you can say *Jackson Pollock*.

3. **Click the Chalk Art brush.**

   Topmost in the palette, this brush looks like what you get by rubbing a stick of black pastel sideways against rough construction paper.

4. **Click and drag with the Paintbrush tool to draw a path where you want your new stroke to be.**

5. **Release the mouse button.**

   The path you drew becomes the stroke of the brush that you chose. In this case, the Chalk Art brush's rough pastel stroke stretches along the entire length of the path. With the path still selected, try clicking on the other brushes to get a feel for how these brushes look.

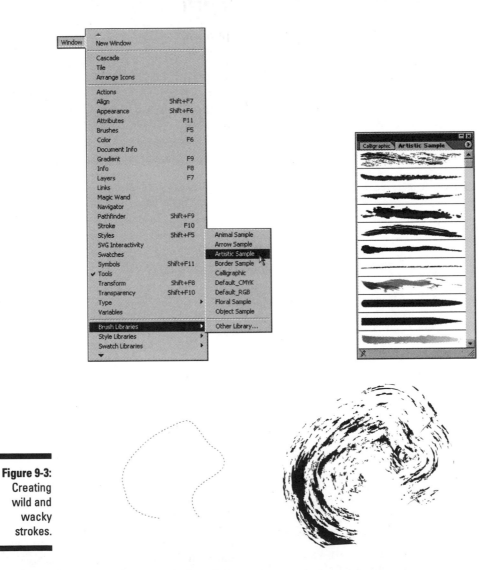

Figure 9-3:
Creating
wild and
wacky
strokes.

Because brushes reside on paths, you can change the position and dimensions of any brushstroke just as you modify any path. You can use the Pencil tool to reshape an existing path, or if you're really brave, you can use the Direct Selection tool to push and pull points and handles around until the brushstroke looks the way you want.

The Paintbrush tool options

The Paintbrush tool offers several options that you can use to customize the way it draws. All these options are found in the Paintbrush Tool Preferences dialog box, shown in Figure 9-4, which appears after you double-click the Paintbrush tool. These preferences function almost identically to the Pencil tool's preferences, with one exception: the Fill New Brush Strokes option. When you leave the check box for this option unchecked (which we recommend), Illustrator automatically sets the Fill color to None. For a more exhaustive and exhausting explanation of the other settings, refer to Chapter 8.

Figure 9-4:
The
Paintbrush
Tool
Preferences
dialog box.

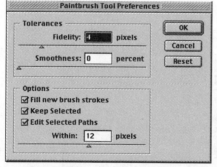

Why set the Fill to None? The path you make with the Paintbrush tool can contain a fill color, but brushstrokes can also be randomly placed pieces of artwork or have unique shapes. The stroke can appear partly inside and partly outside the fill color, which makes the fill seem random and unrelated to your stroke. Brushes work better when you don't use a fill color with them.

Creating a New Brush

Although Illustrator ships with several hundred brushes, obsessively creative folks can't stand to be limited to so few. To create your own brushes, go right ahead by using darn near any set of paths in Illustrator, as shown in Figure 9-5. Furthermore, the process works to create a new Art, Pattern, or Scatter brush.

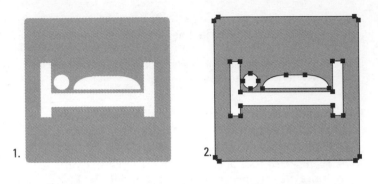

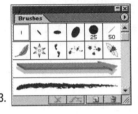

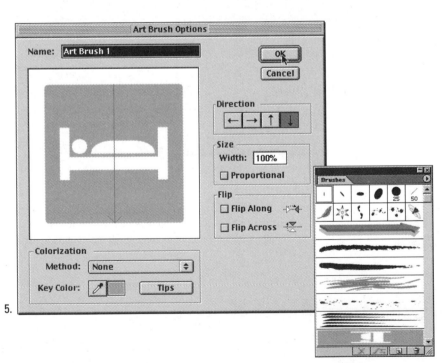

Figure 9-5: 5.
Creating a
new brush.

1. **Create (or open a document with) artwork that you want to use as a brush.**

2. **Using any Selection tool, select all the paths in the artwork.**

3. **Click the New Brush button at the bottom of the Brushes palette (or choose New Brush from the Brushes palette pop-up menu).**

   After you release the mouse button, a New Brush dialog box appears and asks what type of brush you want to create.

4. **Select New Art Brush, New Scatter Brush, or New Pattern Brush; then click OK.**

   (For the purpose of this example, we selected the New Art Brush option.) The Art Brush Options dialog box appears.

5. **Click OK to accept the default settings.**

   If you're concerned about accepting the default settings in the Art Brush Options dialog box, keep in mind that you can always make changes to the Art Brush options by double-clicking the Art brush itself in the Brushes palette. We talk about all those different options in the section "Working with the Different Brush Types" later in this chapter. These options have the same effect whether you're creating a new brush or modifying an existing one.

   The new Art brush appears in the Brushes palette, ready for you to use.

 Create all sorts of interesting effects by using text as Art brushes. Because brushes can contain only paths (not text objects), you must first change the text into paths before you can make it into a brush. Select the text object with a Selection tool and then choose Type⇨Create Outlines.

Working with the Different Brush Types

Here are the four brush types and some options that you can use when painting with them.

Art brushes for times when you're a bit wacky

Art brushes take any Illustrator paths and stretch them along a path. Figure 9-6 shows several examples of Art brushes.

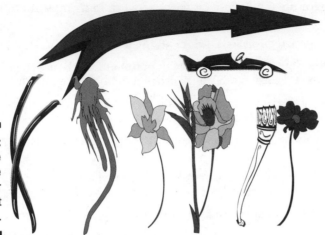

Figure 9-6:
All these
objects are
(believe it or
not) Art
brushes.

You can use several Art Brush Options to make Art brushes look exactly the way you want. Figure 9-7 shows the Art Brush Options dialog box, accessed by double-clicking any Art brush in the Brushes palette.

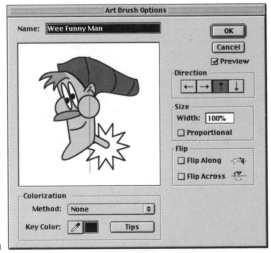

Figure 9-7:
The Art
Brush
Options
dialog box.

In the Art Brush Options dialog box are a variety of options to affect the way the brush makes a stroke. The following list describes how to use some of those options:

- ✔ **Name:** Give the brush a descriptive name here. This name appears when you choose View By Name from the Brushes palette's pop-up menu.

- ✔ **Preview:** Select the Preview option to see any stroke in your artwork that uses the brush stroke you're changing. What you see is what you'll get — the stroke as it will look *if* you apply the new changes. This doesn't alter your actual artwork. This feature is extremely handy because you don't have to remember what all the different settings do — you can just watch what happens after you change them!

- ✔ **Direction:** This option determines whether the graphic rotates clockwise or counterclockwise (relative to the path) as you stretch it.

- ✔ **Size:** With the Proportional option selected, the artwork grows wider as the path gets longer. With Proportional option deselected, the artwork stretches. You can enter a scaling percentage in the Width box.

- ✔ **Flip:** This option resembles the Direction option, except that it flips the artwork upside down instead of rotating it.

- ✔ **Colorization:** Brushes have fill and stroke colors of their own. They are ordinary Illustrator artwork endowed with the power to be brushes, meaning that distinct fill and stroke values are part of the deal. The Colorization setting determines whether the brush keeps the colors of the original artwork or replaces them with Fill and Stroke colors from the Toolbox. A Method setting of None preserves the original artwork's colors. Other settings blend the Fill and Stroke colors with the artwork. How they perform this miracle depends on the colors in the original artwork for the brush and on the specific options you choose.

Click the Tips button for a visual illustration of the various colorization settings.

Figure 9-8 shows the same brush with three different sets of options applied to it.

Figure 9-8:
The same brush changed by only one setting produces variations like these.

Default settings   Different Direction setting   Size Proportional setting   Flip Along setting

Scatter brushes for times when you're a bit wacky

Scatter brushes are similar to Art brushes; they're made up of Illustrator paths. However, the similarities end there. Instead of stretching art along a path, Scatter brushes toss, fling, and *scatter* art along a path. Figure 9-9 shows the result of using a Scatter brush.

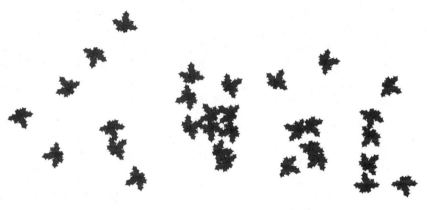

Figure 9-9: This artwork is actually a single path used as a Scatter brush.

Scatter brushes have even more options than Art brushes, but Scatter brushes need more options. Imagine a brush of randomly scattered ladybugs becoming a brush of organized ladybugs that follow the path you create with the brush.

The Scatter brushes repeat and randomize artwork based on four variables: Size, Spacing, Scatter, and Rotation. You set the specific amounts for these options by dragging their respective sliders to the left or right. How the brush uses these values is determined by the method (Fixed, Random, or Pressure) that you select in the pop-up menu to the right of each slider. The following list describes how each method works:

- ✔ **Fixed:** This method uses the exact value in the associated text box, which you previously specified by using the slider.

- ✔ **Random:** This method gives you two sliders instead of one so that you can specify Minimum and Maximum amounts of variance in the associated option. For example, after you set the Size to a Minimum value of 50% and a Maximum value to 200%, the Scatter brush varies the artwork randomly between half its original size and twice its original size.

✔ **Pressure:** Like with Random, Pressure uses Minimum and Maximum amounts of variance in the associated option. This method works only when you have a pressure-sensitive tablet hooked to your computer. This feature is so cool that you may want to run out and buy one of these tablets, which is sort of using a mouse except that you draw with a pen-like stylus. Instead of just painting or not painting (your only options with a mouse), the stylus recognizes just how hard you press. The Minimum and Maximum settings correspond to the amount of pressure. The lightest pressure uses the minimum value; the hardest pressure uses the Maximum value. The values you get vary according to just how hard you press.

Two versions of the Scatter Brush Options dialog box appear in Figure 9-10. Next to each version is a brushstroke created with the option settings shown in the dialog box.

After you determine which method to use, set the sliders on the left side of the dialog box to specify how you want the artwork repeated along the path. Here are the options:

✔ **Size:** This option controls the size of the scattered objects relative to the original.

✔ **Spacing:** This option controls the amount of space that appears between the scattered objects.

✔ **Scatter:** This option controls how far away objects can scatter on either side of the path.

✔ **Rotation:** This option controls how the objects are rotated and whether they're rotated in relation to the path or to the document. Figure 9-11 shows the difference between a Scatter brush rotation based on the path (left) and one based on the page (right).

Pattern brushes — too cool and utterly wacko

Pattern brushes (see Figure 9-12) are too cool for words, so we can just move on. Okay, no weaseling. For openers, you can use five different pieces of art for Pattern brushes rather than just one! Of course, that fact can also make them difficult to create. You need a graphic for straight lines and curves, one for inside corners, one for outside corners, one for the start of a line, and one for the end of a line. The results are worth the time and effort to make sure that these five graphics work together.

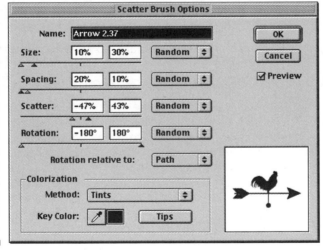

Figure 9-10:
Two
versions of
the Scatter
Brush
Options
dialog box
and the
artwork
resulting
from those
options.

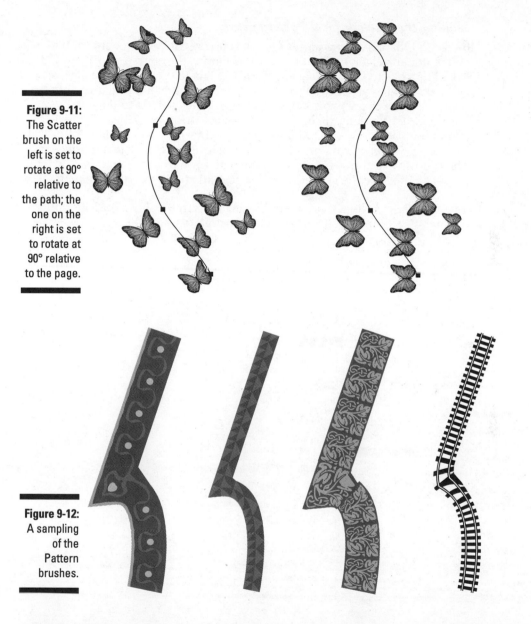

Figure 9-11:
The Scatter brush on the left is set to rotate at 90° relative to the path; the one on the right is set to rotate at 90° relative to the page.

Figure 9-12:
A sampling of the Pattern brushes.

Well, okay, if making five pieces of art is too time-intensive, you can get away with using just one. The Side pattern is the key pattern. If you don't create five different graphics, the Pattern brush just repeats the Side pattern for any missing pattern. But come on, now, that's cheating. If you want eye-popping results, make those five graphics and take full advantage of what this wonderful brush can do.

Making the artwork for a Pattern brush

If you find that creating a Pattern brush is pretty tricky and counterintuitive, you're not alone; a lot of trial and error is par for the course, especially at first. The first step in building a Pattern brush is to create the five pieces of artwork. Before you can do that, however, you need to know just what these pieces of artwork are for. Double-click the Brushes palette to open the Pattern Brush Options dialog box for a peek at the possibilities. Figure 9-13 shows the Pattern Brush Options dialog box, in which you tell Illustrator just where to put the artwork on a path. Pattern brushes are *context-sensitive:* They know what the specific part of the path they are on is supposed to look like — so they use the graphic that corresponds to that part of the path.

You may find it helpful to examine existing Pattern brushes. The Tile Options list in the Pattern Brush Options dialog box offers a sampling.

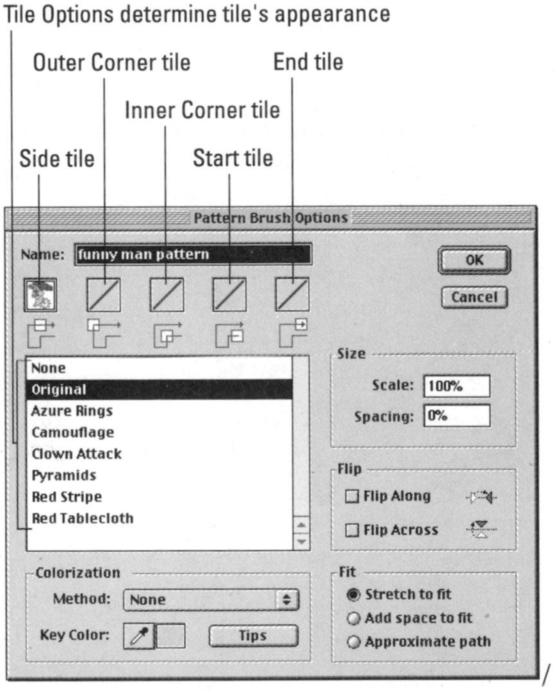

Tile Options determine tile's appearance

Outer Corner tile   End tile

Inner Corner tile

Side tile   Start tile

Figure 9-13:
Each
Pattern
brush title
knows
where it
is on a
path and
uses the
correspond-
ing artwork.

Pattern Brush Options

Name: funny man pattern   OK   Cancel

None
Original
Azure Rings
Camouflage
Clown Attack
Pyramids
Red Stripe
Red Tablecloth

Size
Scale: 100%
Spacing: 0%

Flip
☐ Flip Along
☐ Flip Across

Colorization
Method: None
Key Color: Tips

Fit
● Stretch to fit
○ Add space to fit
○ Approximate path

Setting Pattern Brush options

The Pattern Brush Options dialog box looks more complicated than it really is. Double-click any brush in the Brushes palette, and the Pattern Brush Options dialog box appears, displaying the following features:

- ✔ **Tiles:** These squares are thumbnail representations of each piece of art-work. Beneath each tile, a graphic shows the artwork's position on the path. Click a thumbnail to modify it by using the Tile Options list.

✔ **Tile Options:** Click these options to change your pattern tiles. Click None to remove the selected tile's graphic. (The Original option is already selected if you added your own graphics.) The remaining options correspond to the Pattern swatches in the Swatches palette. This arrangement enables you to use Pattern swatches as an alternative to creating your own tiles. (See Chapter 5 for more details on Pattern swatches.)

✔ **Colorization and Flip:** See the earlier section "Art brushes for times when you're a bit wacky" for details on these options.

✔ **Size:** Use the Scale option to enlarge or shrink the tiles as they run along the path. If they get too big, the Spacing option enables you to increase the distance between tiles.

✔ **Fit:** This option determines how the tiles get distorted to fit around spaces that don't quite match the five different Tile types. Stretch to Fit distorts artwork the most, mashing it into whatever shape it needs to be to fit the path. Add Space to Fit adds space between tiles to distort them as little as possible. Approximate Path only works when the path is rectangular. This option doesn't distort the tiles at all; instead, the tiles "approximately" follow the path.

Positioning the artwork in the Pattern brush

After you create your graphics, think about what position each graphic is going to play. You may find it helpful to create a single guide that actually contains all five positions, as shown in Figure 9-14. Use this graphic as a way of visualizing how each graphic element is going to work at the different points.

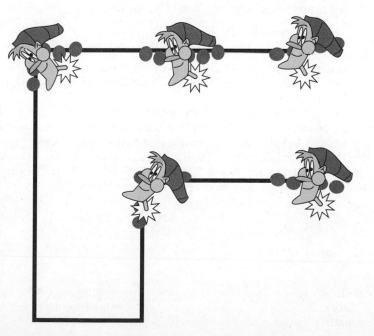

Figure 9-14: Creating a guideline with all five pattern positions can be a big help when you create the artwork for the Pattern brush.

Using the guideline, create five pieces of artwork to correspond to the positions on the path. Knowing exactly how each piece of the artwork needs to change in response to its position takes practice. Some differences can be subtle (such as between the starting art and ending art) or obvious (such as between the side piece and corner pieces), as shown in Figure 9-15.

Figure 9-15:
Left to right:
The start,
side, outside
corner,
inside
corner, and
end pieces.

After you have all the artwork, you're ready to create the Pattern brush. Forward, intrepid artist! Just follow these steps:

1. **Select the Side tile and click the New Brush button in the Brushes palette.**

   The New Brush dialog box appears.

2. **Click the New Pattern Brush option and then click OK.**

   The Pattern Brush Options dialog box appears, with the Side piece in the proper position. (For a refresher on how that looks, refer to Figure 9-13.)

3. **In the dialog box, give the new brush a name and click OK.**

   The new Pattern brush shows up in the Brushes palette. (Don't worry about the other options right now. We come back to those!)

Technically, the new brush is ready to use right now. (The side artwork fills in the other positions.) But true artists (no slackers here!) want to add the rest of the artwork to the brush. Naturally, this part of the process gets tricky. Notice that the brush, as it currently appears in Figure 9-16, has six slots, two of which are filled by the side artwork. The remaining four slots are for the remaining four pieces. The next set of steps creates them.

Figure 9-16:
The new
Pattern
brush,
awaiting the
four
remaining
pieces.

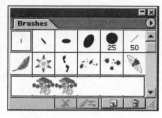

Here's how true artists (the aesthetically dedicated) add the rest of the art-work to the brush, one piece at a time:

1. **Select the artwork and press and hold down the Alt key (Option on a Mac).**

2. **While holding down the Alt key (Option on a Mac), drag the artwork onto the Pattern brush, over the appropriate slot, and then release the mouse button.**

You're over a slot when a bold, dark line appears around the slot. Ah, but how do you know what the appropriate slot is? The brush has no label to tell you what's what. The Pattern Brush Options dialog box obligingly labels the slots, but tragically the order of the Pattern bushes in that dialog box does not correspond to the order in the Brushes palette. The only way to add a new brush to the Pattern brush is to hold down the Alt key (Option on a Mac) and drag it (kicking and screaming) onto the slot in the Brushes palette. But you're in luck! We labeled the slots in the brush for you in Figure 9-17. So feel free to use the Figure as a map.

Figure 9-17:
The Pattern
Brush with
its slots
labeled.

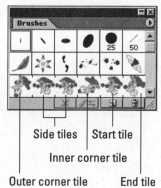

3. **The Pattern Brush Options dialog box appears, displaying the artwork in its appropriate place. Click OK.**

    Don't worry about the other options for now.

4. **Drag all the remaining graphics to their appointed places.**

    Each time you add a graphic, the Pattern Brush Options dialog box appears again. Just click OK and keep going.

Testing your new Pattern brush

When you finally have all your graphics in place, you can test the new brush by applying it to open and closed paths: After making sure that the new brush is selected in the Brushes palette, you create two simple graphics. Anything you create when a brush is selected uses that brush as its stroke, even when you aren't using the Paintbrush tool. Any path will work, but because the Pattern brush uses different artwork at corners, testing the shape on an object that has corners (such as a rectangle) is helpful. In this example, we use the Rectangle tool to create a square. With the new brush still selected, we choose the Brush tool and paint a squiggly line. This procedure shows us how our corner, side, and end tiles look on both curved and straight lines. Testing this way (as we did in Figure 9-18) gives you a good idea of whether all your artwork is working well in the new brush.

If any of your tiles aren't working, tweak the original artwork, select it, and drag it back to the appropriate slot.

If you're suddenly inspired to create more Pattern brushes, a good way to start is by examining the Pattern brushes (nearly a hundred of them) that come with Illustrator. Tinker with them to figure out how they work and how to create them.

Figure 9-18:
The new Pattern brush tested on a square and a squiggle.

Calligraphic brushes for formal occasions

Calligraphic brushes create strokes that emulate the kind of strokes you make with real calligraphic pens; the strokes they make vary in width depending on the direction of the stroke. As the only brushes that aren't created by paths that you can drag into the Brushes palette, Calligraphic brushes are the non-conformist brushes in Illustrator. You set them up by using controls in the Calligraphic Brush Options dialog box, as shown in Figure 9-19.

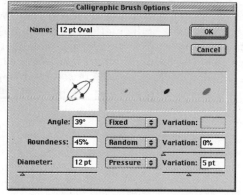

Figure 9-19: The Calligraphic Brush Options dialog box.

Calligraphic brushes are deceptively simple. Don't let the name fool you; you can use them to create any type of artwork, not just calligraphy. (Although they're especially good for emulating traditional pen-and-ink type drawings.)

Yep, the Calligraphic Brush tool seems a lot more like a real pen than the powerful-but-weird Pen tool. A tidbit of international art lore may help you keep them straight: In Japan, calligraphy is an art practiced with brushes.

To create a Calligraphic brush, just follow these steps:

1. **Click the New Brush icon in the Brushes palette.**

   The New Brush dialog box appears.

2. **Select the New Calligraphic Brush option and click OK.**

   The Calligraphic Brush Options dialog box appears — and though it may look intimidating, you have only the following three options to set (after you name the brush):

   • **Angle:** If you were using a real-world brush (or pen, as the case may be), this setting would be the angle at which you're tilting the brush.

- **Roundness:** This setting enables you to change just how round the brush is — from a narrow ellipse to a circle.

- **Diameter:** This setting determines how large the brush is.

The boxes in the middle column determine how (and by how much) those first three options may vary, if at all. Select one of three options in these drop-down list boxes to determine whether the preceding three options may vary not at all (Fixed), randomly (Random), or according to the amount of pressure you apply by using a pressure-sensitive stylus (Pressure).

The boxes in the third column enable you to set the amount by which those first three options may vary (if the method by which they may vary is either Random or Pressure). The higher the numbers, the greater the range of sizes the brush will produce. Figure 9-20 offers a hint of what the Calligraphic Brush tool can do with a pressure-sensitive tablet. The variable width of the stroke adds sophistication to the cartoon.

Figure 9-20:
Artwork created on a pressure-sensitive tablet using Calligraphic brushes.

3. **After you set your options, click OK.**

   The new Calligraphic brush appears in the Brushes palette for you to use.

As you begin creating artwork with brushes, you discover that it's just like painting with real paint brushes — the best artwork requires a combination of several different brushes. Fortunately, you have an astonishing variety of brushes to choose from! The most well-stocked art supply store pales in comparison to the Brushes palette. Best of all, you don't have to pay extra whenever you need a new brush. You can just build your own!

Chapter 10

Extreme Fills and Strokes

● ●

In This Chapter

▶ Creating tone using the Gradient Mesh tool

▶ Making artwork partially transparent

▶ Blending artwork together

▶ Stroking your way to victory over drab art

▶ Creating custom strokes

▶ Way-cool special effects with the Effect menu

▶ Hiding objects with other objects by using masks

● ●

*T*o say that in Illustrator you can create just about anything you can imagine isn't an overstatement. The trick is knowing which buttons to push to make your artistic vision become an Illustrator document. This chapter pushes fills and strokes to their limits, so you can create cool stuff. You know — the stuff that, when you look at it, it makes you scratch your head and say, "How did they do that?" And then you wonder whether you'll ever be able to create anything as artistic.

Well, it isn't so hard. You just need to use some of the more arcane Illustrator tools (the Gradient Mesh tool, for example) and a few cantankerous menu commands that don't want to do anything unless you apply them just right. This chapter shows you how to use them to get good results with the tools and commands that take center stage. Like temperamental sports cars, they're a little tricky to use but worth the effort!

Messing Around with Meshes

Illustrator is really great at filling areas with solid colors, continuous patterns, or gradients. Illustrator gets testy, though, when you try to create a continuous tone — such as the many skin tones that define a human face or the way colors fade into one another in a piece of folded fabric. Illustrator is great at many things, but most artists use paint programs, such as Corel

Painter, whenever they need to do anything with continuous tones. However, the Illustrator Gradient Mesh tool is like a crotchety magician: If you talk nicely to it, it can help you bend the rules a bit.

By using a Gradient Mesh, you can create the shading and tonal effects you expect to find in a paint program. Even so, Gradient Meshes don't replace the need for a paint program. Gradient Meshes can't quite give you the total control over tones that a paint program can, although they can give you cool, painterly effects.

Gradient Meshes overcome the limitations of Gradients, the other Illustrator feature that enables you to blend colors. (For more on Gradients, see Chapter 5.) Simple Gradients fill areas with linear and radial color shifts. Period. Gradient *Meshes* have no such limitation. You can use them to assign colors to the specific points and paths that make up an object. Where the mesh lines cross, you can assign a different color to every line and every point. These colors blend with the colors of the other points. Take a look at Figure 10-1 for a sample of what you can do with a Gradient Mesh.

Figure 10-1:
This cool cat was colored entirely by using the Gradient Mesh tool.

Original artwork   Gradient Mesh added   Gradient Mesh by itself

Figure 10-1 may seem complex, but it's just the same simple steps repeated over and over. The tool seems daunting at first, but you can tackle it if you begin by adding a highlight to a simple shape, as shown in Figure 10-2.

Figure 10-2:
Using the
Gradient
Mesh tool to
create a
highlight in
a path.

To add a Gradient Mesh to a simple shape, just follow these steps:

1. **Create a shape by clicking and dragging with any of the basic object tools (see Chapter 4 for more on basic objects) and fill the shape with a dark color. You can use any shape.**

   For this example, we create a circle and color it black.

2. **Deselect the path. (You can deselect everything by choosing Select⇨Deselect.)**

   Deselecting the path enables you to pick a different color for the Gradient Mesh tool. If you choose a different color with the path selected, you change the color of the object.

3. **Set the Fill color to any light color.**

   Choose Window⇨Color to open the Color palette. Click the Fill box and choose a light color to use as a highlight. (Gradient meshes use only Fill colors and ignore Stroke colors.)

4. **Choose the Gradient Mesh tool from the Toolbox and click the object to which you want to add a highlight.**

   As if by magic, two intersecting paths appear on the object, crossing at the spot where you clicked. This intersection is called the *mesh point*. These paths are the Gradient Mesh. The highlight appears where the paths intersect.

5. **Click other areas within the path to add more highlights — as many as you want.**

The paths that make up the Gradient Mesh can be edited the same as any other path. Click the mesh points in the path with the Direct Selection tool and move them to create different effects. Mesh points also have direction points, just like curved paths. (See Chapter 6 for more on paths.) These direction points can be moved to change the shape of the gradient. You can also change the color of any point or path segment by clicking it and choosing a different color in the Color or Swatches palette. Figure 10-3 shows different effects made by mashing the mesh around.

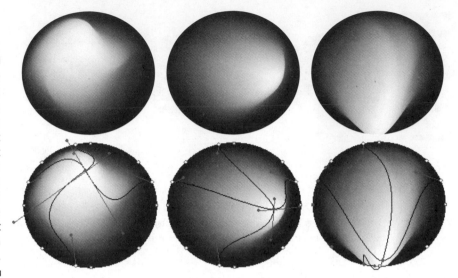

Figure 10-3:
These
objects use
the same
Gradient
Mesh, but
the mesh
points have
been moved
by using the
Direct
Selection
tool.

That's really all there is to this tool! We moved those points by using the Direct Select tool and then tweaked the colors by selecting a point or a path and choosing a new color in the Color or Swatches palette.

You can automate the process by clicking the object you want and choosing Object➪Create Gradient Mesh. This method adds a Gradient Mesh to the object automatically. Illustrator does its best to estimate where the mesh paths should go by looking at the shape of the object and figuring out where the mesh paths should go to shade the object so that it looks three-dimensional. You can even have the Gradient Mesh create the shading for you. Figure 10-4 shows the Create Gradient Mesh dialog box.

```
╔═══════════════ Create Gradient Mesh ═══════════════╗

        Rows: [4        ]          [   OK   ]

      Columns: [4        ]          [ Cancel ]

   Appearance: [To Center      ▼]   ☑ Preview

    Highlight: [100 ] %

╚════════════════════════════════════════════════════╝
```

Figure 10-4:
Set Gradient
Mesh here.

After you select the Gradient Mesh command, the Create Gradient Mesh dialog box opens. Set your options, click OK, and the command does the mesh-y work for you. Here's the all-star lineup of options:

- ✔ **Rows** and **Columns:** These options set the number of mesh paths that the command creates. The higher the number, the more control you have over the colors in your object (but the more complicated the graphic is to work with).

- ✔ **Appearance:** Select one of three Appearance options: To Center, To Edge, and Flat. To Center lightens colors to place a highlight in the center of the object, creating the appearance that the graphic is being pulled outward. To Edge places a highlight at the edges of the object, creating the appearance that the graphic is being pulled inward. Flat doesn't change any colors but still creates the mesh, so you can change colors on your own. See Figure 10-5 for the differences between options.

- ✔ **Highlight:** When you select an Appearance option of To Edge or To Center, the Highlight setting is the maximum amount that the colors lighten to create the 3-D effect.

Figure 10-5 shows an object with a highlight applied to it using Illustrator's automatic highlighting process.

Figure 10-5:
The same Gradient Mesh, with Appearance settings of Flat, To Center, and To Edge.

Making Objects Partially Transparent and Blending Colors

By default, Illustrator creates objects that hide whatever is behind them. However, the Transparency palette enables you to change this situation. By using the Opacity option, you can fade objects so that the underlying objects show through them. You can also blend the colors in the top graphics with the underlying graphics (in an astonishing variety of ways) by using Blend Modes.

One of the powerful features of the Transparency palette is that everything you do in it is *live* — your paths suffer no permanent changes after you make them transparent. You can change opacity again and again — or remove it altogether if you want — without changing your path data. This capability gives you tremendous room to play and experiment with different opacities.

Fade away with opacity

In Figure 10-6, a solid black oval faded-out to 40% opacity partly reveals an angry writer behind it. (Nobody we know, of course.)

Figure 10-6:
The oval at its original opacity (left) and faded to 40% (right) to reveal a disgruntled writer.

To make something partially transparent, follow these steps:

1. **Select the object (or objects) that you want to fade.**

   When you select multiple objects, they all get the same opacity setting.

2. **Choose Window⇨Transparency.**

   The Transparency palette appears, as shown in Figure 10-7.

Figure 10-7:
The Transparency palette.

3. **In the Transparency palette, drag the Opacity slider until it shows the percentage of opacity you want to give to the selected object(s).**

   After you release the mouse button, the selected objects become partially transparent.

By default, transparency applies evenly to both the fill and stroke. To assign the fill and the stroke independent Opacity values, use the Appearance palette. See Chapter 11 for details.

Big fun with math! Blending graphics with Blend Modes

Pssst! Listen very, very carefully while we tell you what's really going on with Blend Modes. Here's the scoop: Forget the math and pay attention to what the resulting artwork looks like.

Illustrator defines every color mathematically. You see that math when you drag sliders in the Color palette. A bright red color may be defined as R:216, G:20, and B:7 (in RGB) or C:20%, M:95%, Y:95%, and K:5% (in CMYK). Each of these numbers reflects a different amount of a component color; every different color has its own color value.

The Blend Modes take the colors in an object and mix them with the colors in underlying objects, performing a mathematical calculation using numbers that identify the colors of the objects. Therefore, if the top object is red, the underlying object is blue, and you have the Blend Mode set to Multiply, red's number gets multiplied by blue's number. The resulting color is what you see. Other modes do more complex calculations. What does that mean? What's blue times red? What's the difference between yellow and mauve? What's the sound of one hand clapping?

In short, it doesn't matter. What the result looks like is what matters! Try this approach for yourself: Select the top object and choose a different Blend Mode. The Blend Modes hang out in the Transparency palette's Blend Mode menu, as shown in Figure 10-8.

Figure 10-9 shows three different Blend Modes at work on the same image — and they're completely changeable. If you try one and don't like it, just choose another from the menu.

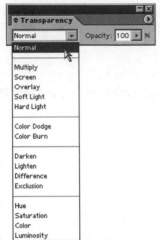

Figure 10-8:
The Blend
Mode
pop-up
menu in the
Transpar-
ency
palette.

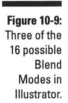

Figure 10-9:
Three of the
16 possible
Blend
Modes in
Illustrator.

Normal   Multiply   Screen

Discovering How Strokes Work

Any path in Illustrator can pick up a stroke (. . . stroke . . . stroke! Sorry. Just daydreaming about going for a nice row on a lake). In Illustrator, a *stroke* is a line placed on a path. A stroke can be of any thickness, which Illustrator calls its *weight*. Strokes can be any color or pattern.

In Chapter 9, we discuss the specialized strokes that you can make with the Paintbrush tool. The Pen and Pencil tools also provide distinctive strokes of their own (Chapters 7 and 8, respectively).

In addition to color and weight, you can give strokes special attributes. These attributes include the specific look of corners (called *joins*) and endings (called *caps*), as well as whether the stroke has a pattern of dashes applied to it. To investigate all the advanced ways you can modify strokes, look at the Stroke palette shown in Figure 10-10. (Choose Window➪Stroke and select

Show Options from the Stroke palette's pop-up menu.) To change the way a stroke appears, select a path and play around in the Stroke palette to see what happens. We won't tell a soul.

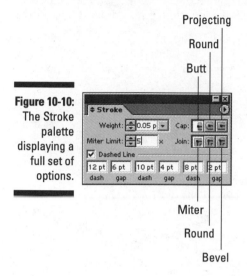

Projecting

Round

Butt

Figure 10-10: The Stroke palette displaying a full set of options.

Miter

Round

Bevel

Strokes are always applied to the center of a path, which means that the strokes, especially those of larger weight, can ooze beyond the path. The path runs along the exact middle of the stroke. For more information on the relationship between strokes and paths, see Chapter 5.

Caps, Joins, and Dashes

A stroke can be (and often is) a continuous line of color that follows a path, even if the path is as convoluted as a strand of cooked spaghetti. But paths can also appear chopped up into dashes. You can tweak the shape of the dashes all at once, without having to fuss over every single one. You can set the shape that an individual *dash* (the basic unit of an *open path*) begins or ends with (its Cap) and the shape of its corner points (its Join).

Strokes can have any of three different caps and any of three different joins applied to them. Combine these with the almost-limitless combinations possible for dash patterns and weights, and you can see the incredible versatility of strokes. To access these additional options, choose Window➪Show Stroke. In the Stroke palette that appears, select Show Options from the palette's pop-up menu; refer to Figure 10-10.

Caps

Shaping the ends of the dashes that make up an open path can change the entire look of the path. For example, imagine a dashed line that's 500 dashes long. Then imagine that all 500 dashes have identical ends, shaped like one of the three shapes in Figure 10-11.

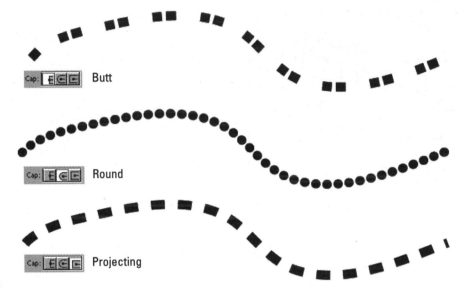

Figure 10-11: Three different caps on three paths.

Depending on which Cap shape you choose, you get three noticeably different capped lines. Here are the options:

- **Butt Cap:** Chops off the stroke at the ends.

- **Round Cap:** Extends the stroke past the ends (or around the dash location) with semicircular ends. (The radius of each semicircle equals half the stroke weight.)

- **Projecting Cap:** Extends the stroke past the ends (or around the dash location) with squared ends. (The amount of each extension equals half the stroke weight.)

To change the way a line is capped, select it with any Selection tool, and then click the desired cap in the Stroke palette.

Joins

The Stroke palette offers three different joins. Figure 10-12 shows how they appear on paths. Joins affect only corner points, not smooth points. (See Chapter 6 for more info on corner points.) They make corners appear sharp and pointy, blunt and rounded, or squared-off.

Figure 10-12:
Three
different
joins on a
path (left to
right): Miter,
Round, and
Bevel.

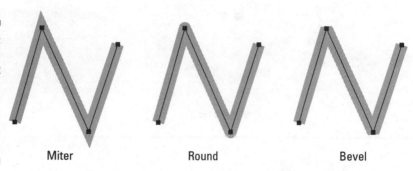

Miter   Round   Bevel

Depending on which Join shape you choose, you get three noticeably different corners. Here are the options:

- **Miter Join:** Causes the outside corner of the stroke to come to a sharp point.

- **Round Join:** Causes the outside corner of a stroke to come to a rounded or smooth curve.

- **Bevel Join:** Cuts off the corner so that the width of the stroke is the same at the bevel as on the rest of the stroke.

If these terms look familiar, then you're probably familiar with woodworking — or you actually paid attention in industrial arts class.

Dashes

Dashes break up the stroke into repeating segments of any length, with gaps between them, also of any length. You can set up to three different dash sizes — and three different gap sizes — in any stroke, as shown in Figure 10-13.

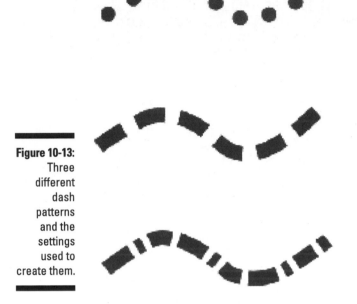

Figure 10-13:
Three
different
dash
patterns
and the
settings
used to
create them.

Dashes work with the Cap settings. (What the heck, call it a labor-saving device.) Whichever Cap setting you use applies to the ends of all the dashes, not just to the ends of the path.

To create a dashed line, follow these steps:

1. **Select the Dashed Line option in the Stroke palette.**

2. **Set a dash size in the first dash box.**

   Remember that the Round and Projecting Cap settings extend the dash from its center by half the width of the stroke. Therefore, if you use the Projecting Cap and your dash setting is 10 points, on a line with a 20-point stroke, the dash will be 30 points long.

   Choose a Butt Cap when you want your dashes to be an exact length that doesn't vary with the width of the stroke. If you want an exact circle for a dash (or a dot), use a 0-point dash. That creates a dot the width of the stroke.

3. **Set the gap size in the first gap box (the distance between the ends of the dashes).**

This setting can be a little confusing if you're using the Round or Projecting Cap settings because these extend the length of the dash past the end of the dash and into the gap, based on the width of the stroke, creating a gap that looks smaller than what you specified. The width of the stroke also affects the gap size. If you want a gap of 20 points and you're using a 10-point stroke, set the gap size to 30 points.

The Effect Menu

The Effect menu contains more amazing things than Area 51. (You know, the place where the government supposedly keeps a crashed alien spacecraft.) Everything that you apply remains *live* — that is, changeable until you tell it to stop changing. Effects change the way an object looks but not the way the object is. Applying effects is like telling the object to put on a specific costume, or changing the appearance of the world when you look through rose-colored glasses. No permanent change takes place.

To put this information technically, instead of rewriting the code for an object (which is what you tell Illustrator to do when you move a point), Effects just tack on extra code, leaving the original code untouched. That extra code can be changed or removed, without affecting the original.

Ah, yes, all things must change — and sometimes you get to change them. Contemplate the concept of *infinite edibility* for a moment. An object in Illustrator is saying, "Turn me into anything." Although Illustrator has always provided the capability of manipulating points, the current version is the first to make such extreme changes possible but not permanent. You can simply get rid of them at any time, without putting a scratch on your original artwork, without having to redo it, without having to resort to Edit⇨Undo, and without having to growl at the dog. Now that's progress.

Applying live effects to objects

Figure 10-14 shows the difference between applying Roughen (gives a distressed look) as a permanent change versus as a live effect. The biggest difference is that the path on the non-live object shows the additional points generated by the permanent Roughen command, found under the Filter menu. The live Roughen command, found under the Effects menu, leaves the path untouched.

Figure 10-14:
Filters versus Effects — a path (left) roughened with the Roughen filter, and the same path (right) roughened with the Roughen effect. (Who would do such a thing to an innocent donut?)

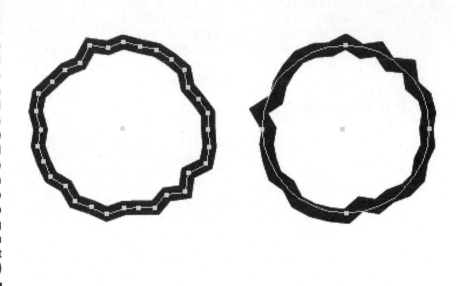

The trickiest part of the Effect menu is that many of its commands share names with commands found under other menus, such as Roughen under the Filter menu. The dialog boxes are even identical! Also, the results look the same; but the way the commands produce those results is different. Keep in mind that if you don't select the command from the Effect menu, you're probably permanently changing the artwork in some way. So pay attention to whether your paths change. That way, if you see a difference, you can use Edit➪Undo and select the same command from the Effect menu.

To apply an effect to a path, follow these steps:

1. **Select a path.**

2. **Choose an effect from the Effect menu.**

   For example, you can choose Effect➪Distort & Transform➪Pucker & Bloat. A dialog box opens for that effect, and you can enter the specific settings.

   You can always go back and change the settings if you don't like the result. (If only we could do that in real life.)

3. **Click OK to apply the effect to the path.**

WARNING!

Many effects only work when the document is in the RGB Document Color Mode (see Chapter 1). If an effect is grayed-out (unavailable) after you select an object, your document is probably in CMYK (cyan, magenta, yellow, and black) mode. You can, however, create your graphics in RGB Document Color Mode and change it to CMYK later. The only catch to this magic trick is that you must first *rasterize* (hang on, we're getting to that) any RGB-specific effects before you convert the document. Rasterizing is the process of transforming vectors into pixels. See Chapter 2 for the lowdown on pixels and vectors, and see the section "Here's the catch . . . rasterization!" (later in this chapter) to find out how to rasterize vectors.

Removing and changing effects

To change or remove effects, use the Appearance palette, as shown in Figure 10-15. The Appearance palette is such an amazing palette that an entire chapter (Chapter 11 to be precise) of this book is devoted to it. For now, though, use the Appearance palette to remove and change effects.

Figure 10-15:
The Gaussian Blur Effect in the Appearance palette.

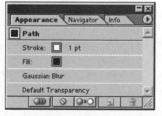

Appearances aside (so to speak), removing an effect is as simple as following these steps:

1. **Select the object that has the effect that you want to remove.**

2. **Choose Window➪Appearance.**

   In the Appearance palette, the selected object is listed as Object or Path. Beneath the object is a list that includes the Stroke and Fill of the object and all the effects applied to it.

3. **In the list, click the effect that you want to discard.**

4. **Click the trash can at the lower-right corner of the Appearance palette.**

   The effect disappears, and the object returns to its former appearance (before you applied the effect).

To change an effect, follow the preceding steps, except instead of clicking the trash can, double-click the effect in the Appearance palette. Doing so opens the particular effect's dialog box, where you can enter new settings. Click OK to apply the effect with the new settings.

Here's the catch . . . rasterization!

All this power comes with a terrible price. By using these effects, you agree to give Adobe your firstborn child unless you can spin a pile of straw into gold. Fortunately, you can escape this predicament by correctly naming Illustrator's product manager in three guesses when he comes to collect his fee — or by figuring out rasterization. (No, that isn't his name.)

Unfortunately, live effects can't always remain live indefinitely. Effects, such as Colored Pencil and Neon Glow, work only when the image is in RGB Document Color Mode. You can create your artwork in RGB, but many times when you're ready to print, you need to change to CMYK mode. (For more information on color modes, see Chapter 1.) After you change to CMYK, though, all those effects disappear! What's a poor artist to do?

Here's where rasterization comes in. Rasterization converts the information into pixels, just like the pixels Photoshop uses. (See Chapter 2 for more information on pixels.) You can no longer edit individual points, but you can convert to CMYK without losing your artwork. After you rasterize an Illustrator graphic, the graphic has all the limitations of any other pixel-based graphic, even though it's in Illustrator.

To rasterize a graphic, choose Effect⇨Rasterize. The Rasterization dialog box appears, as shown in Figure 10-16.

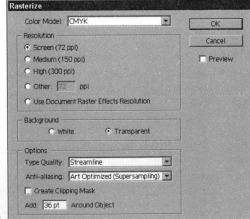

Figure 10-16:
The famous Rasterization dialog box takes a bow.

In the Rasterization dialog box, you can set the following options:

- ✔ **Color Model:** This setting determines the color model used by the resulting graphic. Try to use the color model of your target output as much as possible. If you're creating a graphic print in grayscale, choose Grayscale. If you're bound for the Web, choose RGB.

- ✔ **Resolution:** This setting determines how much information the resulting image contains. Try to match this setting with the graphic's purpose. For the Web, select 72 ppi (pixels per inch). For most ink jet printers, 150 ppi is sufficient. For high-resolution printing, 300 ppi is a good, all-purpose size.

- ✔ **Background:** Pixel-based images are always rectangular. If the graphic you're rasterizing is anything but rectangular, you have to add a background to it to make it rectangular. That space can be White or Transparent. White is fine for a stand-alone graphic, but if that graphic is in front of other objects, the white background will obscure them. When this is the case, choose Transparent.

- ✔ **Options:** The Anti-Alias option adds a slight blurring wherever different colors meet. Believe it or not, this setting usually makes the resulting graphic look better. Results vary from graphic to graphic, of course, so try rasterizing with and without the Anti-Alias option selected. The Create Clipping Mask option matters only if you selected White for the Background setting. In Illustrator, a *Clipping Mask* is a special graphic that hides parts of other graphics. If you select the Create Clipping Mask option, a Clipping Mask is added to hide the white parts added to make the graphic rectangular.

- ✔ **Add:** Tying a numeric value in this option box adds extra pixels around the graphic, just in case you need them. Hey, you never know! Nobody wants to run short of pixels. (Okay, just kidding.) This option actually helps prevent circles from getting clipped on the edges. (Nothing grouchier than a circle that's having a bad hair day.)

After you choose your settings, click OK to convert your graphic to pixels.

Clipping Masks

No, they're not special headgear that the barber wears to entertain young customers. Clipping Masks are a simple, yet incredibly handy, Illustrator feature. Simply put, they hide things. Like Effects and Transparency settings, Clipping Masks are live functions that make no permanent change to path data. They make things look different, but you can take them away with a single command, and your paths remain exactly as they were before.

Clipping Masks use objects to hide other objects, as shown in Figure 10-17. The top object (the masking object) becomes completely transparent. The underlying objects become invisible except for where the mask object is. The number of objects beneath the mask doesn't matter. Only the topmost object functions as the masking object. The top object's fill and stroke also don't matter, because the top object becomes invisible.

Figure 10-17:
The original artwork, the masking object in front of the artwork, and the masked artwork.

To create a clipping mask, here's the drill:

1. **Create an object to be used as a mask.**

   Masks can be any shape or color. You can even use text as a mask.

2. **Position the object in front of whatever you want to mask out.**

3. **Select the object and all the objects behind it that you want to mask out.**

   Shift+click with the Selection tool to select multiple objects.

4. **Choose Object⇨Clipping Mask⇨Make.**

   The masking object and anything outside the mask disappear, leaving just what's inside and behind the masking object.

The things that seem to disappear after you apply the mask aren't really gone. They're just hidden. You can bring them back by choosing Object⇨Clipping Mask⇨Release. Sometimes that's more impressive than pulling a rabbit out of your hat.

Chapter 11

Keeping Up Appearances, with Style(s)

In This Chapter

▶ Looking at the Appearance palette

▶ Adding additional fills and strokes

▶ Combining Effect settings to create different effects

▶ Creating a style

▶ Manipulating existing styles

*L*ong ago (well, okay, in the not-too-distant past), Illustrator was a straight-forward program that offered relatively few (and relatively obvious) choices. You knew when you looked at a pink rectangle that it was made with four corner points joined by four paths and was filled with a single, solid pink color. But those days of blissful innocence are past. Now that pink rectangle may really be a red rectangle that some fiend faded to 50% Opacity by using the Transparency palette. And that rectangle may not be a rectangle at all, but a graphic of an old shoe that has been disguised as a rectangle using the Effect⇨Convert to Shape⇨Rectangle command. In this world of illusions, where anything can appear to be anything else and nothing is as it seems, what's an artist to do?

In this chapter, you discover a wonderful tool for cutting through (and taking control of) the illusions of Illustrator: the Appearance palette. The Appearance palette enables you to see exactly what secrets your artwork is hiding. If that were all it did, it'd be worth its weight in gold. But it does so much more! Beyond just seeing what's been done to an illustration, you also find out how to change the attributes of the illustration. For example, you can alter applied effects — or delete them altogether.

You also discover how to use the Appearance palette to target only the fill of an object (or just the stroke) when you apply Transparency or Effects settings. (If you don't use the Appearance palette, Illustrator applies the same settings to both the fill and stroke simultaneously.) You also use the Appearance palette to perform casual miracles that were impossible in any previous version of Illustrator, such as assigning multiple fills and strokes to a single object.

To make matters even better, you find out how to save all the Appearance settings as a Style. Styles are saved in the Styles palette. You can apply a style to any object you create in the future. In addition to being a quick way to apply all these attributes to objects, styles can be updated in a way that also updates all objects with those styles applied.

The Appearance Palette

The Appearance palette, shown in Figure 11-1, is where you go to see why your artwork looks the way it does. (Although, the palette can't explain why anybody would put neon-pink paisleys all over the place.) You can view the Appearance palette by choosing Window➪Appearance. When the Appearance palette wafts into view, it bears a vast treasure of option information. In its basic state, the palette displays Fill, Stroke, and Transparency settings. In its more complex state, the palette displays additional fills and strokes, and effects applied to those fills and strokes (as well as to the object itself).

Figure 11-1:
The
Appearance
palette.

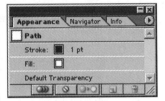

Not to worry: This welter of information isn't nearly as confusing as your income tax form. Here's why: All along, in the course of creating your artwork, you've been putting all these information tidbits into the Appearance palette. You tell Illustrator to add info to this palette every time you set an option that changes the way your object looks (such as Stroke, Fill, and Transparency).

The Appearance palette faithfully records all this information all the time, even if you don't look at it. (Good thing it doesn't record everything appearance related, like that big-bangs shag hairdo you were so proud of in 1976.)

Reading the Appearance palette

The Appearance palette, shown in Figure 11-2, displays accumulated information about a particular object. Now, about this silly matter of reading all that balderdash. . . .

To make sense of all the Appearance palette's information, peruse the following list of its features:

Figure 11-2:
The
Appearance
palette
displays an
array of
information
about the
object, such
as the
stroke and
fill data
shown here.

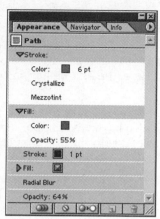

▶ **Target:** This feature identifies the type of graphic that the information in the Appearance palette refers to. Typically this feature reads Object or Path, meaning the information in the palette refers to (or will be applied to) appearance that is or will be applied to a single selected object. When you select a group or a layer, the target reads Group or Layer. If text is selected, the target reads Type. The target section is always at the top. A tiny thumbnail image emulates the appearance of the graphic.

▶ **Global effects:** These effects apply equally to, and affect all aspects of, the entire object. Whenever you apply Effects or Transparency settings (as we describe in Chapter 10) without using the Appearance palette, you apply the effects as global effects. Although they're usually the first attribute you apply, they always appear near the bottom of the list in the Appearance palette.

Another way to differentiate global effects from other effects is the way they line up with other items listed in the palette. Global effects appear in alignment with the Stroke and the Fill listings. Effects applied to a specific stroke are indented beneath the listing for that specific stroke. In Figure 11-2, Radial Blur and Unsharp Mask are the global effects.

▶ **Strokes:** Objects can have more than one stroke only when you add them through the Appearance palette (see "Adding fills and strokes" later in this chapter). Therefore, the first one (listed at the top) is typically the one also shown in the Toolbox. The target may have additional strokes listed here as well. Strokes can have effects applied to them specifically. In Figure 11-2, you see a single stroke with a weight of 6 points. See Chapter 5 for more information on strokes.

- **Stroke and Fill effects:** Effects can be applied directly to strokes and fills, instead of to the entire object, group, or layer. In this figure, the stroke has both a Crystallize and a Mezzotint effect applied to it.

- **Stroke and Fill Transparency:** Each stroke and fill can have various Transparency settings applied to it. Here, the first fill has an Opacity of 55% and a blend mode of Multiply.

- **Fill:** Each object (group or layer) can have multiple fills (as it can have multiple strokes). Each fill can also have any number of effects applied to it. This object has both a solid color fill and a pattern fill applied to it.

- **Transparency:** This feature is the transparency appearance for the entire object, group, or layer. In Figure 11-2, the transparency is set to Object Opacity: 64%, meaning the entire object has been faded to 64%. If no special Transparency settings were applied, this would simply read Default Transparency. See Chapter 10 for more information on Transparency.

The top-to-bottom order of the fills and strokes in the Appearance palette reflect a front-to-back order in the graphic. Strokes and fills on top in the palette appear in front of the strokes and fills that are lower in the palette. Effects run from top to bottom in terms of which effect is applied to the graphic first.

Most of the items in the Appearance palette can be moved up and down through the list into different positions, and this change is reflected in the actual graphic. For instance, you can take the Feather effect applied to a stroke and move it so that it's applied to a fill. You can also take that effect and move it so it applies to the entire object. To move something in the Appearance palette, drag it up and down through the palette, just as you move things in the Layers palette.

If a fill or stroke has an effect applied to it, the little disclosure triangle automatically appears on the left and points down, listing the attributes of that fill or stroke. When you have a whole lot of different effects applied to a fill or stroke, the palette can get cumbersome. Clicking the disclosure triangle hides the list of effects. You can access the list at any time by clicking the disclosure triangle again.

Adding fills and strokes

Chapter 5 explores fills and strokes in greater detail (and if you want to nip back there for more information, we can wait). When you apply a different stroke or fill to an object without using the Appearance palette, the fill or stroke replaces any existing fill or stroke. You don't have to settle for just one of each, though! By using the Appearance palette, as shown in Figure 11-3, you can add as many fills and strokes as you want. This feature offers some interesting possibilities. For example, you can give a path three different colored strokes of different sizes, to create a striped path. Or you can apply a pattern fill over a solid-color fill.

Just follow these steps to apply an additional fill and stroke to an object:

1. **Create an object with a fill color and a thick stroke.**

   In this example, we made a rectangle by clicking and dragging with the Rectangle tool. (See Chapter 4 for more information on the rectangle tool.) We filled it with a gradient by clicking the Fill box in the Toolbox, and then by clicking a gradient swatch in the Swatches palette. We next added a 20-point black stroke to the square by clicking the Stroke box in the Toolbox, and then by clicking a black swatch in the Swatches palette, and finally by choosing 20 points from the Stroke palette. For more info on fills and strokes, see Chapter 5.

2. **Select Add New Fill from the pop-up menu in the Appearance palette.**

   Illustrator adds a fill, but you don't see any difference because the new fill is identical to the fill already there. The new fill is highlighted in the Appearance palette, however, and as soon as you select a new fill color from the Color palette or the Swatches palette, you see the new fill over the old one.

3. **With the new fill still highlighted in the Appearance palette, change the fill to a pattern fill from the Swatches palette**

   For this example, change the fill to the pattern Azure Rings by clicking it in the Swatches palette.

   If you don't know which pattern is the Azure Rings palette, pause your cursor for a moment above each swatch. Its name pops up.

4. **Choose Add New Stroke from the pop-up menu in the Appearance palette.**

   A stroke appears on top of the original stroke. As with the added fill color, the new stroke uses the same settings as the previous stroke, so you don't see an immediate difference.

5. **In the Color palette, change the color of the stroke to White and change its stroke width to 10 points.**

After you add strokes and fills, you can move them around. Simply click them in the Appearance palette and drag up or down. As you drag, a black line appears in the palette, indicating where that fill or stroke will go after you release it.

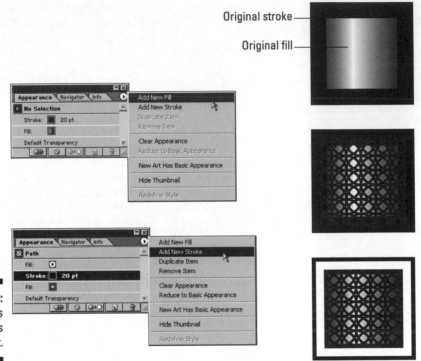

Figure 11-3: Adding fills and strokes to an object.

Multiple fills and strokes work great with the Transparency palette. Each fill and stroke can have its own Transparency settings. This approach is a great way to blend fills and strokes together to achieve unique appearances. For example, if you apply a solid color fill over a Pattern fill and then change the Blend mode of the color fill to Hue, you replace the color(s) in the pattern with the color of the solid color but still maintain all the detail of the pattern. See Chapter 10 for more information on Transparency and Blend modes.

Changing the appearance of groups and layers

You can change the appearance of groups or layers as well as objects. Groups are collections of separate objects that have been grouped together (using the Object⇨Group command) so that they act like a single object when you select them with the Selection tool (see Chapter 3 for more information on the Group command). Similar to grouping, layers are a method of organizing multiple elements of your graphic into separate areas. Chapter 14 discusses layers in depth.

To change the appearance, you need to *target* those groups or layers first. Targeting is a method of selecting a group or layer so that any changes made to the appearance affect all the objects in the group or layer. Changing the appearance of groups or layers creates a global appearance for all objects in the group or on the layer. Objects still maintain their individual appearance settings, but any group or layer changes are added to all the objects.

To change the appearance of a group by adding an effect, just follow these steps:

1. **Select a group by clicking it with the regular Selection tool.**

2. **Add an effect to the group.**

   For this example, add a Gaussian Blur by choosing Effect⇨Blur⇨ Gaussian Blur. In the Gaussian Blur dialog box that opens when you choose the effect, set the Radius to 5 and click OK.

   All the objects in the group become blurred. Just like that. Wow.

On the other hand, targeting a layer to apply an effect is a little more unusual, as shown in Figure 11-4.

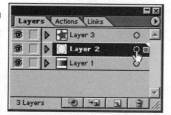

Figure 11-4: Targeting a layer to apply an effect.

Layers are a way to organize and arrange objects in your document. (Chapter 14 talks about layers in depth.) Every time you add an object to a layer, the appearance of that object changes to match the settings of the layer. When that object goes to another layer, with different Layer Appearance settings, the object's appearance changes again.

To target and apply an effect to a layer, just follow these steps:

1. **Choose Window⇨Layers.**

   The Layers palette opens.

2. **In the Layers palette, click the Target Layer Appearance button beside the layer that has the appearance you want to change.**

   The Target Layer Appearance button is the circle to the right of the name of the layer in the Layers palette. Clicking this circle targets the layer, so your changes affect that layer.

3. **Add an effect to the layer.**

   For this example, choose Effect⇨Stylize⇨Feather. The Feather dialog box opens. Set the Feather Radius to 5 and click OK. All the objects in the layer are feathered. (Lay in a large supply of birdseed. Just kidding.)

Applying effects to strokes and fills

Normally, whenever you apply an effect, it's applied to the entire object. However, to keep matters interesting (or confusing), you can also apply any effect to either a stroke or a fill. Whichever one you change, the other remains unaffected, as shown in Figure 11-5.

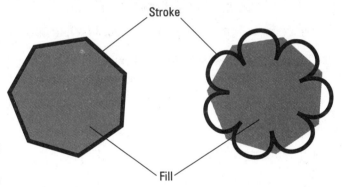

Figure 11-5:
The Pucker & Bloat effect applied to the stroke, but not the fill.

Stroke

Fill

To apply an effect to a stroke only or to a fill only, just follow these steps:

1. **Select an object by clicking it with the Selection tool.**

2. **Choose Window⇨Appearance to open the Appearance palette.**

3. **In the Appearance palette, select the Stroke or the Fill to which you want to apply the effect.**

   For this example, select the Stroke.

4. **Choose an effect from the Effect menu.**

   For this example, choose Effect⇨Distort & Transform⇨Pucker & Bloat. The Pucker & Bloat dialog box opens. Drag the slider towards Pucker (to the left) or towards Bloat (to the right). The effect applies to the path and takes an appropriate place in the Appearance palette.

When you look at your artwork, you see that only the stroke has been Puckered (or Bloated, depending on what you chose). If you want to apply an effect just to a fill, follow the preceding steps, but select a fill instead of a stroke.

Going back to adjust settings

Any effect previously applied to an object, group, or layer can be modified. You can edit the effect by double-clicking it in the Appearance palette. After you do, the effect's dialog box appears, enabling you to edit the current values for that effect. If the effect dialog box has a preview check box, place a check in it and watch your changes in real time!

Don't try to edit an effect you just applied by selecting that effect again in the Effect menu. Doing so applies the same effect a second time over the same path. Instead, double-click the effect in the Appearance palette.

Removing appearances

If you're tired of keeping up appearances (for example, you feel your artwork is too complex and want it to be cleaner and simpler, or you've added so many effects that printing or drawing onscreen takes too long), Illustrator gives you three ways to remove them (from onscreen artwork, that is). You can take an appearance apart (one attribute at a time), trash all the appearance except the basics, or zap everything at once. Here's how you accomplish each of these tasks:

- ✔ **To get rid of a single effect, transparency setting, stroke, or fill:** Select what you want to remove in the Appearance palette and then click the little trash can icon at the bottom right of the palette.

- ✔ **To get rid of all effects, extra fills and strokes, and transparencies:** Click the Reduce to Basic Appearance button (the button with two circles at the bottom center of the palette). This action strips away everything except one stroke and one fill color and resets the Default Transparency to a Blend mode of Normal and an Opacity setting of 100%. (See Chapter 10 for more details on Blend modes and Opacity settings.)

- ✔ **To clear everything away:** Leaving a path with no strokes or fills whatsoever, click the Clear Appearance button (the circle with a line through it at the bottom left of the palette).

Note that the Appearance palette always shows a Fill, Stroke, and Default Transparency for an object, even after you throw them away. Throwing away a fill or stroke automatically sets it to None; throwing away a transparency sets it to the Default Transparency setting, which is a blend mode of Normal and an Opacity setting of 100%.

If you're wondering what the last two buttons in the Appearance palette do, here's the skinny. The icon with the three overlapping circles enables you to specify whether appearance effects are applied to new objects. Click the button so that it becomes highlighted to apply just a single fill or stroke to new objects. You can also choose the New Art Has Basic Appearance option from the

Appearance palette pop-up menu. Click the button so that it isn't highlighted to apply all the appearance effects to new objects. You can also uncheck the New Art Has Basic Appearance option from the palette pop-up menu.

The dog-eared page icon is the Duplicate button. Select the appearance effect or attribute (stroke or fill) you want and click this button to create a duplicate.

Killing live effects until they're dead

Sometimes, you want to preserve the way an object looks, but get rid of all the things in the Appearance palette. One reason to do this is that all these multiple fills, strokes, and effects can take tremendous processing power when they are live. This situation can result in long print times, or long times redrawing whenever you make a change to your graphic. The drawback to live effects is that they are previews and need to be recalculated every time you make a change. You can kill these live effects so that they permanently change your graphic. You can no longer make individual adjustments to them or remove them, but all the calculations have been made and the graphic has been permanently changed. This results in a much simpler, if limited, graphic.

To permanently set all the live effects, choose Object⇨Expand Appearance. The object expands, which is a completely counterintuitive way of saying the object gets simpler. All the settings made in the Appearance palette are really just previews. They haven't been applied to the graphic. Every time you make a change, that appearance needs to be completely recalculated. Expanding the object applies all those changes to it permanently, so the calculations don't have to be made again. The graphic is simpler, if less editable. Figure 11-6 shows the difference between live and, um, dead objects.

Figure 11-6:
A live effect (left) and after Expand Appearance is applied.

Figuring Out Styles

Styles are collections of colors, transparency settings, effects, and additional fills and strokes that can be applied to any path, group, or layer. Think of all that information in the Appearance palette. Saving it and applying it to different objects (without having to recreate all those settings) can significantly reduce the time and effort you spend. That's one advantage of using styles.

Another advantage is that any update in the style changes all the objects to which you apply that style. For instance, if you apply a style with a red fill and black stroke to a path, and later you update the style to an orange fill, the object you previously applied that style to changes to an orange fill and black stroke.

Applying styles to objects

Illustrator comes with a whole slew of premade styles that are stored in the Styles palette (see Figure 11-7), ready for you to use with just a click.

To apply a style to an object, follow these steps:

1. **Select an object.**

2. **Open the Styles palette by choosing Window⇨Styles.**

   The Styles palette appears.

3. **Click a thumbnail style in the Styles palette.**

   Doing so automatically applies all the settings to the selected object.

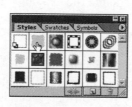

Figure 11-7: Applying a style to a path.

Creating and editing styles

You can create a style from any selected object in the document, as shown in Figure 11-8. You can also create a style based on the current Appearance palette settings. (The Appearance palette contains the settings for the last object selected, even if that object isn't currently selected.)

1. **Select an object (or not, as the case may be).**

   If you don't select a path, the style you create adopts the current settings in the Appearance palette.

2. **Open the Styles palette by choosing Window⇨Styles.**

   The Styles palette appears.

3. **Click the New Style button (the middle button at the bottom right of the Styles palette) or simply drag your object onto an empty space in the Styles palette.**

    A thumbnail representation of the new style appears in the Styles palette.

Figure 11-8:
Creating a
new style.

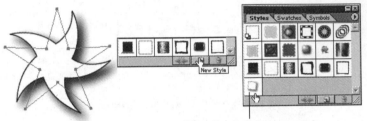

Thumbnail of the new style

You have more than one method available to edit an existing style. Regardless of the method you use, Illustrator automatically updates all the objects that have that style applied to them to match the new style. The basic way to edit an existing style is to redefine it.

After you apply a style to an object, you can click the Break Link to Style button on the Styles palette to prevent Illustrator from updating the object to a new style if you redefine the existing one.

To redefine an existing style, as shown in Figure 11-9, just follow these steps:

1. **Create a basic shape and apply a style to it.**

    In this instance, we created a triangle by using the Basic Shapes tool. Then we chose Window⇨Styles and applied the style Bermuda to the triangle by clicking that style in the Styles palette.

2. **Edit the selected object as you normally would to create the new appearance that you want.**

    Change the fill and stroke, and/or add effects. In this case, we chose a darker fill color and added two strokes of different colors to the triangle by using the Add New Stroke command in the Appearance palette (which we describe in the "Adding fills and strokes" section of this chapter).

3. **After you're satisfied with the changes, open the Appearance palette by choosing Window⇨Appearance. With the altered object still selected, choose Redefine Style *Style Name* from the Appearance palette's pop-up menu, accessed by clicking the triangle in the upper-right corner of the Appearance palette.**

You're replacing a style, but you have to do it through the Appearance palette. Go figure! Because the name of the style we edited in this example was *Bermuda,* the menu reads *Redefine Style "Bermuda."* The menu changes to whatever name the style has been given.

Illustrator updates the style in the Styles palette with the changes — and updates any object in the document that has that same style applied to it.

Another way to edit an existing style is to replace it with another set of Appearance settings. Set the fill, stroke, and effects for an object to make it look the way you want. Then hold down the Alt key (Option on a Mac) and drag the object over the thumbnail of the style that you want to replace in the Styles palette. It may look as if you're dragging that entire object into the Styles palette, but you're just dragging its fill, stroke, and effects settings (in other words, its appearance). To let you know that the object is in the proper position to replace the existing style, a black border appears around the style. Release the mouse to update the style to the Appearance settings of the selected object. Illustrator also updates all objects that share the style.

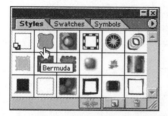

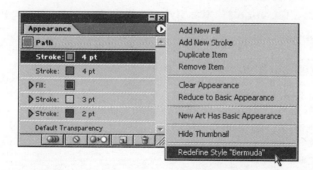

Figure 11-9:
Redefining an existing style.

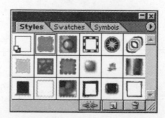

Spotting the difference between graphic and text styles

Illustrator has graphic styles but not text styles. *Graphic styles* specify graphic attributes, such as fill color, stroke color, transparency, additional strokes and fills, and any applied effects. *Text styles* specify text attributes, such as font, size, leading, alignment, and other Character palette and Paragraph palette settings.

Because Illustrator has only graphic styles, you can't save text attributes, such as font and alignment, with your styles. However, you can apply graphic styles to text and text objects; the graphic styles just don't apply any text-specific attributes.

Applying graphic styles to text

Illustrator looks at text as a picture of letters and numbers — not as letters and numbers — and then applies a graphic style to that picture, as shown in Figure 11-10.

To apply a graphic style to text, just follow these steps:

1. **Select text by using the Selection tool.**
2. **Display the Styles palette by choosing Window⇨Styles.**
3. **Click a thumbnail in the Styles palette to apply that style to the text.**

    Illustrator applies the graphic style you select to the text object.

You can quickly apply a style to text or other objects by selecting the style you want and then clicking with the Paint Bucket (which is located in the same slot as the Eyedropper tool) on anything you want to change to that style. (It's so much easier than dragging a real paint bucket. And you don't have to worry about the carpet. Is Illustrator great, or what?)

jeepers

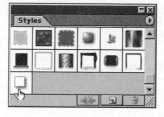

jeepers

Figure 11-10:
Applying a
graphic
style to text.

Part III
Taking Your Paths to Obedience School

The 5th Wave   By Rich Tennant

"Are you sure that's the best way to apply a stroke to a path?"

In this part . . .

Half the battle in Illustrator is creating stuff. The other half is modifying and organizing the stuff you create. This part focuses on manipulating your creations into exactly what you want them to be. You start by selecting and moving pieces of artwork and the individual parts that make up the artwork. Then you can rotate, scale, skew, or mash your art around in a variety of ways. For a really exciting time (adventures in unbridled mutation), you transform one piece of artwork into another by using the Blend tool. Finally, Illustrator reveals a secret of the ages: Organizing is a fun and exciting activity (instead of a tedious chore that devours time like a slo-mo shark) when you use delightful innovations, such as layers, the Align palette, grid tools, and guides.

Chapter 12

Pushing, Pulling, Poking, and Prodding

In This Chapter

▶ Understanding how transformations work

▶ Using the Scale, Rotate, Reflect, and Shear tools

▶ Moving and shaking (even stirring) objects and portions of objects

▶ Blending paths until they're confused and happy

Art that you create in Illustrator can be modified in a number of ways. Perhaps the most powerful of these ways are transformations and distortions. These enable you to bend, move, and manipulate paths and other Illustrator objects like silly putty, shaping them to your every whim. (Power mongers, rejoice!)

In this chapter, you find out how to use the many Illustrator transformation tools to alter the shape of your artwork in any way you desire. In Chapter 13, you dive into distortions.

Understanding the Five Transformation Sisters

You can do five fundamental things to paths: move, scale, rotate, reflect, and shear. Each of these transformations has both a tool and a dialog box associated with it. Move actually has five tools, if you count all arrow and lasso tools (which also are used to move selections).

The key to using all these tools (and their control-freak dialog boxes) is to select what you want to change first and then to apply the transformation. Use the Selection tool when you want to transform an entire object (Shift-click with the Selection tool to transform multiple objects simultaneously) or use the Direct Selection tool to transform just a few points at a time.

Move

Illustrator enables you to move objects simply by clicking and dragging them with any of the selection arrows. Figure 12-1, for example, shows an elaborate object moved from one spot to another.

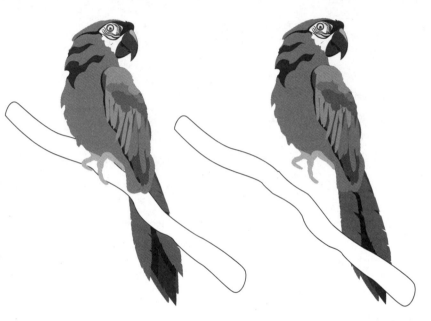

Figure 12-1:
The original illustration (left) is modified (right) by using the Selection tool to move the bird. (Suddenly the parrot seems to defy gravity.)

Sometimes, you need to move a selection a specific amount. Suppose you draw a flower (or a weed, if your drawing skills aren't quite up to par yet), and you want to move this flower exactly one inch to the right.

To specify how much you want to move your object, follow these steps:

1. **Select your artwork and choose Object➪Transform➪Move.**

   The Move dialog box appears (see Figure 12-2).

   You can also double-click any of the three arrow tools to access the Move dialog box.

2. **In the Distance field, type how far you want the object to move; in this case, type** 1 in.

3. **Type** 0 **in the Angle field.**

   Setting the Angle field at 0 ensures that the object moves directly to the right without shifting up or down. Leave the other fields at their default settings.

4. **Click OK to exit the Move dialog box.**

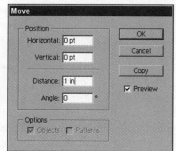

Figure 12-2:
The Move
dialog box.

Okay, so you may wonder how Illustrator knows to move the flower just an inch to the *right*, instead of to the left. Well, Illustrator knows because the number you entered in the text field is a positive number. If you enter a negative number, the object moves to the left. In fact, the only way to move something to the left in the Move dialog box is to enter a negative number in the Horizontal text field. If you do that, the Angle field automatically changes to 180 degrees, which is to the left (0 degrees is to the right).

Tell Illustrator the appropriate measurement unit with these symbols: **in** for inches, **p** for picas, **pt** for points, **cm** for centimeters, **mm** for millimeters, or **px** for pixels.

Scale

To make something bigger or smaller in Illustrator, you *scale* it. Illustrator has a Scale tool, a Scale dialog box, and a scale function as part of the bounding box that surrounds an object after you select it with the Selection tool. Not only can you make an object bigger or smaller, but you can also squish an item to change its size. For instance, you can make an item twice as high but the same width as it was originally. Figure 12-3 shows what happens when you scale an object.

Figure 12-3:
The original
artwork
(left) scaled
smaller
(center) and
larger
(right).

TIP

The easiest way to scale art is not to use the Scale tool but to use the bounding box that appears around objects after you select them with the Selection tool. The bounding box enables you to scale and rotate artwork. To scale artwork, click and drag the handles (big, black squares) around the outside of the artwork.

If you hold down the Shift key as you drag the bounding box handles, you constrain the sizing of the bounding box (and the artwork) so that the width and height are scaled proportionately. This is typically a good thing — it prevents your artwork from getting really, really fat or really, really skinny as you scale it.

TIP

Holding down the Shift key as you use any of a variety of tools keeps the object constrained. For instance, with the Rotate tool, holding down the Shift key constrains rotation to 45° increments (a nice angle sideways, another nice angle upside-down, another nice angle sideways the other way, and finally one more lovely angle straight up).

The bounding box is nice and all, but you don't find Illustrator Knights of the Galaxy using it because they like doing things the hard way (you know, greater evidence of artistic prowess, more prestige). The Scale tool is definitely more difficult to use than the bounding box for resizing artwork, but the Scale tool also has all sorts of capabilities that the bounding box doesn't have, such as scaling from a specific origin, using specific values, and copying as you scale. Locate these buried treasures by double-clicking the Scale tool in the Toolbox.

As a certain short, green, levitating philosopher once said, "Try not. Do. Or do not. . . ." Well, okay, you can just try the technique, as shown in Figure 12-4, if you want to. The galaxy isn't at stake here.

Figure 12-4:
Original artwork selected (left); the hairline preview that appears when you drag with the Scale tool (center); and the final scaled artwork (right).

To scale your artwork by using the Scale tool, just follow these steps:

1. **Select your artwork using the regular Selection tool.**

2. **Choose the Scale tool.**

   The Scale tool icon is supposed to look like a small box being resized into a bigger box. Really. (Call it artistic license.)

3. **Click at the corner of the artwork and drag.**

   By default, the Scale tool scales from the center of the selection. When you drag, a hairline preview of your artwork appears, indicating the size and shape that your graphic will be after you release the mouse.

   Drag away from the graphic to enlarge it; drag toward the center of the graphic to shrink it.

4. **Release the mouse button when the art is the size you want.**

   The artwork scales to that size.

All you accuracy addicts out there (you know who you are) can double-click the Scale tool slot in the Toolbox to indulge your habit: A Scale dialog box appears and offers a nice blank space in which you can type an exact scale percentage. (Some folks just have a hankering to know what an object looks like at 183 percent or 0.5597 percent of its current size.) You can also access these dialog boxes by choosing Object➪Transform and choosing your desired transformation.

But wait, there's more! You also have an option for choosing a Uniform or Non-Uniform scale change. Well, no, choosing Uniform won't dress up the object in khakis. Instead, the object acts as if you pressed some super Shift key and ends up looking like a bigger or smaller version of the original, identically proportioned (nary a squish anywhere). Non-Uniform scale enables you to enter separate scale percentages for Horizontal or Vertical measurements. In addition to scaling objects themselves, you can also scale Patterns, Strokes, and Effects, if your object(s) contains any of these attributes. See Chapter 5 for more on patterns and strokes and Chapter 10 for more on effects.

Not content with scaling from the center? The two-click method of using the Scale tool may soothe your yearning for alternatives. It enables you to move the origin point around the screen before scaling. The *origin point* is a place tacked to the artboard around which the rest of the artwork scales. Normally, the origin point is in the middle of the selection, but you can put the origin point anywhere, even outside the selection! Just select the Scale tool from the Toolbox and click once before you do the click-and-drag routine to scale the object. Illustrator resets the origin point to the location where you single-clicked.

TIP

If you drag back across the origin point (or the middle if you didn't set one) while using the Scale tool, you may well flip the artwork over. That's a little disconcerting, but as long as you don't release the mouse button, you can always drag back and fix it. If you do release the mouse button, you can undo (choose Edit➪Undo).

Rotate

Spinning your artwork around in circles is a good way to whittle away an afternoon. Sometimes, we just sit, click, and spin, watching the artwork rotate on the screen. It's mesmerizing. Then again, we don't really get out all that much.

You can use the funky corner arrows in the bounding box (which shows up when you have something selected with the regular Selection tool) or by using the Rotate tool. The Rotate tool (like the Scale tool) enables you to set the origin point, which is the location the artwork rotates around. Double-clicking the Rotate tool also enables you to set a specific angle of rotation. Figure 12-5 shows artwork before and after it's rotated with the Rotate tool.

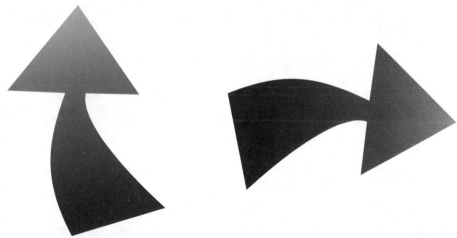

Figure 12-5: The original artwork (left) and after it's rotated (right).

Reflect

Using the Reflect command, you can flip a selection over any axis, making a mirror image. Figure 12-6 shows original artwork before and after it's flipped over a 90° axis.

Figure 12-6:
Reflecting the artwork by using the Reflect tool.

To use the Reflect tool to create a mirror image, just follow these steps:

1. **Select the artwork to be reflected.**

2. **Choose the Reflect tool from the Toolbox.**

3. **Press and hold the Shift key. (Release it after you release the mouse button in Step 5.)**

   The Shift key constrains the reflection to a 45° angle, which makes a horizontal reflection easier to accomplish. (Who knew it took so much work to be a beam of light? Other than Einstein. . . .)

4. **Click the far-right edge of the selected artwork and drag to the left.**

5. **Release the mouse button (and then the Shift key) after the artwork "flips" over.**

But that's not all! If you act now and double-click the Reflect tool, you get the Reflect dialog box (shown in Figure 12-7) absolutely free! Here are its exciting capabilities:

- ✔ **Horizontal:** Select this radio button to flip the image upside-down while you reflect it.

- ✔ **Vertical:** Select this radio button to flip the image over while you reflect it.

- ✔ **Angle:** Select this radio button to rotate the image to a specified, um, angle while you reflect the image.

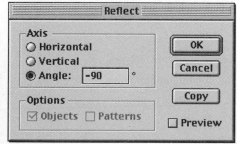

Figure 12-7:
The Reflect dialog box.

Shear

Most programs call this *skew,* but Illustrator takes the high road and uses a lofty aviation term. It's commonly used for creating cast shadows (the kind that fall away from an object, like your own shadow does on a sidewalk on a sunny afternoon, also known as perspective shadows) or cast reflection (like a still lake reflecting autumn trees).

The Shear tool is one of the easier tools to use, but it can be tricky at first. When you click and drag with the shear tool, everything on the side of the origin point moves to where you drag it while everything on the other side of the origin point moves an equal distance in the opposite direction. The artwork in between distorts accordingly, and you get a slanted version of your artwork.

To make the Shear tool easier to use, always use the two-click method. Before you drag with the Shear tool, click at the edge of the selected artwork to set the origin point. When you do this, you only have to pay attention to your artwork shearing in one direction. The overall effects are the same, but you don't have to worry about the artwork shearing in both directions.

To use the Shear tool:

1. **Select the artwork to be sheared.**

2. **Choose the Shear tool from the Toolbox.**

   The Shear tool hides behind the Scale tool in the Toolbox. Click and hold on the Scale tool, and the Shear tool pops out from behind it.

3. **Click once at the edge of the artwork to be sheared.**

   This sets the origin point, making the Shear tool easier to control.

4. **Drag with the Shear tool.**

   The artwork *shears,* or distorts, to look slanted, as shown in Figure 12-8.

Figure 12-8:
Original artwork (left) and after shearing (right). Yeah, that's attractive.

Additional Transformation Tidbits

All this transforming may seem like some pretty amazing stuff. What's really amazing is the bevy of little extras that Illustrator has thoughtfully provided to make transforming easier and faster. The following sections in this chapter show you how to use these extras. Here's a list of what you can do:

- **Use the Transform palette:** This palette keeps all the transformations in one handy place, where you can apply them by typing in numerical values.

- **Copy while you transform:** Rotate a copy of your artwork.

- **Transform each piece of artwork separately:** The Transform Each dialog box enables you to apply transformations to individual objects, instead of to everything at once. This feature is useful, believe it or not.

- **Repeat the last transformation:** Do it again . . . and again . . . all with a simple menu command (or keystroke).

- **Transform a portion of a path:** That's right, you can select just a few points and move, scale, rotate, reflect, or shear them. (This capability is especially useful if you want to give that virtual caterpillar a Mohawk.)

The Transform palette

The Transform palette, shown in Figure 12-9, is a one-stop shopping location for all your transformation needs. Access the palette by choosing Window⇨ Transform. The palette's quite powerful, as long as you don't mind the math.

Figure 12-9:
The
Transform
palette in all
its glory.

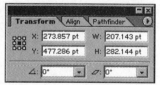

By entering values in the Transform palette's fields, artwork can be moved, scaled, rotated, and sheared. The palette's pop-up menu has options for reflecting (Flip Horizontal and Flip Vertical). This menu also contains options for scaling Strokes and Effects and transforming either the Object, the Pattern, or both. The W and H (width and height) fields can take both *absolute measurements* (sizes specified in inches, centimeters, and so on) or *relative measurements* defined by percentages. Just type the little extra bit after the number that specifies what kind of measurement the number represents — **in** for inches, **cm** for centimeters, or % for a percentage.

If you have to crunch numbers or go nuts, rejoice! The Transform palette does the math for you! For instance, if you want an object to be one-third as wide as it currently is, just type **/3** after the current value in the text box for width, and the artwork will shrink to ⅓ of its original width.

Copying while transforming

All five of Illustrator's transformation functions enable you to copy objects as well as transform them. To accomplish this dazzler, Illustrator applies the transformation to a copy of the original selection, just as if you used cut-and-paste to copy the object, pasted it directly on top of the original, and applied the transformation. In Illustrator, you can do all that in one step.

When using the transformation tools, you can press the Alt key (Option on a Mac) to make a copy of your selection while transforming. Just press the Alt key (Option on a Mac) after you start dragging (not before) and hold it down until after you release the mouse button. Illustrator creates a duplicate of the selection.

Illustrator users do this sort of thing so often that they invented a couple of terms (*Alt-drag* for PCs, *Option-drag* for Macs) to mean *copy an object*. (Nine times out of ten, it means *move a copy*.)

Figure 12-10 shows the way a sample of type looks after you transform it with the Shear tool while holding down the Alt key (Option on a Mac). The result is a cast shadow that appears in front of the original type (which Illustrator treats as an object). For additional information on creating shadows, see Bonus Chapter 2 on cool techniques on the Web at www.dummies.com/extras/Illustrator10/.

If you're using a dialog box to accomplish a transformation, click the Copy button instead of OK to create a *transformed duplicate* of the object. The original artwork stays untransformed.

Figure 12-10:
To get this cool cast-shadow with the Shear tool, we copied the text object and filled with a gradient.

Transform Each

The Transform Each dialog box (see Figure 12-11), accessed by choosing Object⇔Transform⇔Transform Each, does two things: First, it brings most of the transformations together into one dialog box. Second, it applies transformations to each of the selected objects separately, instead of all at once.

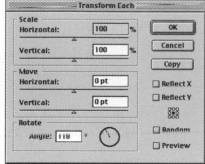

Figure 12-11: The Transform Each dialog box.

Oddly enough, this approach results in an effect that bears almost no resemblance to transforming everything at once. Figure 12-12 shows the results of regular rotation versus the results of rotation using the Transform Each dialog box. (Just don't say we didn't warn you.)

Figure 12-12: Original artwork (left) after it's rotated with the Rotate tool (middle) and using the Transform Each dialog box (right).

Transform Again

After you transform something, you can repeat the transformation quickly by choosing Object⇔Transform⇔Transform Again; the keyboard shortcut is Ctrl+D (⌘+D on a Mac). This action simply repeats the previous transformation — whether by tool or dialog box or palette — and applies that transformation to the current selection. You can even deselect something, select something else, and apply the same transformation to the new selection.

Transform Again also works with copying selections, as shown in Figure 12-13.

Figure 12-13: The tick marks on this clock were made with the Transform Again function by rotating a copy around the center in 6° increments.

Partial transformations

If you select just a section of a path, you can apply the five basic transformations to it, just as you do with an entire object. The result can be quite ordinary (as when you move a few points around) or rather unexpected (as when you scale, shear, or reflect just a few points), as shown in Figure 12-14.

The following steps select, move, and scale *just a few points* on a path (with some interesting results):

1. **Using the Direct Selection tool, click and drag over a portion of a path.**

   As you click and drag with the Direct Selection tool, a rectangular marquee appears. Only the points inside this marquee are selected.

2. **With the Direct Selection tool still selected, click a selected (solid) point and drag.**

   All the selected points move along with the one you click and drag. Be sure to click directly on a point that you've selected (indicated by a solid square); otherwise, you'll accidentally drop the selection and select something else.

3. **Release your mouse, choose the Scale tool, and then click on the same point as Step 2 and drag.**

   Dragging toward the middle of the selected points brings them closer together. Dragging away moves them farther apart.

   Don't click too near the middle of the points, or they get all cantankerous and hard to control.

Figure 12-14:
Moving and
scaling a
portion of
a path.

Blending: The Magic Transformation

This section covers what may well be the oddest feature in Illustrator. Illustrator can blend one path into another. For instance, you can blend the shape of a fish into a lowercase letter *f*. The result is a series of paths that slowly transform from one path into another. In addition to the shape changing from one path to another, the color (and style, if one exists) changes as well.

Sound familiar? No surprise. The results look a lot like the morphing effect you see in every werewolf-vampire-alien-shapeshifter movie made in the last ten years.

Only paths can be blended together. The paths can be open (lines, curves) or closed (shapes such as circles and squares). They can also contain either solid colors or gradients. You can select any number of paths (no more than three, though, for the best results) and blend them together, as shown in Figure 12-15.

To create a blend that takes the artwork from one path to another, just follow these steps:

1. **Create two paths on opposite sides of the document.**

2. **Choose the Blend tool from the Toolbox.**

3. **Click one path, click the other path, and watch the blend appear.**

   The number of objects between the two original paths depends on how different the colors are.

4. **(Optional) To specify the number of steps between the paths, double-click the Blend tool.**

5. **In the Blend Options dialog box that appears, select Specified Steps from the Spacing pop-up menu and enter the number of steps you want between the two paths. Click OK.**

   Illustrator creates the number of objects you specify between the two original paths.

Other options are available in the Blend Options dialog box besides Specified Steps. The Smooth Color option lets Illustrator automatically calculate the number of steps for the blend. This allows for a smooth transition of color and shapes. The Specified Distance option specifies the distance between steps in the blend. This is based on the edge of one object to the edge of the next object. You can also specify the orientation of your blend — either align to page or align to path. The icons for each give you a visual of each orientation.

You can also edit your blends with selection tools, such as the Arrow or Lasso tools, or with the Rotate or Scale tools. If the blend still doesn't meet your expectations as you make your edits, you can undo a blend by choosing Object➪Blend➪Release. You also find the Blend command under the Object menu. To use the menu command, select the objects you want to blend first and choose Object➪Blend➪Make. The Blend Options can also be found under this menu, as well as more advanced blending features.

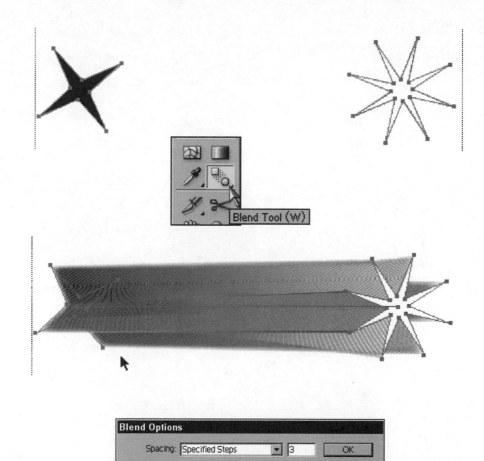

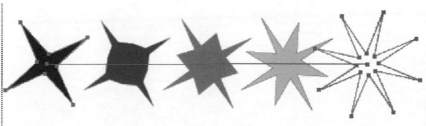

Figure 12-15:
Creating
a blend
between
two paths.

Chapter 13

Taking Images Out of the Realm of Reality

In This Chapter

▶ Applying unusual distortions to artwork

▶ Using the new Liquify tools

▶ Enveloping with ease

▶ Warping images for fun and money

A s you can read in Chapter 12, transformations — those critters that scale and rotate — can truly transmogrify your art. In this chapter, we venture into a universe where things are just a wee bit off kilter. Okay, to be honest, things are way strange. But cool!

Hang with us while we traverse the more esoteric world of distortions, oozing liquidations, and all things warped. Be prepared to pucker up — and try not to become too bloated along the way.

Applying Simple Distortions

In this section, we cover the tried-and-true distortions that have been part of Illustrator for quite a while. If you've worked with Illustrator before, you'll recognize some old pals, such as Bloat, Roughen, and Zig Zag. Although these techniques are easy to understand and use, a little goes a long way with these distortions. Resist the temptation to over use these tools.

Pucker & Bloat

No, this isn't what happens after overdosing on lemonade during a heat wave. The Pucker & Bloat filter (formerly called Punk & Bloat), accessed by choosing Filter⇨Distort⇨Pucker & Bloat, squeezes and bulges paths by moving points and handles in the opposite directions from each other. Check out Figure 13-1 to see what happens to text outlines when they get puckered and bloated.

Figure 13-1:
Pucker &
Bloat. Can
you guess
which is
which?

pucker pucker
bloat bloat

Figure 13-1: Pucker & Bloat. Can you guess which is which?

The Pucker & Bloat filter is related to the number of points on a path. The more points, the more pucker spikes and bloat bubbles. You can add points via the Add Anchor Point tool (in the slot with the Pen tool) or by choosing Object⇨Path⇨Add Anchor Points. For more on paths and anchor points, see Chapter 7.

Roughen and Scribble & Tweak

For making artwork look messy, the Roughen filter and the Scribble & Tweak filter are your best bets. (To access these filters, choose Filter⇨Distort and then choose either Roughen or Scribble & Tweak.) Roughen adds additional points to your paths and moves those points around, making the artwork look, well, rougher, as if it were drawn with a very shaky hand. Use Scribble & Tweak to move existing points and handles around to make the artwork look a lot looser, as if it were hastily scribbled. What's unique about these filters is that the results are totally random so that the graphic they produce appears much less rigid and more natural. As you can see in Figure 13-2, applying these filters to existing artwork can result in unique effects, such as a hand-drawn appearance.

Figure 13-2:
This artwork
has been
roughened
to give the
appearance
of hand-
drawn
artwork.

Zig Zag

Using Zig Zag adds points to your artwork and then moves every other point in and the remaining points out, giving an evenly saw-toothed appearance. That may sound contradictory, but hang with us. See the results of using Zig Zag in Figure 13-3. To access the Zig Zag filter, choose Filter⇨Distort⇨Zig Zag.

Figure 13-3:
Use the Zig Zag filter to create effects like this. (Another espresso, please.)

Free Distort and Twist

The remaining two filters, Free Distort and Twist (Filter⇨Distort⇨Free Distort and Filter⇨Distort⇨Twist), perform pretty much as you would expect. Use Free Distort to surround an object with a box and independently pull the handles of the box to distort that object. The Twist filter twirls your object based on the value that you enter in the Angle field in the Twist dialog box.

Creating Graphic Ooze with Live Distortions

This next level of distortions is so much fun to play with that you may never get any work done. What we like best about these distortions is that they're "live;" that is, your images remain fully editable, even if you've distorted your image into something totally unrecognizable. What's even more amazing is that you can use some of these distortions to distort text, and that same text still remains editable. Very cool, indeed. (We promise that these live distortions will not result in your artwork mysteriously appearing next to your desk like some eerie hologram.)

Liquifying without a blender

The new Illustrator 10 Liquify tools enable you to easily apply distortions to objects directly on your page. In other words, you aren't confined to the confines of a dialog box with sliders, like you are with the Distort filters that we describe in the earlier section "Applying Simple Distortions." Liquify tools offer you the freedom to pull, twist, and otherwise wreak havoc on your image with total liberty and creative abandon.

To perform the rite of liquification, first select your artwork and then select your torture tool of choice from the Toolbox. Check out Figure 13-4 for an illustration of each liquification tool/type and name. We created each of these cartoons with default settings, applying different Liquify tools to adjust the hair curl and nose of our poor victim. (Is this how plastic surgeons and hairdressers get started?)

Here are the Liquify tools and how to use them for maximum fun. Just click the tool that you want and follow our instructions from there. Refer to Figure 13-4 to match each tool with its effect.

- **Warp:** Drag your mouse to push the pixels forward — they move with your cursor.

- **Twirl:** Drag or hold your mouse down to rotate the pixels. The longer you hold your mouse down, the greater the twirl.

- **Pucker:** Hold your mouse to move the pixels towards the center of your cursor. Holding your mouse down longer results in more of a pucker.

- **Bloat:** Hold your mouse to move the pixels outwards from the center of your cursor. Holding your mouse down longer results in a bigger bloat.

- **Scallop:** Drag or hold your mouse down to create a rounded, scalloped edge. The longer you hold your mouse down, the more intense the scallop.

- **Crystallize:** Drag or hold your mouse down to create a spiked edge. Holding the mouse down longer creates a spikier effect.

- **Wrinkle:** Drag or hold your mouse down to create a distressed, "shaky-hand" edge. I know you've probably caught on that if you hold the mouse down longer, the effect will be increasingly wrinkled.

Using a pressure-sensitive tablet with the Liquify tools gives you even more control over their effects.

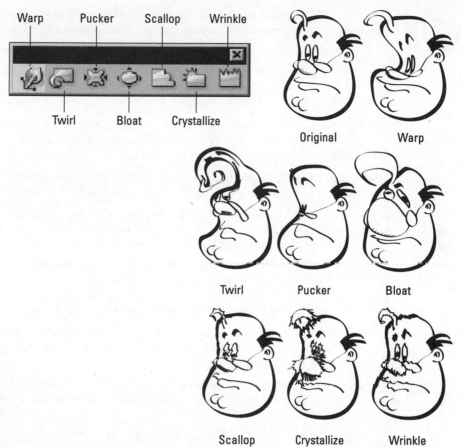

Figure 13-4:
One poor
schmoe
who's gone
through the
Liquification
mill.

Liquify options

Each Liquify tool has a corresponding Options dialog box that controls the tool's settings. This dialog box can be accessed by double-clicking any of the Liquify tools in the Toolbox. And although we recommend experimentation to get a real feel for how the Liquify tools operate, peruse the upcoming list for guidelines on how the various settings affect the tools' behavior.

✔ **Brush options:** Use these three options to define your brush size, angle, and intensity.

  • **Global Brush Dimensions:** Select the size of your brush from a range of 1 to 1,000 points (pt). Set Width and Height sizes independently to create oval-shaped brushes.

TIP

Hold down the Alt key (Windows) or Option (Mac) before clicking with a Liquify tool to change the brush size on the fly.

- **Angle:** Specify the angle of your oval brushes — from –360° to 360°.

- **Intensity:** Establish the intensity of your brush from a range of 0 to 100%. The greater the percentage, the greater (or more intense) the tool's effect.

✔ **Use Pressure Pen:** For those fortunate owners of pressure-sensitive tablets, select (check) this option to take advantage of greater control and finer tuning offered by these devices.

✔ **Warp/Twirl/Pucker/Bloat options:** That's a mouthful, eh? Use these options to set anchor points and edge smoothness.

- **Detail:** Use Detail to control how many additional anchor points that you add to the path. A higher Detail value (10 is the max) results in more anchor points.

- **Simplify:** Check the Simplify options in conjunction with the Detail option to eliminate unnecessary anchor points (those that don't contribute to the shape) added by a higher Detail value. The higher the Simplify value, the smoother the edge.

✔ **Twirl Rate:** A ballerina's dream. The higher the rate, the quicker the twirl appears and the curlier it is. See Figure 13-5 for an example of two different Twirl Rates.

✔ **Scallop/Crystallize/Wrinkle options:** In addition to the Global Brush Dimensions and Detail options, these last three tools also offer a few additional options.

- **Complexity:** The higher the Complexity value (1-15), the more anchor points are added to the object during the distortion, as shown in Figure 13-6.

- **Brush Affects Anchor Points:** Use the Brush Affects Anchor Points option to apply the distortion to the anchor points, as shown in Figure 13-7.

- **Brush Affects In Tangent Handles:** Use this option to apply the distortion to the first Bézier curve directional handles.

- **Brush Affects Out Tangent Handles:** Use this option to apply the distortion to the second Bézier curve directional handles.

We recommend keeping the Always Show Brush Size options selected (checked). Doing so enables you to view the actual size of your brush while you work rather than just seeing a cross-hair icon. *Note:* The Horizontal and Vertical options appear only in the Wrinkle Tool Options dialog box. Enter a percentage from 0% to 100% to adjust whether the wrinkles appear up and down or sideways or somewhere in-between. (So this *is* how plastic surgeons get started!)

Figure 13-5:
Different
twirl rates
affect the
speed and
curliness of
the twirl
distortion.

Default Twirl Rate
of 40 degrees

Twirl Rate
of 180 degrees

Figure 13-6:
A Scallop
distortion
with two
different
Complexity
settings.

Complexity of 1

Complexity of 5

Figure 13-7:
A Crystallize
distortion
using three
different
brush
settings.

Brush Affects
Anchor Points

Brush Affects
In Tangent Handles

Brush Affects
Out Tangent Handles

In order to distort text by using the Liquify tools, you must first convert it into outlines by choosing Type⇨Create Outlines. After the text has been converted, select it with the Selection tool and use the Liquify tools like you would with any other Illustrator object. Be aware that although the Liquify tools are indeed cool, use them sparingly on type. Your type must still be legible. How else are people going to find their way to your groovy garage sale of 1960s-era black-light posters? For more on creating and working with type, see Chapter 15 and the Bonus Chapter 1 on typography on the Web at www.dummies.com/extras/Illustrator10.

Pushing the Envelope

One of the best new features of Illustrator 10 is enveloping. Powerful, varied, and downright fun, enveloping can be applied to virtually everything — vector objects, text, pixel-based images, gradient meshes, patterns, and more. What's even better is that the envelopes remain live so that you can keep revising your distorted objects to your heart's content.

You have three ways to apply an Envelope distortion to your artwork: from a warp, a mesh, or a path. Depending on what kind of effect that you're going for, one may be more suitable than the others.

At warp speed

To create an Envelope distortion by using a warp, follow these steps:

1. **Select your artwork with the Selection tool.**

   Your artwork can be path- or pixel-based, or even text. This example includes a line of text and a pixel-based image of some cheesy Groucho-esque disguise glasses. We opened the image of the glasses, created the text with the Type tool, and then positioned it under the glasses with the Selection tool.

2. **Choose Object⇨Envelope Distort⇨Make With Warp.**

   The Warp Options dialog box appears, offering an array of options.

3. **Select your desired style from the pop-up menu.**

   Each of the 15 styles offers a corresponding icon giving you an idea of the warp effect. Make sure to select (check) the Preview option so that you can see the results.

Note how the envelope grid appears over the artwork. For this example, we chose Squeeze, which creates an hourglass effect.

4. **In the Warp Options dialog box, choose Horizontal or Vertical (if available and if you want to distort the proportions of the warp) and adjust the Bend and Distortion options.**

Our mutation includes selecting Horizontal and boosting the Bend to 100%. Adjust the Horizontal and Vertical percentages to skew the style to the left, right, top, or bottom. Adjusting the Bend to either end of the scale intensifies the effect. For this example, these options are at the default settings of 0.

5. **Click OK and admire the results.**

See the distortion in Figure 13-8. Note how both the image and the type were distorted with the warp. If an image could stand a little tweaking, select the Direct Selection tool and click on your Envelope path. Choose an anchor point on that path and drag to adjust the Envelope. Your artwork will distort to fit the revised envelope.

Figure 13-8:
Putting the
squeeze on
Groucho.
Oucho!

Original   Squeezed

What a mesh

The Make From Mesh method of Envelope distortion applies a grid of specified rows and columns over your artwork. Select the points on the mesh with the Direct Selection tool to distort the artwork underneath. See Figure 13-9 to view the Envelope Mesh in action.

TIP

You can add additional points on the mesh grid with the Gradient Mesh tool. See Chapter 10 for more on Gradient Meshes.

Figure 13-9:
Use an
Envelope
Mesh to
distort your
image by
manipulating
points on a
grid.

Pathways

The last method of Envelope Distortion enables you to use any path as the Envelope for the distortion. This can be very handy when creating logos because objects, scans, and type can all fit neatly into a specified shape, such as an oval. Follow these steps to find out how to use a path for the Envelope:

1. **Create a path for your envelope and place it over your artwork.**

   The Envelope path must be the front-most object.

   In Figure 13-10, a circle for the Envelope path is placed over the text and pixel-based apple image.

2. **Select the path and your artwork with the Selection tool and choose Object➪Envelope Distort➪Make With Top Object.**

   Your artwork is distorted to fit inside the path, as shown in Figure 13-10.

Here are a few other pertinent details regarding Envelopes:

- ✔ **To change the contents within the Envelope rather than the Envelope itself,** select your Envelope and choose Object➪Envelope Distort➪Edit Contents. Then feel free to modify your artwork — change the color, edit the text, and so forth.

- ✔ **To release (undo) the Envelope,** choose Object➪Envelop Distort➪Release.

- ✔ **To permanently apply your Envelope,** choose Object➪Envelope Distort➪Expand. Your art will look the same, but you're no longer able to edit the contents or release the Envelope.

- ✔ **To be able to apply Envelope Distorts to linear gradients, pattern fills, or appearance attributes,** you must select these options in the Envelope Options dialog box (Object➪Envelope Distort➪Envelope Options).

Figure 13-10:
Fitting an
apple and
some text
nicely into
a circle.

Inflicting Warps without Harm

The last of the new live distortion weapons are warps. Again, any type of Illustrator object — vector- or pixel-based images — or text can be warped. The 15 kinds of warps may look familiar because they share the same names as those that appear under the Envelope Distort ⇨Make With Warp style pop-up menu. (Read the earlier section "At warp speed.") Although these distortion warps may seem to apply the same results, you will see in a moment that there are some differences.

Applying a warp

To apply a warp, simply select your artwork, choose Effect⇨Warp, and then select your desired warp from the submenu (a menu that extends out from another menu). Because they're a type of Effect and Effects are a type of Appearance attribute, warps distort the look of the object without altering the actual object itself, as shown in Figure 13-11. If this revelation is totally confusing to you, check out Chapter 11 for more about Appearances and Effects.

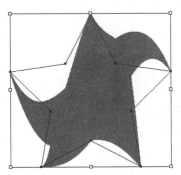

Figure 13-11:
A star appears warped, but its underlying skeletal structure remains unchanged.

Warped beyond belief

Here are some other juicy tidbits on warps:

- **To edit a warp,** double-click the warp name in the Appearance palette (Window⇨Appearance).
- **To reuse a customized warp,** save it as a Style, which can then be applied to other objects. For more on Styles, see Chapter 11.

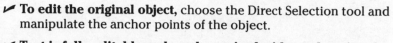

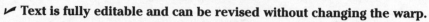

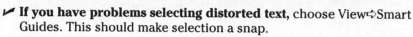

✔ **To edit the original object,** choose the Direct Selection tool and manipulate the anchor points of the object.

✔ **Text is fully editable and can be revised without changing the warp.**

✔ **If you have problems selecting distorted text,** choose View⇨Smart Guides. This should make selection a snap.

Chapter 14

Organizing Efficiently

- -

In This Chapter

▶ Arranging and stacking images

▶ Using the Layers palette

▶ Changing stacking order of objects with the Layers palette

▶ Naming objects, groups, and layers

▶ Organizing artwork with groups

▶ Using the new Grid tools

▶ Letting Smart Guides do the work for you

▶ Working with guides

▶ Aligning objects

- -

*I*llustrator is not a 3-D program, but oddly enough, you may spend a lot of time trying to place objects in front of one another correctly. A good way to think about how Illustrator relates to the 3-D world is to consider Illustrator objects like construction paper cutouts. You can arrange them any way you want, but in all likelihood, some will overlap. Each piece of paper can then be tucked behind another piece or pulled out in front of another piece. Doing so results in totally different effects.

In this chapter, we focus primarily on stacking objects — tucking them behind each other or bringing them forward to upstage each other — and show you how to deal with stacking as easily as possible. In addition, a later section scrutinizes precision placement and aligning of objects (in normal 2-D space).

Stacking Illustrator Artwork

Illustrator automatically accomplishes front-to-back positioning for you in a straightforward, logical way. Each new object that you draw, place, or paste is positioned in front of the last object that you drew, placed, or pasted, resulting in a stack of artwork.

Unless you apply Transparency (as we detail in Chapter 10), objects positioned in front of other objects tend to knock out the portions of the objects that they overlap. Figure 14-1 shows Illustrator objects stacked in three different arrangements. The objects are in the same locations, but their stacking order is different. The result is completely different artwork in each example.

Figure 14-1:
These arrange-
ments of artwork are a result of changing the stacking order of the objects.

Stacking order

Illustrator treats onscreen objects as if they were playing cards stacked neatly on a table. (Think of yourself as standing next to the table and looking straight down on them. All of the individual cards cannot be seen. You only see the topmost card.) *Stacking order* is the order of objects in the stack. The order of the objects in the stack is typically determined by when they're created or placed in the document, although you can change this order by using an Object⇨Arrange command. Read more on the Arrange commands in the upcoming section "Moving art up (front) or back (down) in the stacking order." The first object created sits at the bottom of the stack. In Illustrator, this is referred to as the *Back*. The next object created is in front of that object, and the most recent object created sits on top of all the others. The topmost position is considered to be the *Front*.

Figure 14-2 shows a basic illustration and an imaginary side-edge view of that artwork as it would appear from the side.

Even when two objects appear visually side-by-side and do not overlap in any way, Illustrator still considers one object to be in front of the other — as if each object that you create in Illustrator were painted on a separate piece of transparent plastic. Often, the only time you can know the stacking order is when you move one object in front of another. That's the only time you need to know the stacking order because stacking order makes a difference only when objects overlap. When objects overlap improperly (like if a big yellow triangle hides the word *YIELD* that you really want in front of the triangle), you can use the Arrange commands to change stacking order.

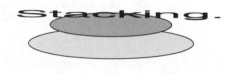

Figure 14-2: The illustration (left), shown from a sideways view (right).

Moving art up (front) or back (down) in the stacking order

Illustrator offers the following five commands to move objects up and down through the stacking order:

- ✔ **Object⇨Arrange⇨Bring to Front:** This command brings selected artwork to the top of the layer you're working on (more about layers in the next section) by putting that artwork in front of the other objects.

- ✔ **Object⇨Arrange⇨Send to Back:** This command moves selected artwork to the bottom of the layer you're working on by putting that artwork behind the other objects.

- ✔ **Object⇨Arrange⇨Bring Forward:** This command brings selected artwork forward (that is, upward in the stack) one step at a time.

- ✔ **Object⇨Arrange⇨Send Backward:** This command puts the selected artwork farther back (that is, downward in the stack) one step at a time.

- ✔ **Object⇨Arrange⇨Send to Current Layer:** This new command moves the selected artwork from the layer it resides on to the layer selected in the Layers palette. For more on layers, see the section "Using the Layers palette" coming up in this chapter.

Illustrator uses stacking order to keep track of all the objects onscreen, even when they don't overlap. The Bring Forward and Send Backward commands affect the stacking order, regardless. Whether you send an object backward or bring it forward, you may not see any difference if nothing's overlapping. Don't panic! The object really did move in the pecking order.

Managing the Mess

Although the commands for moving artwork may seem fairly flexible at first, that's only true if you keep the number of objects limited. After you start creating artwork with dozens (or even hundreds) of objects in it, the first four commands start showing their limitations and causing frustration. For instance, think of the hassle of putting an object in a precise order when you have a hundred different levels in the stack ("Move it from level 94 to level 63? Sure, no problem." Right.), not to mention the challenge of selecting one object from among hundreds!

That situation is where the Layers palette comes in. Not only does it enable you to organize your artwork into layers, but it also gives you a much more flexible method of arranging your artwork within the stacking order. You can also do fiendish things to layers, such as hiding them so you can't see them or locking them so you can see them but can't change them or duplicate them (along with their artwork) in a different document. This flexibility brings a great deal of sanity to working with complex illustrations.

Imagine that you're creating an image of a flock of birds in a maple tree. Your client wants to see the tree change according to the four seasons. She also wants to see the tree with and without the birds. You have one tree, fifty birds, and hundreds of leaves — and the whole image is set in spring. Oh, and the client is coming over to see the finished artwork in fifteen minutes! Do you panic? No, you use layers! You separate the tree, birds, and leaves into separate layers. Then you can hide and reveal the bird layer to show the tree with and without the birds. Hide the layer with the leaves on it, and you have your maple tree in winter! To simulate seasons, duplicate the leaves layer twice. Then, again using the Layers palette, you can select all the leaves in one layer and change the Fill colors to summer colors. Then go to the third leaf layer and change those colors to fall colors. By showing one layer while hiding the other two, you can create your fall, spring, and summer trees. There you have it! Eight pieces of artwork from one piece, in about as much time as it takes to describe it!

Using the Layers palette

The Layers palette, shown in Figure 14-3, provides you with the means to do as much (or as little) organization as you want. You can split your artwork into layers, sublayers, and sublayers of those sublayers. Then you can view, hide, select, rearrange, or delete any number of the layers and sublayers.

Thumbnails

The thumbnails on the Layers palette show what objects are on each layer. You can quickly select everything on that layer by clicking the Target circle once. Double-clicking the Target circle enables you to apply Transparency settings and effects to that layer, as we discuss in Chapter 10.

Figure 14-3:
The Layers
palette with
multiple
layers.

Is the thumbnail too small to get an accurate view of the artwork? Choose Palette Options from the Layers palette pop-up menu. The thumbnail size is determined by the Row Size. Choose from small, medium (the default size), or large; or choose Other and type in any pixel size for your thumbnails.

We call it Layer Cake . . .

If you haven't opened the Layers palette before, you may be surprised to find that you've been working with layers all along. Whenever you create a new document, Illustrator automatically creates a layer to contain your artwork.

When you work with multiple layers, you may have to get accustomed to the Arrange commands, such as Bring Forward and Send to Back. These commands work within layers but don't move objects from one layer to another. After you select an object and choose Object⇔Arrange⇔Bring to Front, Illustrator brings the object to the front of the layer that it currently occupies — but not all the way to the front of the document. So if another object is hanging around in a layer in front of the selected object and you use Bring to Front, the selected object may still be behind another object in the document. If this happens, you can use the new Object⇔Arrange⇔Send to Current Layer command, or you can use Steps 3 and 4 in the following list to move artwork into another layer.

A good way to get a feel for the Layers palette is to break a piece of existing artwork into several layers, as shown in Figure 14-4.

To separate your artwork into multiple layers, just follow these steps:

1. **Decide how you want to organize your artwork.**

   You may want to split it into similar elements — such as type, pixel images, graphics, and a background.

2. **Create the additional layers you need for your artwork by clicking the Create New Layer button — click once for each additional layer.**

   The Create New Layer button is the third button from the left at the bottom of the Layers palette; it looks like a sheet of paper with the bottom-left corner folded up to reveal a second sheet of paper underneath it. You can also choose New Layer from the Layers palette pop-up menu.

3. **With the Selection tool, select the graphic element in your artwork that you want to move to one of the other layers.**

   After you select the art, a little square appears to the right of the layer that currently contains the selected artwork.

4. **To move the art to another layer, click and drag the little square up or down in the Layers palette to the layer you want.**

   When you release the mouse button, the artwork has already changed layers. You may not see any apparent change in the artwork, but moving the artwork into a new layer changes the color of the selection highlights (the tiny, onscreen squares and lines that appear along the points and paths after you select something with any Selection tool). The color changes to the selection highlight color for the new layer. It's a dead giveaway.

5. **Repeat the previous two steps until all your artwork is in the correct layers.**

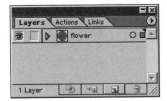
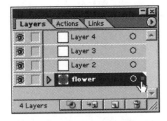

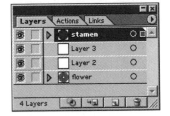

Figure 14-4: Placing existing artwork into multiple layers.

Changing the stacking order of layers

Layers, like individual objects, have a stacking order. This order is reflected in the Layers palette. The contents of layers at the bottom of the palette appear in back of the contents of layers at the top of the palette. To change the stacking order of a layer, click the name of the layer or its thumbnail and drag upwards or downwards in the Layers palette. As you drag, a black bar appears between layers to indicate where the layer will be moved to after you release the mouse. When this black bar is at the position you want the layer to occupy, release the mouse. The layer and all its contents move to that position.

Lock and Unlock, View and Hide

Well, no, we aren't suddenly writing rhythm-and-blues lyrics. You can lock layers by clicking the Lock/Unlock toggle button (the square just to the left of the Thumbnail). Clicking it causes it to do the opposite of whatever it's currently doing. If a layer is unlocked, for example, clicking the Lock/Unlock button locks the layer. If a layer is already locked, clicking the Lock/Unlock button unlocks the layer. So far, so good. But potential frustrations lurk.

When a layer is locked, you can see it, but you can't select it or alter it in any way. If you try to select anything in a locked layer, you select only the object behind it. After you get accustomed to this state of affairs, you find that layers are a great way to get things out of the way that you aren't working on and to preserve any artwork that you don't want accidentally changed.

Just to the left of the Lock/Unlock button is the View/Hide button (which looks like an eye). Why hide all that work? One word: safety. This button not only hides the artwork in the layer, but it also locks the artwork so you can't accidentally change it. The View/Hide button is also a great way to get things out of the way and to prevent accidents. It's also a great way to create multiple versions of artwork by showing and hiding different elements. (You know — trees with several sets of leaves for different seasons, or football players with several uniforms, depending on their contracts. . . .)

Hidden artwork is always locked artwork. If it weren't locked, you could change that poor, hapless object without meaning to — because you can't see hidden artwork. (Wow. Sometimes obvious stuff is so comforting.)

Copying layers (quickly and completely)

You can copy a layer — along with all the artwork it contains — by clicking the layer and dragging it on top of the Create New Layer button, which is just waiting around at the lower edge of the Layers palette, hoping that somebody will give it something to do. This technique is also a great way to create multiple versions of artwork. You can duplicate one element many times, and then change the appearance for each layer. Show and hide the layers to compare and contrast the different versions.

To create a new sublayer (a layer within a layer), click the Create New Sublayer button at the bottom of the Layers palette, or choose New Sublayer from the Layers palette pop-up menu.

Viewing objects and groups

After you click the little triangle to the left of a layer's name, you see an instant panorama of the groups and objects on that layer, as shown in Figure 14-5.

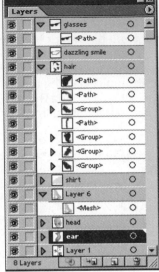

Figure 14-5: You can see the contents of a layer in the Layers palette by clicking the triangle to the left of the layer's name.

Using your options on layers, groups, and objects

You can give each layer, group, and object in Illustrator a name. If you don't name them, they wander around despondently, lugging their default names (such as <path> and Layer 1). Naming layers can be a great help for locating different objects. (Those teensy thumbnails can be awfully hard to distinguish.) Naming the layers provides you with instant recognition.

To change a layer's name, double-click that layer in the Layers palette. To change the name of a group, double-click that group in the Layers palette. And finally, to change the name of an object, double-click that object in the Layers palette. (Is there an echo in here? Nope, just consistency — part of good software design.) The Layer Options dialog box appears, as shown in Figure 14-6.

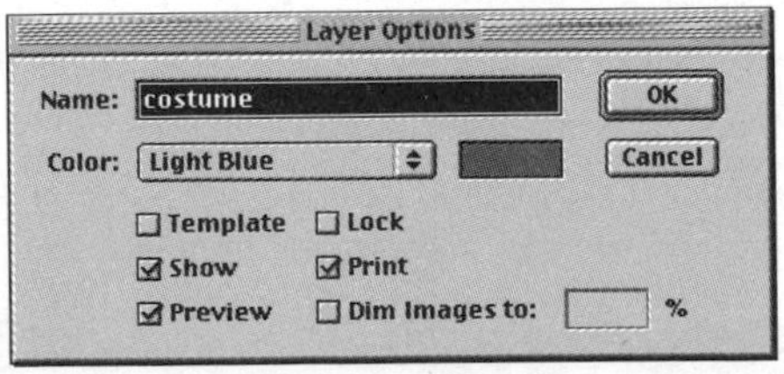

Figure 14-6: The Layer Options dialog box.

Layer Options

Name: costume

Color: Light Blue

☐ Template ☐ Lock
☑ Show ☑ Print
☑ Preview ☐ Dim Images to: ___ %

OK   Cancel

The Layer Options dialog box offers several other options beyond just naming layers:

- **Name:** Use this text box to type in a descriptive name for the layer.

- **Color:** Set the selection highlight color here. Changing this option doesn't change any color in the artwork — just the color used to show that something is highlighted.

- **Template:** Selecting this check box enables you to give the layer a special designation and the following unique set of behaviors (which tells you that the layer is a template):

    - The layer is automatically locked so nothing on it can be selected or changed.

    - By default, pixel-based artwork shows as dimmed, which allows you to focus on your own artwork better while still being able to see the template artwork. Think of the layer as virtual tracing paper. You can, however, uncheck (deselect) this option if you so desire.

    - The names of the Template layers are italicized, so they're easy to spot in the Layers palette.

    - Template layers do not print, and they aren't included with your artwork when you use the Save for Web command.

    - You can create a different version of a particular piece of artwork and put the existing artwork in a Template layer where it's out of the way. It won't print, but you can still see it.

- **Lock** and **Show:** These options can be checked and unchecked to enable you to perform the same function as selecting the Lock/Unlock and View/Hide buttons in the Layers palette.

- **Preview:** Selecting this check box allows you to see your artwork in Preview mode. When unchecked, it displays the current layer's artwork in Outline view; all other artwork in the document remains in Preview view.

- **Print:** This option can be checked or unchecked to make the layer printable or not printable.

- **Dim Images to:** This option enables you to dim pixel-based artwork to any set percentage. You may want to do so for tracing purposes so that you can focus on your Illustrator artwork while using the faded pixel artwork as a guide.

You can move objects, groups, and layers around inside the Layers palette, doing all sorts of strange things to your artwork. You can move objects from one layer to another, move groups inside other groups, and even nest layers by dragging them inside each other. Try doing this and watch out for surprises.

Imposing Slavish Conformity with Groups

Grouping objects is a great way to organize your artwork; it gives several objects a common address, so to speak, where Illustrator can find them. After you click any one of them with the Selection tool, you automatically select all the objects in the group.

To create a group of objects, select the objects that you want to include and then choose Object⇨Group. You won't see any physical change in the artwork, but from that point onward, all objects in the group are selected at once (provided that you use the regular Selection tool to select them).

The main difference between layers and groups is that grouping organizes objects by *their relationships to other objects* rather than by their position inside a layer. As any former high-school student can tell you, belonging to a group means having to conform to its rules. Consider these rules, for example:

- **Grouped objects must exist in the same layer:** You accomplish this by selecting two objects in different layers and grouping them. The bottom-most object gets moved into the layer that the topmost object inhabits.

- **Groups can be grouped together:** You accomplish this by selecting two or more groups and choosing Object⇨Group. If you have two groups called *Football Team* and *Cheerleaders*, for example, you can group them in another group called *Stadium*.

- **Grouped objects can be ungrouped:** You accomplish this by selecting the group and choosing Object⇨Ungroup. (Or maybe you could get an object in the group to do something uncool. . . .)

See Chapter 6 for more information on selecting groups.

Lining Up

Illustrator provides several ways to make things line up as neatly as possible. Instead of just eyeballing the things in the line (which sounds sort of icky), you can have Illustrator help you make sure everything lines up just right. In fact, so many ways to align things exist that you don't need to figure out all the different methods. Just pick the one that makes sense to you and use it.

Two of the more-arcane-but-useful functions in Illustrator are tricky to find and use, but are worth the effort:

- **Snap to Point:** This function (choose View⇨Snap to Point) snaps your cursor to a nearby point (on a path) whenever you're near to it. This function is perfect for butting objects up against each other.

✔ **Constraining via Shift:** This function (hold down the Shift key after you make your selection) constrains movement of objects to 0, 45, or 90 degrees (and all sorts of combinations thereof).

If you want your objects to move in a constrained fashion, make sure that you hold down the Shift key after you make your selection and keep holding it down until after you release the mouse button. If you hold the Shift key down before you make your selection, you add that selection to anything else that you've already selected. If you let go of the Shift key before you let go of your mouse button, you release the constraint, and the object is positioned someplace far from where you want it to be.

Electronic graph paper

The new Rectangular Grid tool, which shares a toolslot with the Line tool, allows you to create grids of any size and configuration. Double-click the Rectangular Grid tool or simply click the tool on your Artboard to access the Rectangular Grid Tool Options dialog box. Enter values for the size of the grid and the number of columns (called Horizontal Dividers) and rows (called Vertical Dividers). You can also enter a skew value that progressively increases or decreases the size of the rows and columns. The Fill Grid option when left unchecked creates a grid without a fill, and the Use Outside Rectangle As Frame surrounds the grid lines with a rectangle.

The Polar Grid Tool operates in a similar manner as the Rectangular Grid tool. In the Polar Grid Tool Options dialog box, you find options for Size and the number of Concentric Divides (smaller circles that appear within the largest outer circle) and Radial Dividers (the lines that radiate from the center of the smallest circle to the edge of the largest circle). The appearance of the grid when you have both radial and concentric dividers is that of a spider's web, as shown in Figure 14-7. You also have the same Skew and Fill Grid options that you do with the Rectangular Grid tool. The Create Compound Paths From Ellipses option creates a polar grid where every other concentric circle is transparent. The effect created a bull eye's target, as shown in Figure 14-7.

In addition to the grids created by the Rectangular Grid and Polar Grid tools, you can also have Illustrator transform your background into electronic graph paper. Choose View⇨Show Grid. To change the settings for the grid, choose Edit⇨Preferences⇨Guides and Grid. In the Guides and Grid Perferences dialog box, you will find options for changing the color, style, and increments of the grid. If you choose View⇨Snap to Grid, your objects snap to the grid corners whenever you move them or whenever you create new objects. When we say *snap,* we don't mean that the objects automatically jump to the grid corners. What happens is a lot more subtle: When you drag an object by using any selection tool, it sort of sticks a little when an edge of the object is over a grid corner. If you don't want the object to reside at that point, you can keep dragging. The stickiness is just enough to help you align the object. Figure 14-8 shows a document with a Grid behind it.

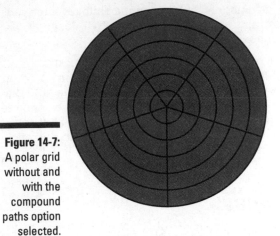 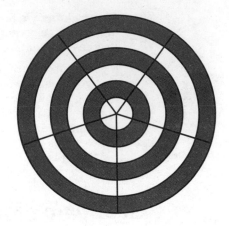

Figure 14-7:
A polar grid without and with the compound paths option selected.

Without compound paths   With compound paths

Figure 14-8:
A document (in this case, a cartoon) with a grid behind it.

Guides that are truly smarter than most of us

What if Illustrator knew what you were thinking? Science fiction? Maybe. But Illustrator is smart enough to know what you want to align — if you turn on Smart Guides, that is (by choosing View➪Smart Guides). These little helpers come out and start drawing temporary guides for you all over the place. Suddenly you can align objects in all sorts of ways.

Here's how this feature works. When the Smart Guides feature is on, it watches you work. As your cursor passes over different objects, Smart Guides draws lines from the points that you drag over, showing you how they align.

Although Smart Guides come in handy, they cause enough busy blinking of objects and lines to compete with the Saturday morning cartoons. We advise that you keep them turned off unless you're doing some serious organizing or drawing and can use the visual cues.

Let the rulers guide you . . .

You can create a guide of your own if you drag out from one of the rulers (click the ruler and drag it into the document). Think of these guides as individual grid lines. You can use them to align artwork horizontally or vertically wherever you want without having your whole screen become littered with grid work like you do whenever you choose View⇨Show Grid.

Unlike Smart Guides, Guides give you no additional information about your artwork. They're just lines that hang out behind your artwork to use as a point of reference. When View⇨Snap to Grid is turned on, objects snap to Guides as well (even if you aren't using a grid).

You can drag out as many of these guides as you want or need. To move a guide that you've dragged out, choose View⇨Guides⇨Lock Guides and toggle the option off. Then click and drag the guide that you want to move. You can also press the Delete key after clicking a guide to remove it altogether. This action lets you customize your guides so that they're in the exact position you need to help you with the specific artwork you're creating.

Lock your guides after you move them by choosing View⇨Guides⇨Lock Guides and toggling the option on.

I'm a path, I'm a guide

You can turn any path into a guide by selecting the path and choosing View⇨Guides⇨Make Guides. That means circles, squares, wavy lines, or an entire logo can be used as a guide. You can also turn any guide back into a path (even the ruler guides) by selecting them and choosing View⇨Guides⇨ Release Guides. Guides need to be unlocked and selected for this to work.

If you need to move or delete a single guide, you can press Ctrl+Shift (⌘+Shift on a Mac) and then double-click the guide to unlock it and change it into a path. (Just press Delete afterward to make it disappear.)

You can always clear out all the guides in a document by choosing View⇨ Clear Guides.

Alignment

Illustrator's Align palette enables you to align and distribute selected objects just by clicking a button. Open the Align palette by choosing Window⇨Align. The little pictures on each button in the palette show what the button does after you click it.

The top row of buttons aligns objects. You can align objects horizontally or vertically. If you align objects horizontally to the left, Illustrator aligns the left-most points in the objects. If you center objects horizontally, Illustrator aligns the centers of the objects.

The final location of the objects may seem a little random at times because the Align command aligns them to a point that is the average of the locations of the objects. For instance, if you align two objects vertically by their centers — and one object is on the right side of the page and the other is on the left side — the objects will align somewhere near the center of the page. To get them exactly where you want them, you may need to click and drag the objects with the Selection tool after you align them. Still, the Align palette saves you a whole lot of time getting there.

The bottom row of buttons distributes objects. In other words, these buttons move selected objects so that they are the same distance apart. The Distribute Objects option takes the two objects that are the farthest apart and distributes the remaining objects between these two objects.

The Align palette is a good way to align things that you've already created in Illustrator and simply need to straighten up a bit. If everything you've created is all helter-skelter (or just helter work with), Align adjusts your artwork until it looks just right. Or left. Or centered. (It's pretty handy and politically neutral.)

Part IV

Practically Speaking: Type, Print, and Files

The 5th Wave — By Rich Tennant

"OK, TECHNICALLY, THIS SHOULD WORK. JUDY, TYPE THE WORD 'GOODYEAR' IN ALL CAPS, BOLDFACE, AT 700-POINT TYPE SIZE."

In this part . . .

In our visually oriented culture, the way that words look can be as full of meaning as what they say. Small wonder that creating fancy, artistic type is one of the most popular uses of Illustrator. Illustrator offers easy (and practically limitless) ways to create wow-look-at-that artwork with a few simple steps.

In this part, we cover all the basics (and some of the beyond-basics) of type, from aligning your characters and changing their size to making type flow around a circle or inside a shape. You also discover how to unlock the secrets of mastering the appearance of your type from editing the most minute part of a letter to using the Create Outlines command.

Also, don't miss the scoop on printing your creations, putting them on the Web, and how to move files in and out of Illustrator 10.

Chapter 15

Introducing Letters and Such (Type 101)

In This Chapter

▶ Uncovering why Illustrator has so much type stuff

▶ Understanding type terms

▶ Mixing fonts effectively

▶ Measuring type

▶ Spacing out lines of type

▶ Changing the space between letters

▶ Stretching and squishing type

▶ Aligning type to one side or another

Type is undoubtedly one of Illustrator's strongest areas. All the things that Illustrator does best — logos, advertisements, posters, Web-page graphics — depend on text and typography. Many Illustrator features interact with type in some way; and the program's type capabilities are pretty straightforward after you know where they are and what they can do.

In this chapter, we introduce the basics of Illustrator type. (If you're already familiar with controlling type in Microsoft Word or some other piece of word-processing software, you're already familiar with many of these terms.) To ease the journey, this chapter covers locating the Illustrator controls — and deciphering the Illustrator way of doing things. Bonus Chapter 1 on typography on the Web (www.dummies.com/extras/Illustrator10/) takes off from there, getting into nifty tricks, such as type-on-a-path, which Illustrator is (typographically speaking) famous for.

Using the Word Processor from Outer Space

If you think of Illustrator's type capabilities as an extended word-processing program, you're in the right ballpark; people frequently mention Illustrator's amazing typographical control. The basics of type (such as fonts, size, and alignment) work much the same in Illustrator as they do in most software programs. But Illustrator also packs some advanced typographical capabilities — such as saving files in three of the most universally recognized file formats (EPS, GIF, and JPEG). What sets this program apart from the rest is that you can do wonderful things with type and use it just about anywhere.

Controlling type in Illustrator

Illustrator has three places where you can work with type options: the Type menu, the Character palette, and the Paragraph palette, as shown in Figure 15-1. These three locations are essential knowledge for Illustrator users; so is a good grasp (so to speak) of the Type tool in the Toolbox.

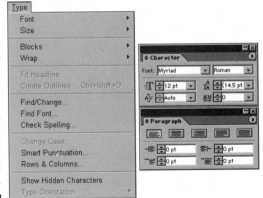

Figure 15-1:
The Type menu, the Character palette, and the Paragraph palette.

The Type tool

You don't need anything but the Type tool to create type (as shown in Figure 15-2) — although the Type tool by itself won't let you change anything about your type.

Figure 15-2:
Creating
point type in
Illustrator.

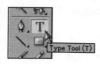

Point type

Starting with the Type tool, follow these steps to create type:

1. **Choose the Type tool (which looks like a letter *T*) from the Illustrator Toolbox.**

2. **Click where you want the text to start.**

   A flashing insertion point appears. (If you accidentally click and drag at this point, you create a text box that contains your type. For more information on the text box, see the next series of steps.)

3. **Start typing.**

This process is the most basic way to create type. What you actually do in the preceding steps is create *point type*, which is a single line of type that doesn't wrap (move to the next line) automatically. You have to press Enter (Windows) or Return (Mac) if you want to add a line beneath this line; otherwise, the line you're typing continues to infinity.

You can also create rectangle type (type that's confined within a rectangular area) with the Type tool, as shown in Figure 15-3. Just follow these steps:

1. **Choose the Type tool from the Illustrator Toolbox.**

2. **Click and drag with the Type tool.**

   As you drag, a rectangular marquee grows from the cursor. Text can only be typed inside the area of the marquee.

3. **Release the mouse button.**

   A flashing insertion point appears in the upper-right corner of the text box.

4. **Start typing.**

   As you reach the right edge of the text box, the text wraps to the next line.

Figure 15-3:
Creating
rectangle
type in
Illustrator.

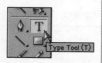

This is a perfect example of rectangle type in Illustrator. Note how the text wraps automatically.

In both cases, you create a type object. You can treat this type object like any other Illustrator object. (After you select it, the familiar path and point symbols show up to indicate the selection.)

With both point type and rectangle type, you can always get to the next line by pressing Enter (Windows) or Return (Mac) on the keyboard.

The Character palette

The Character palette, found by now selecting Window⇨Type⇨Character, is the place where you make changes to individual characters (letters, numbers, and punctuation). Figure 15-4 shows the Character palette with all the pieces labeled.

To make text changes by using the Character palette, you first need to select the text you want to change. You can select text in three ways:

- **Click the text with a selection arrow.** This action selects all the text in the text object. Even though the text isn't highlighted (rather, it has a simple underline, or the outline of a rectangle), you can still change the size, font, and alignment.

- **Click and drag the Type tool across the type that you want to select.** When you click and drag, a black box appears behind the selected text to indicate that the text is selected. This is what Illustrator means by *highlighting*. Only highlighted text is changed. But watch out! If you click and drag too far away from your targeted text, you make a new text box instead of selecting the text.

  Pay attention to the Text tool's cursor; it always alerts you about what the tool is going to do. When the cursor is in position to create a new text box, a dotted rectangle appears around it. If it's in the right place to select text, the dotted rectangle disappears. To select text, click and drag when you see only the I-beam text tool cursor with no box around it.

- **Double- or triple-click with the Text tool.** Double-clicking a word selects the entire word. Triple-clicking selects the entire paragraph in which the word appears.

The Paragraph palette

The Paragraph palette (shown in Figure 15-5) is the place to make type changes that affect whole paragraphs. If you haven't dealt with this feature in other software, you may be in for a bit of a tussle. At least the palette is easy to summon; simply choose Window⇨Type⇨Paragraph. Then things start to get a little strange.

Font Size

Font Family   Leading

Font Style

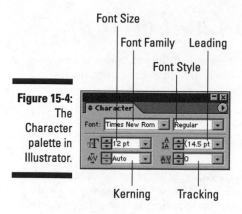

Figure 15-4:
The
Character
palette in
Illustrator.

Kerning   Tracking

Align Left

Align Center

Align Right

Justify Full Lines

Justify All Lines

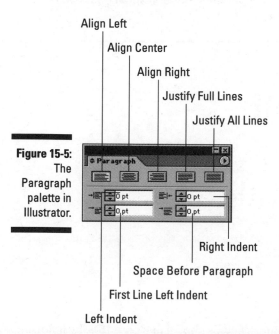

Figure 15-5:
The
Paragraph
palette in
Illustrator.

Right Indent

Space Before Paragraph

First Line Left Indent

Left Indent

To Illustrator, a paragraph consists of the type contained between two returns. Even if you type only one letter and then press Enter (Windows) or Return (Mac), Illustrator considers that single letter a paragraph.

You don't have to select an entire paragraph for the Paragraph palette functions to make changes. Paragraph palette changes affect the entire paragraph, regardless of what you select. For instance, even if you highlight only a single letter, changing a paragraph option affects the entire paragraph, not just that single character. Most of the options on the Paragraph palette work this way, so applying them to individual characters simply wouldn't make sense.

Introducing the Strange Land of Type

Although much of Illustrator may seem new and different, it describes type with a language steeped in centuries of tradition, so some of the terms may sound strange.

Fonts, typefaces, and font families

You often hear these terms used interchangeably. Fonts, typefaces, and font families actually have distinct meanings; for this book's purposes, you deal primarily with fonts. *Fonts* are sets of common letterforms that give consistent, distinct designs to the entire alphabet, all the numbers, and a boatload of symbols. Figure 15-6 shows a variety of fonts.

Helvetica
Arial Black
Courier
New Baskerville
Sand
Skia

Figure 15-6:
Several
different
fonts.

You change fonts in Illustrator quite easily, as shown in Figure 15-7, by following these steps:

1. **Using either the Type tool or a Selection arrow, select the type you want to modify.**

2. **Choose Window⇨Type⇨Character.**

   The Character palette appears. The family name of the currently selected font appears at the upper left of the Character palette. Beside the Font Family name is the Font Style box, with a downward-pointing triangle just to the right.

3. **Click the downward-pointing triangle next to the Font Style box.**

   A pop-up menu presents you with a list of all the fonts on your computer.

4. **Pick a font from the list and click its name.**

   After you release the mouse button, the selected text changes to the font you chose.

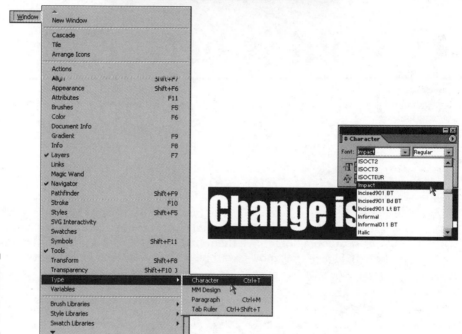

Figure 15-7: Changing fonts in Illustrator.

You may discover that Illustrator refuses to fake a font. Some Illustrator newbies who have worked with type in word-processing and page-layout programs are miffed to find that Illustrator doesn't have buttons for making fonts bold and italic. Programs with such features are usually faking it. Not every font family has genuine bold and italic versions. If a program takes the non-italic version and tilts it (or the non-bold version and thickens it), the resulting false impression can waste money. The *faux* bold and italics may look okay onscreen — and even print out okay on an inkjet printer. But when an imagesetter (a professional high-resolution printer) rejects them as fake, they show up on the page as the ordinary non-bold, non-italic fonts that they are — *after* you've had costly films made.

As you peruse the list of fonts, notice that the font styles appear in submenus of the main list. This feature shows you related versions of a particular font. For instance, Figure 15-8 shows samples of three font styles in the same family. Top to bottom, they are Times Roman, Times Bold, and Times Italic (first two words of the third line). All are in the same submenu of the Times menu item. Font styles in the same font family have a similar look and work well together.

Figure 15-8:
These font styles are part of the Times font family and look good placed together.

Change is good.
Bold is better.
I agree, he thought.

Serif and sans serif

Fonts are generally divided into two categories: serif and sans serif. *Serif* fonts have little doohickeys called serifs on the tips of letters and numbers; *sans serif* fonts don't have them (in this case, *sans* means "not gonna happen here"). Figure 15-9 shows examples of serif and sans serif fonts.

Figure 15-9:
Serif (top; serifs are circled) and sans serif (bottom) fonts.

Goodbye.
Hello.

Why choose serif or sans serif? Traditionally, serif fonts are used for large areas of text because the serifs make the text easier to read. Sans serif fonts are used for headlines because they stand out more boldly. However, as wider ranges of fonts have become available to wider ranges of users, more people are breaking the traditional font-choice rules. Traditional usage isn't always the case anymore. Books and magazines still use serif fonts (more than sans serif fonts) for long passages of text, but you can find many exceptions to the rule. Sans serif type is often easier to read onscreen; those little serifs are frequently just too small to display properly on low-resolution computer screens.

When you're creating for print, a wise idea is to print your Illustrator text throughout the creative process. The printed page can differ substantially from what you see onscreen. If you're creating text for Web graphics, consider yourself lucky; when you've got your graphics and the text looking good onscreen, mission accomplished!

To make Illustrator show as closely as possible what your text will look like on the Web, choose View⇨Pixel Preview.

The biggest Don't Do It that we can think of

Back in 1987, when Illustrator and PageMaker had just hit the scene, many computer users without an artistic bone in their bodies created documents and graphics. They got carried away with the computer's magnificent ability to mix and match fonts. The printed results often looked short of professional: busy, trashy, and hard to read. Lately, font madness has struck again — with Web pages — so your loyal authors make this impassioned plea:

Don't use too many fonts on the same page the way **we just did**.

What's too many? Well, the awful no-no we just inflicted on the page has five. If you run out of fingers (on one hand) while counting fonts, you have too many. The classic limit is three fonts (including any bold or italic versions of the main font you're using).

Exploring Size, Leading, and Other Mysterious Numbers

The world of type has a lot of measuring associated with it. You have to keep in mind point size, leading, x-height, kerning, baseline shift, tracking, horizontal scale, vertical scale, em-width, and other arcane matters that only the Secret Brotherhood of Typesetters really cares about. All these numbers affect the appearance of your type. Some of these measurements are important; some of them aren't. The following sections let you in on which is which — and on how to understand and use each type setting in Illustrator. Figure 15-10 shows where to find some of these measurements on the letters themselves.

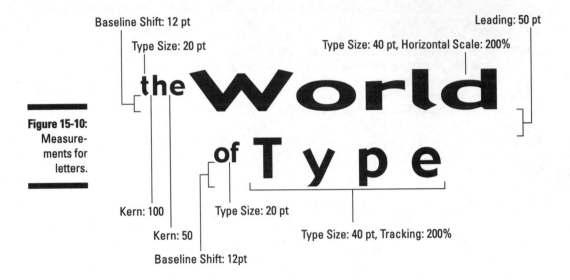

Figure 15-10:
Measure-
ments for
letters.

Baseline Shift: 12 pt

Type Size: 20 pt

Leading: 50 pt

Type Size: 40 pt, Horizontal Scale: 200%

Kern: 100

Kern: 50

Type Size: 20 pt

Type Size: 40 pt, Tracking: 200%

Baseline Shift: 12pt

Measuring can be just plain odd

The size of type is measured in *points*. An inch has 72 points. A quarter-inch has 18 points. That's the easy part. The hard part is that type isn't measured from top to bottom. Rather, type is measured from its ascenders and descenders for the entire font. You know those cute little tails that hang down from the lowercase *g*, *j*, *p*, *q*, and *y*? Well, those tails are called *descenders*; the *ascenders* are the upper parts of letters, such as the tall parts of lowercase *d* and *k* and of UPPERCASE letters.

Words, such as *anon* (all lowercase, no ascenders or descenders), seem to have a smaller type size than words such as *Mr. Ripley*, even though they're the same type size. Type is measured from the uppermost point to the lowermost point that is possible to create using that font. Even if you aren't using any ascenders and descenders in the words that you're typing, the font size has to leave room for them (see Figure 15-11) in case words, such as *Rumpelstiltskin* or *syzygy,* show up in the sentence.

Things get really wacky when you mix different fonts. Each font can have completely different heights for its ascenders and descenders, creating the appearance of completely different font sizes, even though the actual space from the topmost point to the lowest point for both entire alphabets is identical.

Figure 15-11:
Font size
has to allow
enough
space to
accommo-
date all the
possible
ascenders
and
descenders
in a font.

Ascenders

asdfjpABCJQ

Descenders

TIP

For another example, sneak a peek at the mishmash of fonts we stuck in "The biggest Don't Do It that we can think of" section (earlier in this chapter): They're all 12-point fonts.

You can set the point size of your type in the Character palette, right below the font. Pick a value from the pop-up menu or type in a value in the field provided and press Enter (Windows) or Return (Mac).

A good guideline is that capital letters are about two-thirds the point size, and that lowercase letters without descenders or ascenders (like the lowercase *a*) are about one-half the point size. So if you want a letter *a* that's one inch (72 points) high, you have to specify it as 144 pt (two inches) tall.

Measuring can be just plain annoying

The space between rows (lines) of letters has an even stranger story. First, the space is called *leading*. Second, the space is measured not between the descenders of the line you're on and the ascenders of the line below (which would make sense), but rather between the *baseline* of the line you're on and the baseline of the line above the line you're on. The baseline is the line on which most letters rest (those that don't have descenders). Figure 15-12 shows how leading appears in a typical paragraph.

You set the leading in the spot to the right of the font size in the Character palette. If a number appears in parentheses, that's the automatic value of the leading — 120 percent of the point size, rounded up to the next half point.

TIP

If the amount of leading matches the point size, the descenders of one line touch the ascenders of the line below. In the majority of cases, that's a *large* no-no.

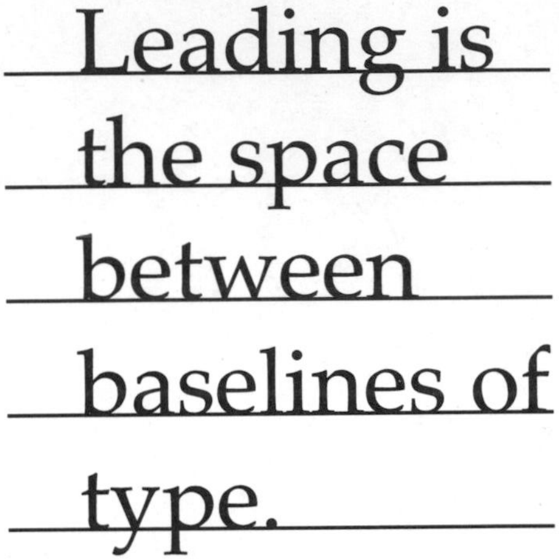

Leading is the space between baselines of type.

Figure 15-12:
Leading is
the space
between the
baselines
of type.

Spacing out while staring at type

Yet another thing to worry about (or ignore, if you choose to) is the space between individual letters that are next to each other. This space can be called two things (specifically to confuse the novice):

- **Tracking:** The space between letters in a series of letters
- **Kerning:** The space between two specific characters

Figure 15-13 shows the difference (sorta) between these two.

Change the kerning by placing your cursor where you want to change the space between two characters. Change the tracking by highlighting a series of characters. Then change the appropriate field in the Character palette, as indicated in Figure 15-14.

Typically, you can leave these values alone. However, when setting short sets of large type, for example, the type can look much better when it's kerned more tightly. Many rules and guidelines exist for proper kerning and tracking, but the best designers set these by eye. If the type looks good, it's probably kerned correctly.

Putting type on the rack

You can stretch your type to make it wider or taller. By changing the values in the Vertical Scale and Horizontal Scale boxes (shown in Figure 15-15), you can reshape type into all manner of oddness.

Figure 15-13:
Tracking and kerning in Illustrator.

Tracking

Kerning

Figure 15-14:
Changing the kerning and tracking values in the Character palette.

Kerning   Tracking

TIP

In general, this sort of modification is frowned upon, unless used sparingly and only to produce a small degree of change.

Figure 15-15:
Vertical Scale and Horizontal Scale text boxes in the Character palette, along with examples in type.

Vertical Scaling

Horizontal

Scaling

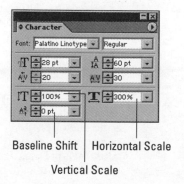

Baseline Shift   Horizontal Scale

Vertical Scale

Moving on up and down

Whereas leading sets how far apart the lines of text are, the baseline shift controls the vertical position of the text after it's been moved via the leading value. Use the field at the bottom of the Character palette to change the baseline shift. Positive numbers move selected text up; negative numbers move selected text down. Figure 15-16 shows a paragraph with a word of text that has a shifted baseline.

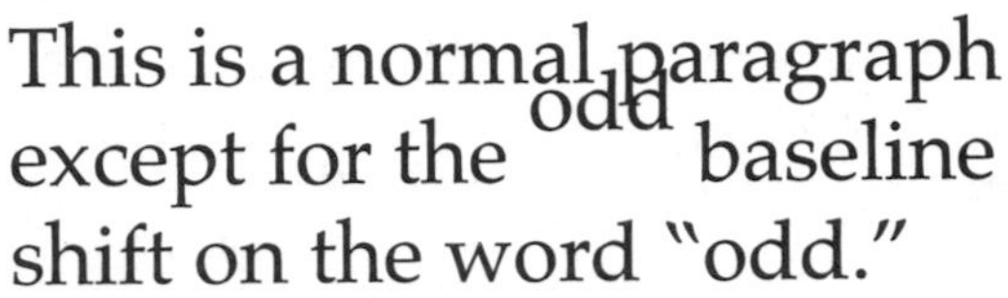

Figure 15-16:
Using
baseline
shift within a
paragraph.

This is a normal paragraph except for the odd baseline shift on the word "odd."

Adjusting Entire Paragraphs

The Paragraph palette provides controls for modifying all the text in a paragraph at once. These controls are quite different from those in the Character palette. (Don't want any silly old consistency to spoil the fun, now do we?)

Changing the alignment of a paragraph

At the top of the Paragraph palette are five buttons that set the alignment of paragraphs. Although the buttons are tiny, if you squint hard enough at them, you can see that the tiny graphic image on each one mimics the alignment that they create. Position the cursor over the button without clicking and a tooltip appears and tells you what it is.

To align a paragraph, click anywhere inside it with the Text tool; then click the alignment button in the Paragraph palette. By default, paragraphs are aligned to the left side with their right edge ragged and uneven. Choose Align Right, and the opposite is true (right edge smooth, left edge ragged). Try Align Center for ragged left and right edges with centered lines of text. Use the Justify Full Lines setting for straight left and right edges (except for the last line if it's not a full line). Finally, the Justify All Lines setting keeps all lines (including the bottom one) even on both the left and the right. Figure 15-17 shows examples of these alignments (and which buttons to click to get them).

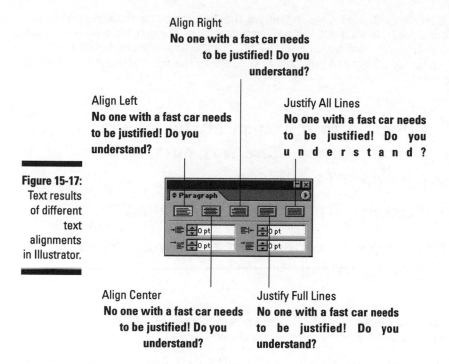

Align Right
No one with a fast car needs to be justified! Do you understand?

Align Left
No one with a fast car needs to be justified! Do you understand?

Justify All Lines
No one with a fast car needs to be justified! Do you u n d e r s t a n d ?

Figure 15-17:
Text results of different text alignments in Illustrator.

Align Center
No one with a fast car needs to be justified! Do you understand?

Justify Full Lines
No one with a fast car needs to be justified! Do you understand?

Changing the space around the paragraph

The Paragraph palette in Illustrator offers three options for adjusting the space around a paragraph, plus an option to set how far from the left edge of the paragraph the first line starts. Figure 15-18 shows these options.

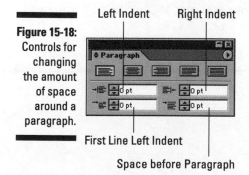

Figure 15-18:
Controls for changing the amount of space around a paragraph.

Left Indent   Right Indent

First Line Left Indent

Space before Paragraph

The Left Indent setting is for modifying the position of the left edge of the paragraph. The larger the number, the farther to the right the left edge moves.

The First Line Left Indent setting moves the first line of the paragraph left or right relative to the left edge of the paragraph. Use a negative number to make the first line come out from paragraph's left edge, as shown in Figure 15-19. Use a positive number to push the first line in to the right of the paragraph's left edge.

Figure 15-19:
Bringing out the left edge of a paragraph with a negative number.

He appeared to a woman in the parking lot of a grocery store. She was putting her groceries into her car.

He asked: "Do you have the time?"

She looked up and there he was. Elvis. The King! Alive!

The Right Indent setting adjusts the paragraph's right edge. The larger the number, the farther to the left the edge moves.

The Space Before Paragraph setting adjusts the amount of space before the current paragraph. If you select a bunch of paragraphs, changing this setting puts space between each one of the paragraphs.

Using the basic options available in Character palette and the Paragraph palette, you can create astounding feats of typestry. These two palettes provide the core for nearly everything you do with type in Illustrator. Using them, you can equal or surpass just about anything you can create on a single page in any word-processing or page-layout application. (For a crash course in how to do just that, fasten your seat belt and take a look at Bonus Chapter 1 on typography on the Web at www.dummies.com/extras/ Illustrator10/ — which grabs these basics and pushes them to their limits, creating the fanciest type tricks this side of the Typesetters' Inner Sanctum.)

Chapter 16

Printing Your Masterpiece

In This Chapter

▶ Working with printing in mind

▶ Sizing artwork to fit a page

▶ Printing black-and-white illustrations

▶ Printing color illustrations

▶ Understanding the strange issue of color separations

*W*hen designing your artwork, keep in mind how it will look if it's going to be printed. If you know what medium you're going to print your artwork on, you can save yourself time in the long run. For instance, if you create a stunning logo, full of vibrant colors and subtle hues and reflections, you probably can't use that logo in a black-and-white context. In this chapter, I provide some great ideas to keep in mind while you create your artwork — and you can also refer to this chapter when you arrive at the printing process.

If you just want to print, read the next section. If you want to discover all the stuff behind what goes into printing, check out the upcoming section "What You See Is *Roughly* What You Get." Or, if you want the nitty-gritty about setting up Illustrator for printing (plus even more details on printing), skip ahead to the section "Setting Up Your Page to Print (You Hope)."

Printing Quickly

If you have a printer hooked up to your computer or network, you can print just about anything that you can create in Illustrator.

Before you print, make sure that your artwork is inside the printable area. A dotted gray line indicates the printable area; anything outside the dotted line doesn't print. If you don't see a dotted gray line, choose View➪Show Page Tiling. To hide the line, choose View➪Hide Page Tiling.

To print your artwork, Choose File➪Print. When the Print dialog box appears, press Enter (Windows) or Return (Mac), or click the Print/OK button. You now have a printed version of your Illustrator creation. Pressing Enter

(Windows) or Return (Mac) without adjusting any settings in the Print dialog box is known in the trade as *running with the defaults. Defaults* are settings that are made automatically when you install Illustrator — and they work just fine for printing artwork from Illustrator. When your creations don't print as you expect them to, however, you need to adjust the other settings, which I discuss throughout this chapter.

What You See Is Roughly What You Get

Whatever you create onscreen, you can print (theoretically). And what you print looks pretty much like what you see on your monitor. Note that we say *pretty much* and not *exactly*. Here's why:

- **Resolution differences:** Your monitor resolution is much lower than your printer resolution. You may think that everything you print will look better than it does onscreen — in most cases, you'd be correct. Sometimes, however, that extra resolution makes problems that you can't see onscreen, such as dust, dirt, scratches and other pesky artifacts, stand out in print.

- **Aliasing differences:** By default, Illustrator displays art and text on your monitor as *anti-aliased* (the edges where colors meet blend together, producing a more visually appealing image onscreen). Printed pages are not anti-aliased, and images print smoothly and cleanly.

- **Color differences:** Your monitor displays color images by lighting up little red, green, and blue phosphorescent squares called *pixels*, whereas printing produces color images by applying dots of ink on paper. Creating colors by completely different physical processes causes a major difference between what you see onscreen and what you get in print.

With these points in mind, you should regularly print your artwork during the creation process to make sure that the printed result is as close as possible to what you're designing onscreen. That way, you can modify your artwork to avoid surprises when you print the final product. After some practice, you develop an eye for what a printout will look like, even when you're working entirely onscreen.

Setting Up Your Page to Print (You Hope)

Long ago in the Dark Ages, people slaved over drafting tables, among matte knives and ink bottles, struggling to create graphics while gagging on glue fumes. At last, at the dawn of the new millennium, computer systems forever replaced those ancient torture devices. These days you can whip up a document in Illustrator, feed pure white paper into a printer, and *let 'er rip!* (Uh, maybe we ought to rephrase that.) Just keep in mind that even a killer graphic has one more hurdle to clear — the leap from electronic file to hard copy. Sometimes artwork prints vertically on the page when you intend it to print horizontally. Sometimes the artwork doesn't fit on the page. Although we can't cover every problem that can occur in printing, in this section we look at a few of the major causes of printing problems in Illustrator and how to handle them.

Printer type and page size

Use the Page Setup or Print Setup dialog box to set up your page so that it prints properly. You can view your Page Setup or Print Setup dialog box by choosing that option from the File menu.

The easiest way to print is to choose File⇨Print and press Enter (Windows) or Return (Mac) after the Print dialog box appears. This process works fine nine times out of ten. But then there's that pesky tenth time when things don't print quite the way you expect. Often you can correct the problem by using options from the Page Setup or Print Setup dialog box, as shown in Figure 16-1 and Figure 16-2, respectively.

The dialog boxes in the figures may look different from what appears on your screen depending on the specific printer you're using, but the basic options remain pretty much the same.

Figure 16-1:
The Page Setup dialog box on a Macintosh.

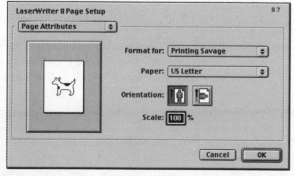

For Mac users, Page Setup contains the information that Illustrator needs about what type of printer you're using, how big the pages are, and other information, such as whether the printer is color or black and white. Print Setup does the same song and dance for Windows. You have dozens of options, but don't panic — some are specific to the Macintosh and others to the PC using Windows.

Figure 16-2:
The Print
Setup dialog
box in
Windows.

The only options you need to care about

Imagine establishing an oasis of simplicity in the sea of everyday confusion. Well, you can, if you focus on these few options in the Page Setup or Print Setup dialog box:

- **Name (Windows) Format For (Mac):** The top of the Page Setup or Print Setup dialog box indicates the printer you want to use. Click the printer name, and a pop-up menu appears listing all the printers that you have access to (in an ideal world, where your software and networked hardware are set up properly). If you have access to only one printer, this setting remains the same all the time. The printer that you are currently printing to should always be selected because it sends important information to the rest of the Page Setup or Print Setup dialog box, such as the page sizes that are available with the currently selected printer.

- **Size (Windows) Paper (Mac):** This pop-up (or drop-down) menu enables you to see the available page sizes for the printer that is selected in the Format For or Name pop-up menu. Make sure that you select the right page size for the paper you plan to print on.

- **Orientation:** This setting determines whether your page prints the tall way (represented on the Mac by button with an androgynous human figure standing upright, and in Windows by the Portrait radio button) or the wide way (represented on the Mac by the button with an androgynous human lying down, or in Windows by the Landscape radio button).

- **Scale to Fit or % of Normal Size (Windows) Scale (Mac):** This value (located in Page Setup on the main panel and in Print Setup after clicking the Properties button and then the Graphics tab) controls the size of the illustration. The value is defined as a percentage of the artwork's size inside Illustrator. For example, if you have a logo that's 1 inch x 1 inch in Illustrator, changing the scale to 250 percent results in the logo scaling up to 2.5 inches x 2.5 inches when printed.

Check the Page Setup or Print Setup dialog box settings whenever you choose a different page size or print to a printer other than the one you were previously using. Doing so will save trees, frustration, and nearby delicate ears.

Printing Mechanics

After you make sure that your Page or Print Setup settings are correct (typically they're fine unless — ahem — somebody mucks them up), you're ready to commit your masterpiece to paper.

Printing composite proofs

Printing a composite proof is really printing what you see onscreen to a single sheet of paper. You do this kind of printing all the time. If you have a color printer, your result looks really close (hopefully) to what's onscreen. If you have a black-and-white printer, you get a black-and-white version of what's onscreen.

The other kind of printing is called printing separations. Printing separations means generating a separate sheet of paper (or, more likely, film) for each ink to be used when the artwork is printed. We discuss separations in more detail in the section "All about Way-Scary Separations" later in this chapter.

You can print composite proofs by following these steps:

1. **Choose File⇨Print from the menu.**

   The Print dialog box appears.

2. **Select the appropriate printing options (as we detail in the next section "Important printing options").**

3. **Click OK (Windows) or Print (Mac).**

Important printing options

The Print dialog box (Figure 16-3 is a mug shot of the Mac and Windows versions) has all sorts of options, but only a few of them are worth noticing. Fortunately, the default settings are usually what you want anyway — for example, one copy of whatever you send to the printer of your choice. However, for situations in which the current setting is not what you want, the following handy options are lurking in the Print dialog box:

- ✔ **Printer:** The top of the Print dialog box indicates the printer that you intend to use. If you have only one printer, this setting is most likely correct all the time. If you have more than one printer, you can see which one you're currently using. You can change the printer setting here as well.

- ✔ **Number of Copies (Windows) Copies (Mac):** This option shows the number of copies of your artwork that you want to print, each on a separate sheet.

- ✔ **Print Range (Windows) Pages (Mac):** Illustrator can't really have multiple pages (a page one, two, three, and so on). It can, however, print one page across several pages (in effect, a very large single page). Before you print, choose File⇨Document Setup and then select the Tile Imageable Areas radio button in the Document Setup dialog box. Artwork that hangs outside the Artboard prints on separate pages. You can then print the artwork on multiple pages, tiling it so that you can cut and paste the artwork by hand into a big poster, if you want. (Using these options, you can make your artwork larger than your page size by as much as 18 feet!)

Unfortunately, the implementation of this feature is abysmal (which is why we don't mention it anywhere in this book beyond this paragraph). For instance, you have no way of telling which pages your artwork is on, even though you have to specify the pages in the Print Range option in the Print dialog box. This inevitably leads to paper waste. Even when you do get the thing to print out properly, you still have to cut up your pages and tape them together. If you need poster-sized output, you're much better off printing it at your local service bureau on a large-format output device.

In addition, you want to consider three other options. These are found in the main Print dialog box in Windows. On the Mac, you need to click the pop-up menu in the upper-left corner of the Print dialog box just beneath the Printer selection pop-up menu (this menu has no name but usually displays the word *General*) and choose Adobe Illustrator 10. Either way, you get three options:

- ✔ **Output:** This option controls whether you print composites or separations.

- ✔ **PostScript:** If you're printing to a PostScript printer, change this to the correct version of PostScript in your printer. (You can find out what version is in your printer by printing a test page from the printer.) Illustrator 10 is designed for PostScript 3 printing. Keep in mind that each version of PostScript adds features and enhancements. Illustrator can still print to lower levels (and even to non-PostScript printers). However, some features, such as Gradient Meshes and Object Blends, print out at a lower quality than with PostScript 3 printers — and everything prints a lot slower. So if you have the option, print to PostScript 3 printers, or, when the time comes to buy a new printer, lobby for one that supports PostScript 3. The increased speed and quality quickly offset the extra cost.

✔ **Separation Setup:** If you want to print separations, you can access the Separation Setup dialog box by clicking the Separation Setup button. After you make your changes, you return to the Print dialog box.

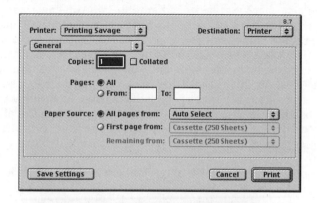

Figure 16-3:
A typical
Print dialog
box for a
Mac (top)
and for a
Windows
PC (bottom).

All about Way-Scary Separations

Separations print a separate page for each color of ink that you use in a document. Printing separations is a good way to double-check your work before you send it to a service bureau to be made into film or plates. If you never do that, skip this section.

If you do send your work to a service bureau to be made into film or plates, printing separations can save you a lot of time. For example, suppose you plan to print a job using black ink and the spot color Pantone 185. After printing separations, you get pages for cyan, magenta, yellow, and Pantone 185, rather than just pages for black and Pantone 185. You know immediately that some of the colors you used were created as cyan, magenta, yellow, black (CMYK) process colors, not as spot colors. (Read more on spot colors later in this section.) On closer examination of the pages, you see that the black type you used exists on all pages, and you know that the type was specified as Registration, not as Black. Registration and Black look identical onscreen, but Registration is a special color that's used exclusively by printers (for those little marks that help center the content on the page). Registration is totally unsuitable for artwork. (Ack! No! Don't print that ink drawing in Registration! You'll only get a page full of gunk.)

We could fill a book with information about looking at separations to find out information about potential problems in your artwork. The book would be painfully long and boring, however, and one we don't want to write. Our advice: Print separations and leave it at that. Perhaps the best place to find out more about separations is your service bureau. The people there can help you examine your separations. In fact, many service bureaus require that you provide laser print separations when you place a print order so they know the file is properly prepared.

The concept behind printing separations from Illustrator is straightforward. Because printing in color requires different inks, which are applied to paper sequentially on a printing press, each ink gets its own printing plate. Illustrator generates film, paper, or even the individual plates themselves — one for each color of ink.

Traditionally, full-color artwork is printed using four different inks (and therefore four plates): cyan, magenta, yellow, and black (CYMK). If you have a CMYK document in Illustrator, you're working in the environment that's perfect for full-color printing. Check out Figure 16-4 for a composite image and the four separations used to create it. (All are shown here in black and white, of course.)

In addition to standard full-color printing (also known as *process printing*), you have the concept of spot-color printing. Spot colors are colors that print on their own plate. A good example is a can of Coke. Rather than full-color printing, the Coca-Cola Company uses several spot colors, which are typically red and black (sometimes they add another color for highlighting). Doing this saves the cost of an extra color of ink and ensures that the shade of red on a can is the exact same red as every other Coke can in the world. You can set any named color swatch to be a spot color in the Separations Setup dialog box.

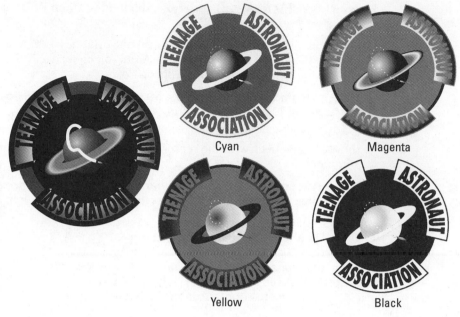

Cyan

Magenta

Yellow

Black

Figure 16-4:
The original
artwork
(left) shown
as four
separations
(right

Remember, separations are not in color

Separations don't print in color; they print in black and white. It doesn't matter to the printing press what color each plate is; the color is determined by the ink that's used with a particular plate.

Looking at Separations Setup

Okay, anybody except a jet pilot may find the Separations Setup dialog box (shown in Figure 16-5) a bit intimidating. But don't panic at the sight of all those controls. Instead, create the artwork that you want to separate. (Be sure to save any changes before you continue.) Then use the following steps to set up your document for separation printing:

1. **Choose File⇨Separation Setup.**

   The Separation Setup dialog box appears.

   If most of the fields are grayed out, that means you have not yet selected a PPD (Printer Prep Document). Every printer has a PPD (unless some vile knave deleted it or never installed it on your computer). The PPD contains information that applications need to print to it properly.

2. **Select the PPD for your printer by clicking the Open PPD button and choosing your printer's PPD.**

   If you can't find the PPD that matches your printer, you can find sample PPDs in the Adobe Illustrator folder. After you choose a PPD, you can change the other settings in the dialog box.

3. **Make sure that the settings (Page Size, Orientation, Emulsion, Halftone, and Image) are correct.**

   If you aren't sure whether they're correct, leave the default settings as they are and check with the representative from your offset printing company.

4. **In the text area beside the scroll bar (where the colors appear), click the printer icon to the left of any color that you want to keep from printing.**

5. **Click OK after you finish making changes.**

To print separations (rather than a composite), be sure to choose Separations (not Composite) in the Output field in the Print dialog box (on a Mac, you have to choose Adobe Illustrator 10 Settings to change this).

By the way, if you need a quick refresher on the uses of CMYK and RGB (red, green, blue), sneak a peek at Chapter 1. We won't tell a soul.

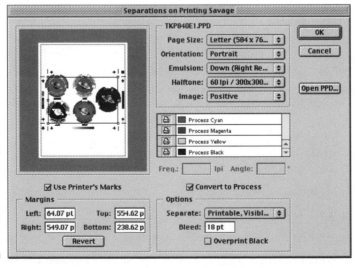

Figure 16-5:
Use the Separations Setup dialog box for printing separations.

Chapter 17

Putting Your Art on the Web

● ●

In This Chapter

▶ Designing for the Web in Illustrator

▶ Differentiating between raster and vector formats on the Web

▶ Saving JPEG, GIF, and PNG for the Web

▶ Exporting Flash and SVG

▶ Using the new Symbolism tools

▶ Creating and optimizing slices

● ●

*1*llustrator is the perfect tool for creating and designing graphical elements for Web pages. That statement may surprise you because most Web graphics are pixel-based, whereas Illustrator is a vector-based graphics tool. In Illustrator, however, the big advantage to creating Web graphics is in the resolution independence of vector graphics (as we discuss in Chapter 1). You can create a graphic once, scale it to be any size you need it to be (even use it for print in addition to the Web), and it will always be a high-quality rendition of your creation.

In this chapter, you peer into the myriad ways of preparing Illustrator graphics for the Web and figure out how to determine the options that best meet the needs of individual graphics. You also find out about how some new file formats, such as Flash and SVG, help you put vector graphics on the Web — preserving the advantages of vector graphics (such as small file size and maximum quality, no matter at what size you view or print the graphics).

From Illustrator to the Web

When you create a graphic in a pixel-based program, such as Photoshop, you have to decide how big you want the graphic to be from the very start. If you want to enlarge the graphic, you add pixels; if you want to make the graphic smaller, you throw away pixels. Either way, you get a blurry, lower-quality image. But with Illustrator, you don't have these problems. Even though you ultimately create pixel-based graphics, your graphics don't become pixel-based until you save or export them. You can save the Illustrator file many times at different sizes, and each one will be at the best possible quality!

The differences between creating for the Web and creating for print happen when you save your graphic. Whenever you create artwork in Illustrator for the Web, you work just as always. The key difference is in how you save your work after you create it. The only other difference that you may find is in the color choices whenever you create a graphic for the GIF file format. (More on that in a moment.) Otherwise, the creative processes for Web and print are identical.

Because you view Web graphics onscreen, you have a much better idea of how they will look after you put them on a Web site than you would if you were going to print them. Colors onscreen (and on the Web, which is always displayed on a screen) consist of red, green, and blue (RGB) pixel combinations. So if you create graphics just for the Web, RGB documents (for more on RGB see Chapter 1) are your best bet. If you create things for both screen and print, RGB gives you the greatest flexibility.

Using Web colors only

Suppose that you're in a room full of Web designers and you hear them talk about *Web-safe color space* and the *Web palette*. You look around discreetly. A dapper man in a dark suit steps out from behind the potted plant and tells you, "You're traveling through another dimension . . ." and a weird piano riff starts to play. . . .

Granted, Web design can seem pretty weird. At least the number of colors are relatively small. *Web-safe color* refers to a set of 216 colors that look the same in all Web browsers and on all computer platforms. If you've been creating for print for any length of time, you may be used to using an almost unlimited range of colors. A mere 216 colors may seem limited at first, but there's method in the madness.

One key benefit of the GIF-file format command is that you can specify exact colors to use in your artwork *after* the artwork is created. The catch is that you can only choose from the 256 colors that the GIF format supports. (Other formats, such as RGB support up to 16.7 *million* colors. Yikes!) So how do you get 216 out of 256? Well, unfortunately, only 216 colors actually display the same on all Web browsers and computer platforms. That's what makes them Web-safe.

What happens if you use a color outside of those 216? Whenever a computer encounters a color it can't display, it *dithers* the colors. The computer takes the colors that it can display and tries to emulate the missing color, putting alternating squares close together of the colors that it can display. If you look at the monitor from a distance and squint, you see a color that looks very similar to your original color.

Dithering is especially noticeable in large areas of solid color. The effects vary from computer to computer and browser to browser. Sometimes the effects aren't noticeable at all. Sometimes you get an obvious plaid or striped pattern. Other times, you get plaids and stripes together (and that is such a fashion *faux pas*).

Bottom line: If it's critical that your colors display consistently (and without dithering) to as many viewers as possible (as in the case of a corporate logo on a home page), use Web-safe colors. Use these Web-safe colors when you save your Illustrator graphic for the Web or when you first create your graphic in Illustrator. You can change the colors in your previously created Illustrator artwork by choosing File⇨Save for Web. Or you can start out using Web-safe colors to build your artwork (which may save some hassle down the line) by choosing Window⇨Swatch Libraries⇨Web. The Web color palette is shown in Figure 17-1.

Figure 17-1:
The
Illustrator
Web color
palette.

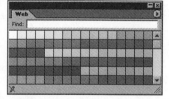

Just click any color in this palette and add it to your Swatches palette so that you can use it just as you do any other color. If you use colors only from this palette, you ensure that your artwork uses only Web-safe colors. However, many Illustrator features (such as blends, color filters, and transparencies) can quickly turn even these colors into unsafe colors. Illustrator likes millions and millions of colors. . . .

Don't let all this talk of Web-safe colors make you gun-shy. In some situations, Web-safe colors are vital (for example, in logos and large onscreen areas of solid color) — in other situations, they just don't matter. Dithering is most obvious in large areas of solid color; if your graphic is made up of many small parts, the dithering won't really be noticeable.

The Save for Web command enables you to decide at any time whether to use Web-safe color when you save your illustration.

Working in Pixel Preview mode

The majority of graphics created for the Web are pixel-based. The two most widely supported graphics file formats on the Web are JPEG and GIF, and these formats save only pixel data, not vector data. (See Chapter 2.) When your graphics are in either of these formats, the majority of Internet users will be able to view your graphics. Fortunately, Illustrator can save graphics as both JPEGs and GIFs. Because pixel-based and vector-based images can look quite different, Illustrator has a special preview mode designed for when you're creating graphics for the Web: Pixel Preview mode. In Pixel Preview, you can see what your vector artwork will look like when it's turned into pixels for display on the Web. That way, you get a better idea of what the final artwork will look like on the Web (rather than waiting to be surprised when you see it on the browser for the first time).

To turn on Pixel Preview mode, choose View⇨Pixel Preview. You may not notice anything different onscreen until you zoom in closer than 100%. Try 200% to really see the pixel detail. Figure 17-2 shows Pixel Preview turned off and turned on at 200%.

Figure 17-2:
Pixel
Preview
turned off
(left) versus
Pixel
Preview
turned on
(right).

This approach is much more convenient than using the File⇨Save for Web command to convert your graphic into pixels to see how it will look, and then having to resave it if it looks awful. With Pixel Preview mode, you can edit the graphics "live" while you're viewing the pixels.

Choosing a file format

Deciding what file format to use is almost as perplexing as picking between paper or plastic in the checkout line. Annoyingly, no single correct answer exists when you have to decide which file format to use for the Web. What works best for your purpose normally turns out to be a compromise between what you want and what you can have.

Well, okay, what can you have? You can use any of five file formats to put your graphics on the Web: GIF, JPEG, PNG, Flash (SWF), and SVG. The basic difference is in how each format presents your artwork. Consider this thumbnail comparison:

- **GIF, JPEG, and PNG** require that path-based files be converted to pixel-based artwork. The results look sketchier but load faster.

- **Flash (SWF) and SVG** preserve the paths you create in Illustrator — sometimes complete with gigantic file sizes.

Each format has unique benefits and drawbacks. And here they come now.

GIF file format

GIF is a great format for traditional Illustrator graphics — which means almost no gradients, blends, or fine details. GIF (Graphics Interchange Format) uses a maximum of 256 colors, but typically you want to use even fewer. The fewer colors you use, the smaller your files.

GIF works best with simple graphics that have large areas of solid color. GIF compression encodes an area of solid color as if it were one big pixel. The more solid colors you have (almost regardless of how much onscreen area they cover), the smaller the file size. But if you use gradients, soft drop shadows, or really complex graphics, you introduce more instructions into the file, and the file gets a lot bigger.

In the process of compressing all the different colors in your image (sometimes thousands or millions) down to 256 or fewer, you can get banding and dithering. *Banding* happens when a range of different colors gets compressed into one solid color and looks like a big stripe in your image where you didn't intend to put one. *Dithering* is Illustrator's way of simulating missing colors by putting tiny squares of the remaining colors close together. This type of dithering is separate from any additional dithering that happens when you don't use Web-safe colors; see previous section "Using Web colors only."

GIF files differ from JPEG files in two important ways: They can have transparent areas, and you can specify the exact colors you want (such as Web-safe colors) when you save the file.

GIF is one of the most widely recognized graphics formats for the Web. If you use a GIF file, you virtually guarantee that all your site's visitors can open it in their browsers.

JPEG file format

JPEG is among the most widely recognized graphics formats for the Web. Anything that you save in JPEG format can be viewed by almost everyone. The JPEG format (created by the Joint Photographic Experts Group) provides the best compression possible for digitized photographs by throwing information away. Don't fret too much about this situation. JPEG does so intelligently — examining the image and removing data where the human eye is least likely to notice the absence. What this amazing feat of mathematics means to you as an artist, however, is that your graphics files should start out with a lot of information — so that if you have to throw out a lot of the information, you still have a lot left. Unlike GIFs, JPEGs can't have transparent areas and offer no way to specify exact colors.

Complex images with lots of gradients, blends, and soft shadows make good JPEGs. Alas, this format is really lousy for graphics that have big areas of solid color. You can't hide the loss of information. Basically, if the image looks good as a GIF, it may look bad as a JPEG — and vice versa. Fortunately, you can decide which format works best by using the Save for Web command.

PNG file format

PNG (Portable Network Graphics) format has a split personality — PNG-8 and PNG-24. The graphics quality that you can get with simple GIFs is also available with PNG-8 graphics. PNG-24, on the other hand, is as adept at handling complex images as JPEG. PNG-8 and PNG-24 files can have transparent areas — and PNG-24 compression is *lossless,* which means no reduction in image quality.

Why don't we just use PNG for everything? Well, first, PNG offers no way to control how much compression is applied to the image; you can't make the image smaller (as you can with a JPEG). More importantly, PNG is not as universal as JPEG and GIF; you don't see PNG format nearly as often on the Web. If you use this format, not all your visitors can view the graphic on their browsers. Some may need to install a special piece of software called a *plug-in* so their browsers can read PNG graphics. This situation creates enough hassle that some visitors turn away from Web pages using PNG graphics to avoid downloading and installing the PNG plug-in.

If your primary concern is image quality, use PNG-24. If you want the maximum number of people to view your work on the Web and the maximum control over file size, use GIF or JPEG.

Macromedia Flash (SWF) file format

The Macromedia Flash (or SWF, for Shockwave File) file format, created by Macromedia, is one of the cooler things to happen on the Web in recent years. Flash is the current standard for vector graphics on the Web. Not only does it support vector-based graphics, but it also supports animation, sound, and interactivity. Of course (as per Murphy's Law of Innovation), something so cool can't be perfect, and Flash has its blemishes, too. First, nearly every browser requires a plug-in to view a Flash file, which limits your audience from the start. Second, Flash doesn't support cool Illustrator features, such as transparency, object blends, and gradient meshes. Last, Flash files don't play well with others. If you try to tie the Flash files into other non-Flash aspects of your Web site, you may run into difficulty.

SVG file format

SVG (Scalable Vector Graphics) format is the upcoming standard for vector graphics. It's the coolest thing that will happen to the Web in the near future — which means that you still have a while to wait. As with Flash graphics, the current versions of most browsers need a plug-in in order to be able to read SVG files.

Ah, but the upside is tantalizing. SVG supports anything that you can create in Illustrator, as well as animation and interactivity. SVG files can interact with HyperText Markup Language (HTML) pages and work in conjunction with eXtensible Markup Language- (XML) driven Web sites. A long list of companies, including Adobe and Corel, are fully behind SVG. It may well become the dominant vector-graphics format in a few years (perhaps by the time the International Space Station is complete). Watch out for the following pitfalls:

- ✔ **I'm waiting:** Although the industry has great expectations for SVG by 2005, it may not seize the vector-graphics crown on schedule.

- ✔ **I'm still waiting:** Although SVG is one of the coolest formats out there, it's so new that only a few people have the plug-in and hardly any support exists for SVG right now (although it's included with Illustrator 10).

Still, you optimists can take heart: Illustrator 10 is one of the few applications that can create SVG files. Whenever the touted SVG revolution comes, you (as an Illustrator user) can say you knew it all along.

So which file format is best, already?

Sorry, but we can't tell you which file format is the best choice for you to use. That answer depends on what you need the file format to do and what trade-offs you're willing to live with. That's the most practical answer for now. However, a summary may help ward off the Too-Many-Choices headache, so here goes:

- ✓ **Maximum compatibility:** Use GIFs and JPEGs if you want maximum compatibility with as many people as possible.

- ✓ **Simplicity:** Use GIFs for simple graphics with large, solid colors or for transparency.

- ✓ **Complexity:** Use JPEGs for more complex graphics with gradients and so forth.

- ✓ **Maximum quality:** Use PNG for maximum-quality complex graphics when compatibility isn't an issue.

- ✓ **Web considerations:** Use Flash when you need to publish vector-graphics on the Web and want as much compatibility as possible (but don't require as much compatibility as with GIFs and JPEGs).

- ✓ **La vida loca:** Use SVG when you want as many bells and whistles as possible and are willing to throw compatibility to the wind.

If we're all lucky, everyone will eventually adopt SVG as the standard, and we won't have to worry about issues, such as which file format to use. (Of course, you gotta ask yourself: Do I feel lucky?) Until then, choosing the right file format is a juggling act that balances features, quality, and compatibility.

Creating Web-Specific Pixel Graphics

Most graphics on the Web are not vector-based but pixel-based because of compatibility issues. Regardless of which pixel format you use, Illustrator gives you the same dialog box from which to export your artwork. Choosing File⇨Save for Web displays the Save for Web dialog box, as shown in Figure 17-3.

The Save for Web dialog box may appear a bit intimidating at first, but it's actually quite easy to use. Although you do have to wade through a lot of settings, the dialog box provides you with a preview of the image, so that you can see how the settings affect the image's quality. The dialog box also gives you the file size and an estimate of how long the graphic will take to download — important considerations in creating graphics for the Web.

The dialog box is slightly different, depending on the file format you're working with, but the following few features remain consistent in any format you use:

- ✓ **Original, Optimized, 2-Up, 4-Up:** These tabs let you view the image at different settings. Click the Original tab to view the image before any settings are applied. Click the Optimized tab to see how the image will look after you save it with the current settings. Click the 2-Up and 4-Up tabs to see the image at multiple settings at once. These last views are the most useful. Your goal when saving your image, no matter what format you use, is always to resemble the original as closely as possible while maintaining the smallest file size (and lowest download time). The ability to compare the image at different settings with the original is vital to achieving this goal. To use the 2-Up and 4-Up settings, click either of the tabs. Then click one of the images to select it. Any settings you make apply only to that selected image. Click a different image to apply different settings. Illustrator saves whatever image is selected (at whatever settings) after you click OK.

✔ **File Size and Download Time:** These features tell you how large your file is and how long that file will take to download over a 28.8 modem. This information is very important. Think of every second required for a graphic to download as another second the viewer has to get bored and click away from your page. Weigh this download time against the quality of the graphic and ask yourself whether having those extra colors, a little less banding, or a better-looking graphic is worth the download time.

✔ **File Format:** This pop-up menu is where you choose the format — GIF, JPEG, PNG-8, PNG-24, SWF, or SVG.

✔ **The remainder of the settings:** The remainder of the fields around the File Format pop-up menu are the file settings and the unique settings of that format. After you choose a format, the remainder of the settings change to match the features of that format. These are covered in-depth under each file format in the next few sections of this chapter.

✔ **Color Table:** This tab shows you the exact colors used when you save the file in GIF or PNG-8 format. Here you can delete colors (or shift non-Web-safe colors to Web-safe colors).

✔ **Image Size:** This tab lets you set the size (in pixels) of the image as you save it. This setting is the actual physical size of the image as it displays in the browser, not the file size.

✔ **Layers:** Illustrator 10 enables you to export your file as Cascading Style Sheet (CSS) Layers. An advanced feature, CSS Layers enable you to selectively hide or show layers on your Web page. They also allow for transparent overlapping slices. More on CSS Layers in the section "Cascading Style Sheets Layers" later in this chapter.

✔ **Slices:** A new tool has been added to the Save for Web toolbox. The Slice Select tool enables you to select slices you made to your object in Illustrator. Slicing your artwork divides your artwork into individual pieces allowing your file to load in sections on your Web page. Slices also enable you to assign features, such as rollovers and links, to individual slices. More on slices in the section "Cascading Style Sheet layers" later in this chapter.

Dithering Algorithm

Color Reduction Algorithm

Slice Select tool   File Format

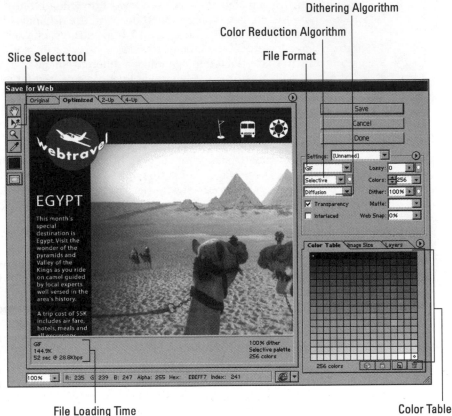

Figure 17-3:
Preview
your image
in the Save
for Web
dialog box.

File Loading Time   Color Table

Saving a graphic as a GIF file

To save your graphic as a GIF, follow these steps:

1. **Choose File⇨Save for Web.**

   The Save for Web dialog box appears.

2. **Select GIF from the File Format pop-up menu (refer to Figure 17-3).**

3. **Click the 2-Up or 4-Up tab at the top of the graphic.**

   After you choose either 2-Up or 4-Up, the first graphic is your original image, and the second is selected as the Optimized image. As you change your file settings, this graphic updates to preview those changes. Clicking the third or fourth graphic (in 4-Up view) lets you make different settings and simultaneously compare and contrast them to find the best settings. Adjust your settings to find the best balance of small file size and best image quality. Every setting you change affects both of those things. Watch the image carefully to see how the changes affect it.

4. **Adjust the settings for the graphic:**

   • **Color Reduction Algorithm:** This delightfully descriptive setting simply means that you take the many colors in your image and reduce them to 256 or fewer colors. How do you want to do that? Your choices are Perceptual, Selective, Adaptive, Web, or Custom. The first three are pretty much the same. *Perceptual* makes the colors as close as possible to whatever colors the human eye perceives in the original image (so they say). *Selective* does the same thing but uses as many Web-safe colors as possible. *Adaptive* makes the remaining colors as mathematically close to the original as possible. *Web* uses the closest Web-safe colors to the colors that are in the image. *Custom* is for power users who want to create their own color-reduction algorithms.

   • Your choices are really between Perceptual and Web. Perceptual gives you an image as close as possible to your original creation. Web gives you an image that looks the same no matter what computer or Web browser it's on. Unfortunately, Perceptual usually looks great, whereas Web dithers things substantially. But look at the Web choice this way: This is as bad as the image is going to look. With any other setting, the graphic is going to look better or worse unpredictably. With the Web setting, you know exactly how much dithering is going on, and nothing more will happen to the image. Compare the second image in Figure 17-4 with the third, which is selected. The only difference between the two is the Color Reduction algorithm. Although noticeable dithering appears in the Web-safe image, it doesn't look unacceptably bad, and the file size is a little smaller.

   • **Dithering Algorithm:** This is the actual shape of the dithering pattern. *No Dither* won't dither the image at all. *Diffusion* randomizes the dithering pattern to make it less noticeable. *Pattern* dithers in a fixed grid. *Noise* is even more random than Diffusion, making any dither even less noticeable. Sadly, the settings that produce the least noticeable dithering also create the highest file sizes. Noise produces the largest files, and Diffusion the second largest. Pattern produces small files with noticeable stripes. No Dither produces obvious bands of color in the image. Notice the sky in Figure 17-4. A No Dither setting causes the stripes. Here again, your goal is to strike a balance between the smallest size and the best quality.

   • **Transparency:** How do you want to treat the parts of your image that have no graphics? Do you want them to be transparent or filled with the Matte color (explained later in this list)? Check this box to make them transparent.

Figure 17-4:
Saving a GIF
in the Save
for Web
dialog box.

- **Interlaced:** This setting makes the file larger so that it seems to be downloading faster, which seems like a contradiction. When a graphic is interlaced, it first loads a very low-resolution version to the Web browser, then the full-resolution version. It seems to load faster, but it's just soothing the user by showing something useful happening. Without Interlacing, the whole page has to download before you can look at it. (It actually loads faster this way; it only *seems* to take forever.) Impatient people may want to select this box (unless, of course, they already skipped this list).

- **Lossy:** This setting reduces file size by as much as 40 percent by eliminating pixels (at the expense of image quality). Use as much Lossy as you can get away with but don't ruin your image.

  Lossy won't work with Interlacing turned on.

- **Colors:** This setting is the total number of colors used in the image. Sometimes, reducing the number results in a smaller image, but doing so doesn't usually have as much effect as the Dither and Lossy settings.

- **Dither:** If you select Pattern, Noise, or Diffusion for a dither method, you can use this setting to turn down the amount of dithering. Lower amounts result in smaller graphics with more noticeable dithering patterns.

- **Matte:** If you don't choose Transparency, the Matte color fills areas of your image where there are no graphics. If you're using transparency and know what color you plan to use for the background of the Web page, you can set the Matte to that color and the pixels at the edge of your graphic will blend with the background, creating a more visually appealing image. If you don't know what the background color will be, set the Matte color to None. Otherwise, the edge pixels may blend to a different color from your background, producing an obvious fringe around the graphic, as if it were snipped hastily out of a different background.

- **Web Snap:** If you aren't using Web for your color reduction algorithm, you can use Web Snap to convert some of the colors (starting with those used most in the image) to Web-safe colors. This setting is a great way to achieve a balance between quality and compatibility. By changing just the largest areas of color to Web-safe, you can avoid the dithering problem in places where it will be most noticeable. The higher the setting, the more colors Illustrator converts to Web-safe.

After you make your settings on several images and decide which image works best for you, click that image, and then click OK. The graphic saves as a GIF, ready for you to use on your Web page.

Saving a graphic as a JPEG file

In Illustrator, JPEGs are easier to make than GIFs. You only need to worry about one setting: Quality. Of course, quality can be specified in two ways. (Simplicity? Well, almost.)

To save your artwork as a JPEG, follow these steps:

1. **Choose File⇨Save for Web.**

   The Save for Web dialog box appears.

2. **Choose JPEG from the File Format pop-up menu.**

3. **Click the 2-Up or 4-Up tab at the top of the graphic.**

   For more on viewing options, see the earlier section "Saving a graphic as a GIF" in this chapter.

4. **Choose a Quality setting.**

   You can choose the Quality setting in two ways, but the effects are identical: by choosing it from the Quality pop-up menu or by entering a number into the Quality field.

   - **The Quality pop-up menu:** Offers you a choice of four preset values: Maximum, High, Medium, and Low. These options refer to the quality level of the image, not the amount of compression applied. A Maximum quality level produces (as you may expect) the largest file sizes and the highest-quality images.

- **The Quality field:** In this field, just to the right of the pop-up menu, you type in any value from 100 (maximum quality) to 0. Use the lowest Quality setting possible that doesn't destroy your image. You may notice that the loss of quality in your image shows up as weird patterns that weren't there before. These patterns are especially noticeable where two large areas of different colors meet. Notice the weirdness (called *artifacting*) in the fourth image in Figure 17-5. A little of this is tolerable in the name of smaller files, but too much becomes distracting. Note that entering settings in this field is identical to choosing values from the pop-up menu. In the pop-up menu, the values of Maximum, High, Medium, and Low correspond (respectively) to settings of 80, 60, 30, and 10 in the Quality field.

5. **Adjust the other settings.**

   - **Progressive:** Like Interlacing for GIFs, Progressive creates the illusion that the image loads faster on Web browsers by loading a low-resolution version of the graphic first and then turning it into a higher-resolution image. In actuality, the image takes longer to load because Progressive files are larger, but viewers feel as though the download is going faster because they see things happening while they wait, rather than waiting for the whole download before they see anything.

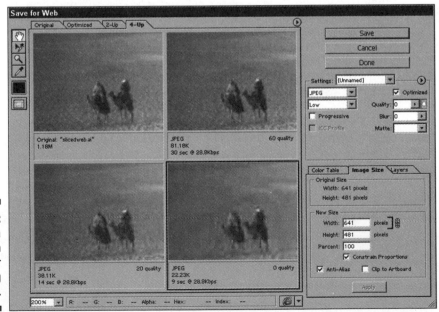

Figure 17-5:
Saving a
JPEG from
the Save for
Web dialog
box.

- **Blur:** Blur is a fairly useless setting. The goal is to reduce the artifacting in the image by blurring it. Unfortunately, the setting blurs the whole image, not just the artifacts, creating problems where none existed before. Leave this set to zero and ignore it. (Unless, of course, you're feeling a little misty.)

- **Matte:** JPEGs can have no transparent areas, so wherever no graphic exists, Illustrator fills in with this color. A setting of None fills in with white.

Saving a graphic as a PNG-8 or PNG-24 file

The settings for PNG-8 are identical to those for GIF except you don't get an option for Lossy. (Read through the earlier section "Saving a graphic as a GIF file.") Put PNG-8 wherever you see GIF. No settings exist for PNG-24, except options for Transparency, Interlacing, and Matte; what you get is what you get. Choose that file format, and the compression scheme does its thing. Either you like the result (and click OK), or you don't (and choose GIF or JPEG instead).

Creating Web-Specific Vector Graphics

Vectors have several advantages over pixels. One of the chief advantages is their small size, especially for basic graphics such as logos and buttons. Another advantage is their ability to be scaled without any loss of quality.

Saving a graphic as a Macromedia Flash file

Flash is a very versatile format developed by Macromedia. Not only can you use Flash to show vector graphics on the Web, you can also animate and add sound and interactivity to them. In Illustrator, you can create the graphic and do limited animation with it. (See Bonus Chapter 2 on cool techniques on the Web at www.dummies.com/extras/Illustrator10/.) Beyond that, you have to use another application (such as Adobe LiveMotion or Macromedia Flash) to take full advantage of the format. For this reason, the Export to Macromedia Flash (SWF) command is really intended to prepare artwork for export to one of these other applications, rather than to create artwork to go directly to the Web. Not that you can't put a Flash file created in Illustrator directly on the Web. You certainly can, but then you're tapping into just a fraction of what Flash can do.

Still, if you want your Illustrator artwork on the Web as vector data, Flash is currently the way to go. The one drawback to the format is the previously mentioned need for a browser plug-in in order for people to see your graphic in their browsers. This situation can make your graphic inaccessible to some people. However, Flash is such a popular format that many people have the plug-in installed in their browsers. Chances are quite good that many people will be able to see your work without problems.

So if your primary concern is that your graphic appear on the Web with no-holds-barred top quality (and print with the best possible quality to boot), use the Flash format.

To save a graphic in Flash format, just follow these steps:

1. **Choose File⇨Export.**

   The Export dialog box appears.

2. **Specify a name, location, and file format for your document.**

   In this case, choose Macromedia Flash (SWF) from the file format pop-up menu.

3. **Click Export or OK.**

   The Macromedia Flash (SWF) Format Options dialog box appears, as shown in Figure 17-6.

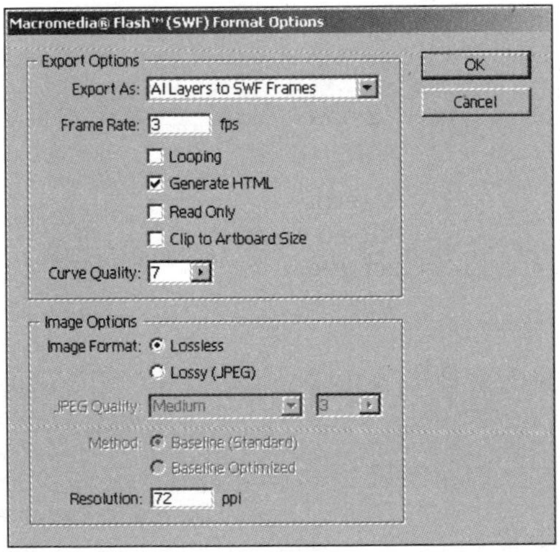

Figure 17-6:
Exporting an AI File to an SWF File with the Macro-media Flash (SWF) Format Options dialog box.

The Macromedia Flash (SWF) Format Options dialog box gives you the following options.

✔ **Export Options:** These options enable you to establish, among other things, how the layers in your file are handled and how fast those layers appear in the animation.

- **Export As:** This is a pop-up menu with three options: AI File to SWF File, AI Layers to SWF Frames, and AI Layers to SWF Files. (*AI* is short for Adobe Illustrator and refers to the file you're currently saving. *SWF* is another term for a Flash file.) This option determines how Illustrator layers (see Chapter 14) are handled when you save them. AI File to SWF File flattens all the layers into a single image, just as if you were printing the illustration. AI Layers to SWF Frames builds a special file that, when loaded to a browser, displays each layer in sequence starting with the first layer and stopping with the last. You can use this option to create a slide show by putting a different graphic on each layer, or to do simple animations. (For more information on animations, see Bonus Chapter 2 on cool techniques on the Web at www.dummies.com/extras/Illustrator10/ — it will move you.) The final option, AI Layers to SWF Files, exports each layer as a separate Flash file.

- **Frame Rate:** This setting determines how fast the Flash file flips through the different Illustrator layers after you choose AI Layers to SWF Frames in the Export As option. Each layer is considered a frame, and the number you enter here is the number of frames you want to appear every second.

- **Looping:** Select this setting to create a file that plays repeatedly when you export AI Layers to SWF Frames. For more on Layers to Frames, see Bonus Chapter 2 on cool techniques on the Web at www.dummies.com/extras/Illustrator10/.

- **Generate HTML:** Select this setting to generate a HyperText Markup Language (HTML) file so that your Flash (SWF) file appears in your browser at its correct and original size rather than filling the window. No more additional editing hassles.

- **Read Only:** Select this setting to create a file that people can view but not change in any way. Also, the file cannot be edited in any Flash application.

- **Clip to Artboard Size:** Select this setting to crop out any artwork that is off the Artboard.

- **Curve Quality:** The higher this setting (from 1 to 10), the closer the graphic is to your Illustrator file and the larger your file size. Lower settings provide lower quality with smaller file sizes. Yet again, you're plagued by the agonizing compromise between file size and image quality!

✔ **Image Options:** These options are a subset of the options in the Flash (SWF) Format Options dialog box. They may never come into play in the graphic you're exporting; they only matter if you have a pixel-based image (such as a scan) incorporated into your Illustrator file or if you create your artwork using features such as Transparency settings, *complex gradients* (gradients with more than eight colors), gradient meshes, or Effects. (See Chapter 10 for more info.) The Flash format doesn't support these features, so it turns them into pixels in the final Flash file (your other Illustrator graphics remain vector-based). The following Image Options determine how to handle these pixel graphics:

- **Lossless:** Select this radio button to save the pixel graphics in PNG-24 format. Don't worry; the Flash plug-in takes care of any compatibility issues with the PNG format. Use this option if you're exporting your graphic for further editing in Flash because you can apply further compression settings in those programs. Lossless lets you start with the highest possible quality.

- **Lossy:** Select this radio button to save the graphics as JPEGs. Choosing Lossy enables you to choose a corresponding JPEG quality. See the "JPEG file format" and the "Saving a graphic as a JPEG file" sections earlier in this chapter for more on JPEGs and compression settings.

- **Method:** Stick with Baseline (Standard) to ensure a format that's recognized by most browsers. Selecting Baseline Optimized optimizes the color but isn't recognized by all browsers.

- **Resolution:** This setting determines how much information the graphics contain; 72 ppi (pixels per inch) is perfect for onscreen display, but if you want people to be able to print your graphics, you may want to go up to 150 ppi, or even 300. Watch out, though, because this high setting results in huge file sizes.

After you complete all your settings, click OK to save your file in Flash format.

With the introduction of symbols (which we discuss later in this chapter in the section "Legal Graffiti") in Illustrator 10, you can export Flash (SWF) files that include symbols. When opened in a Flash application, the symbols are included in the Symbol library of the application.

Saving a graphic as a SVG file

Scalable Vector Graphics (SVG) are great, but . . . well . . . futuristic. Look at it this way. You go to your local car dealer and you find the car of your dreams, with every feature that you ever wanted and some that you didn't know even existed. The gas mileage is great, the color you want is in stock, and you can drive the car off the lot today! And the price? It's about half the price you're willing to pay! But just as you're about to sign on the dotted line, the dealer informs you that there's one little catch: The car runs on a special kind of gas. All the major gas stations have committed to start carrying the special gas in the future, but right now the special gas is not available. What do you do? Take the risk and invest the money, or purchase a car for which you know you can get gas?

SVG is technically great. It offers everything that Flash does, with promises for a whole lot more, such as total support for everything you can create in Illustrator. Also, the format is much more "open" than the Flash format. To create Flash files, you must use an application that specifically supports Flash format, such as Illustrator or LiveMotion. However, if you knew how, you could write SVG files in any word-processing program. In the future, SVG files may integrate seamlessly with Web pages without requiring plug-ins or anything else, meaning that you may get maximum quality and maximum compatibility, and issues such as file formats, dithering, and Web-safe colors, would become concerns of the past.

Unfortunately, for now you may still have a hard time finding that special gas. All the major software companies have pledged support for SVG, but that support isn't there yet. The industry moves so fast that no one can say how long SVG may take to catch on. By the time you read this, that transformation may have occurred. As a matter of fact, Adobe has begun this transformation. Illustrator 10 provides some SVG enhancements, as you'll see in this section. But it may be years until SVG rolls off the tongue as easily as JPEG. (PNG has been around for years and is only just beginning to be adopted.)

So if you want to live a life of action and adventure on the leading edge of technology, start saving your files as SVG right now. Create graphics so insanely great that people are forced to risk computer crashes and other frustrations to download and use the unstable plug-ins that they need to view your SVG files. Go on. We dare you. We double-dare you. We double-*dog* dare you. If you can pull it off, you're the coolest kid in town and will be far ahead of everybody else. If you can't, you still have GIFs and JPEGs and Flash files to fall back on.

To create an SVG file, just follow these steps:

1. **Choose File⇨Save.**

   The Save dialog box appears. For the first time in Illustrator, the SVG file format can be saved directly rather than exported. You can also open an SVG file directly into Illustrator. And if that isn't enough, Illustrator 10 lets you open SVG files that were created in other SVG-savvy applications.

2. **Choose SVG (SVG) from the Format pop-up menu. Specify a name and location for your document.**

3. **Click Save.**

   The SVG Options dialog box appears, as shown in Figure 17-7.

4. **Establish your desired settings and click OK.**

Check out the following list to get the low-down on each option.

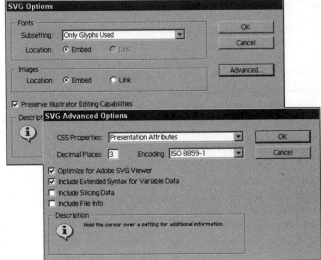

Figure 17-7:
Saving an
SVG file
with the
SVG Options
dialog box.

The SVG Options dialog box offers the following options:

✔ **Fonts:** This option enables you to embed various font groupings in your SVG file.

• **Subsetting:** The SVG format lets you embed the fonts that you use in the document in the SVG file. Fonts have been one of the major stumbling blocks for designers on the Web. Simply put, whoever has different fonts from yours installed on his or her computer may see your text, but not necessarily as you created it. Your font subsetting choice eliminates this problem by making the fonts you used part of the SWF file. You have seven choices for subsetted fonts.

Choose the subsetting option None (Use System Fonts) if you don't want to embed any fonts, if you didn't use text in your graphic, or if you converted your text to outlines. (For more information on converting text to outlines, see Bonus Chapter 1 on typography on the Web at www.dummies.com/extras/Illustrator10/.)

Choose Only Glyphs Used to embed just the font info for the specific letters you used. This option creates a smaller file, but the graphic is less editable than when you include All Glyphs because you can use only letters that are already used in the file. If you just want people to see the graphic the way you created it, choose Only Glyphs Used.

Glyph is just a weird name for letter; you've seen it before in the word *hieroglyphics*.

- **All Glyphs:** Includes all the characters of all the fonts you used. Even if you used just one letter out of Futura Condensed, all the letters, upper- and lowercase, and all special characters are included. If you want people to be able to make changes to your text, choose All Glyphs.

  Like All Glyphs, the other values — Common English, Common English Glyphs Used, Common Roman, and Common Roman Glyphs Used — are useful when the textual content of the SVG file may change.

- **Location:** You can choose to have your fonts built directly into the file (Embed) or collected in another location (Link). Embed results in a larger file, but you have only one piece to take care of. Link results in multiple files.

✔ **Images:** Like with fonts, you can choose to have any placed pixel images in your document built into the SVG file (Embed) or stored externally (Link). Embed creates a larger file that is completely self-contained. Link creates a separate folder for pixel graphics.

✔ **Preserve Illustrator Editing Capabilities:** Select this check box to include a fully editable Illustrator file with your SVG file so that you can make revisions easily and more efficiently. Beware that checking this option will increase your file size.

The following options appear when you click the Advanced button in the SVG Options dialog box.

✔ **CSS Properties:** This option lets you determine where your Cascading Style Sheet (CSS) properties are located. *Cascading Style Sheets* are a standard method of imposing consistent display characteristics on HTML documents. Many Web sites use CSS as a dynamic and flexible way to format Web pages. Talk with your Webmaster about the best settings to use. (To find out more about Cascading Style Sheets, consult *Cascading Style Sheets For Dummies,* by Damon A. Dean, published by Hungry Minds, Inc.)

✔ **Decimal Places:** Higher values (from 1 to 7) for this setting result in better image quality with (what a big surprise!) larger file sizes.

✔ **Encoding:** The SVG format provides several Encoding methods to support alphabets in different languages, such as Kanji.

✔ **Optimize for Adobe SVG Viewer:** Select this check box to optimize the image (you see the image faster) for the Adobe SVG Viewer (a plug-in you use to view SVG files in your browser).

- ✔ **Include Slicing Data:** Select this check box to preserve all slicing information. Slicing carves up your image to allow for better optimization and the ability to assign separate animation features to each chunk. For more on slicing, see the section "Slicing and Dicing Your Graphics" later in this chapter.

- ✔ **Include File Info:** Includes metadata, such as author and creation/revision dates.

Forget about the last option here on variable data (Include Extended Syntax for Variable Data). It's way above the scope of this book. But if you have a need to know, check out *Illustrator 10 Bible* by Ted Alspach, published by Hungry Minds, Inc.

Illustrator 10 has added the live SVG effects feature in which effects, such as shadows and blurs, can be added to vector objects. These effects are great because they aren't *rasterized* (turned into pixels) until the file is actually viewed in the browser — the quality is maintained, regardless of size. File sizes are still small, and the new effects can be created and edited, although some XML expertise is needed.

Although all this razzmatazz is great, you still need a plug-in to view SVG files. The SVG Viewer plug-in is installed when you install Illustrator. You can also get the latest version of the plug-in at www.adobe.com/svg.

Although we focus in this chapter on a very specific part of Web graphics production (getting your graphic into a file format that can be displayed on the Web), this is just the start. Actually putting that graphic where people can see it is another saga entirely, one that involves Web-authoring tools (or hand-coding HTML), service providers, and a whole alphabet soup of FTPs, URLs, and other confusing TLAs (three-letter acronyms). As you may have guessed, actually getting the graphic onto the Web in a real-live Web page goes beyond the scope of this one book. (For more information on that end of things, refer to *Creating Web Pages For Dummies,* 5th Edition, by Bud E. Smith, published by Hungry Minds, Inc.)

The critical step in creating a Web graphic is saving the file. After you save a graphic for the Web, you have many, many options, all of which affect your graphic in different and significant ways. If you aren't producing the Web site yourself, have a discussion with the site's Webmaster before you save the graphic to find out what formats and options work best for the site.

Legal Graffiti

The new Symbol Sprayer and its family of Symbolism tools, shown in Figure 17-8, are Adobe's latest gift to you to make your job of producing Web graphics easier and quicker. Feel like a kid (okay, a bad kid) and spray onscreen repeating graphics all over the place to your heart's content. No clogged spray nozzles, no paint drips, no fumes. Who could possibly resist that intriguing spray can sitting there in the Toolbox just begging to be picked up?

Symbol Sizer — — Symbol Spinner

Symbol Scruncher — Symbol Stainer

Symbol Shifter — Symbol Screener

Symbol Sprayer — Symbol Styler

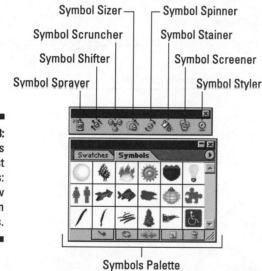

Figure 17-8:
He who has the best toys wins: The new Symbolism tools.

Symbols Palette

Symbols are reusable and repeatable elements that are used in animation. Although they can be graphics, buttons, movie clips, sound files, and even fonts, in Illustrator they can be comprised of any Illustrator objects — vector- or pixel-based images or text. Each individual symbol is referred to as an *instance*. The beauty of symbols is that although you may have multiple instances of a symbol in your file, each instance references a single symbol in the Symbols palette, thereby keeping the file size extremely small.

Symbols provide a quick and easy way to create a large group of similar objects and an easy means to collectively edit these objects. Symbols can be used for most anything but are especially handy in creating navigation buttons, borders, map icons, and masses of graphics, such as foliage, snowflakes, and stars.

Using the Symbol Sprayer

We like it when tools like this work the way that we think they should (unlike the tedious Pen tool). Follow these steps to become the master of your personal digital spray can:

1. **Select the Symbol Sprayer.**

   Note that the sprayer icon is surrounded by a circle, which represents the diameter of your sprayer. (Read the upcoming section "Setting the Symbolism Options" to discover how to change that size.)

2. **Choose Window⇨Symbols.**

   The Symbols palette appears with a default library of symbols to choose from.

3. **Select a symbol from the Symbols palette, click it, and drag it across your artboard.**

   A trail of symbols (of the one you chose) appears, mirroring the movement of your cursor while you drug it across your artboard. (Check it out in Figure 17-9.) Unless you feel the need to edit your symbols or create your own custom symbol, you're done!

Figure 17-9:
Pssst:
Graffiti
never had it
so good (or
legal).

Creating a custom Symbol

If you're the creative type, create your own symbol. First create the artwork, which can include any Illustrator objects — vector- or pixel-based images or text. You can even use a combination of objects, as shown in Figure 17-10. Next, select your artwork and do one of these three things: click the New Symbol button; choose New Symbol from the Symbols palette menu; or drag and drop the art onto the Symbols palette. Voilà — a symbol is born.

Figure 17-10: Combine object types to create custom symbols. Just ducky.

Editing your Symbols

The other Symbolism tools enable you to tweak your symbols to graphic perfection. To edit your symbols, first select the symbols with the Selection tool. Note how you select the bounding box (a temporary border surrounding objects) of the symbols and not the individual instances. That's because symbols are a unique breed of graphic that require a unique kind of editing.

- ✔ **Symbol Shifter:** Click and drag your mouse to shift the position of the symbols in relation to each other.

- ✔ **Symbol Scruncher:** Click and hold down your mouse to move the symbols closer together or farther apart. Hold down the Alt (Windows) Option (Mac) key to move the symbols apart.

- ✔ **Symbol Sizer:** Click and release or hold your mouse down to size the symbols larger or smaller. Hold down the Alt (Windows) Option (Mac) key to reduce the size of the symbols.

  You can also use the Rotate and Scale tools to rotate and size symbols.

- ✔ **Symbol Spinner:** Click and drag your mouse to rotate the symbols.

- ✔ **Symbol Stainer:** Click and release or hold your mouse down to tint the symbols by using the current Fill color.

- ✔ **Symbol Screener:** Click and release or hold your mouse down to increase the transparency of the symbols.

- ✔ **Symbol Styler:** Applies a style from the Styles palette onto the symbol. With the Symbol Styler, select and drag a style from the Styles palette onto a symbol instance.

Feeling extra productive? Press Alt and right-click (Windows) or Option+Ctrl and click (Mac) to have the palette of Symbolism tools appear right under your cursor for quick and easy access.

Setting the Symbolism options

Double-click any of the Symbolism tools to bring up the Symbolism Tool Options dialog box, as shown in Figure 17-11. Here you adjust the behavior of each tool.

Select your tool icon from the row and then adjust its Diameter (1–999 points), the Intensity (1–10), and the Symbol Set Density (1–10). Most of the tools provide shortcut keys with which you adjust settings while you draw. We recommend keeping the Show Brush Size and Intensity and Preview Bounding Boxes of Symbol Instances options selected (checked) so that you get a good idea of your tool coverage (and you get a box rather than a bazillion anchor points as your symbols spew forth).

Like the Symbol Sprayer, each of the Symbolism tools applies its effects on the symbol instances based on the diameter setting.

In the Method option of the Symbolism Tools Options dialog box (see Figure 17-11), choose the User Defined setting to apply the settings within your Illustrator application to the Symbolism tools. For example, if you choose User Defined for your Stain setting for the Symbol Sprayer, the symbols will appear with your current Fill color, regardless of the original color of the symbol.

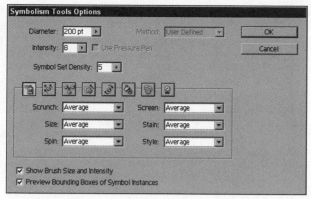

Figure 17-11:
The
Symbolism
Tool Options
dialog box:
Grand
Central for
controlling
the look
of your
symbols.

Here are some other handy tips to keep in mind when working with symbols:

- **If you export your file as a Flash (SWF) file,** (see the section "Saving a graphic as a Flash file" earlier in this chapter), your symbols are included in the symbol library of your Flash application.

- **To place a single instance of a symbol,** choose Place Instance of Symbol from the Symbols palette menu, or click the Place Symbol Instance button at the bottom of the palette.

- **To convert a symbol into a regular Illustrator editable graphic,** select the symbol instance and click the Break Link to Symbol button at the bottom of the Symbols palette, or select the command from the palette menu. You can then modify the graphic, select it, and click the original symbol in the Symbols palette. Then, choose Redefine Symbol from the palette menu. Not only is the symbol revised, but any symbol instance on your artboard is revised as well. Imagine having to change 1,000 little leaves on a tree if they were regular graphics and not symbols!

- **Symbolism tools can take advantage of a pressure-sensitive tablet.** Select Use Pressure Pen in the Symbolism Tool Options dialog box.

- **To name or rename your symbol,** either double-click the symbol in the Symbols palette or choose Symbol Options from the Symbols palette menu.

- **To delete a symbol,** select it in the Symbols palette and click the Delete Symbol at the bottom of the palette, or choose the command from the palette menu.

- **To duplicate a symbol,** select it in the Symbols palette and choose Duplicate Symbol from the palette menu. Duplicating is handy for making variations of symbol.

No matter how many instances of a symbol you have on your artboard, they all reference the single, original symbol in the Symbols palette. Thus you get extremely small file sizes — a big plus when creating graphics for the Web or for animation.

Slicing and Dicing Your Graphics

If you're an avid Web surfer, you've probably encountered a site or two where the graphics appear onscreen in separate chunks. In the Web world, these chunks are referred to as *slices*. Slices are useful for a number of reasons. They can provide a better experience for viewers by allowing them to immediately see portions of the image while it loads rather than having to wait for an entire large image to load. Another benefit is that slicing the image into sections that appear in multiple places on your site makes it load more quickly on the next place after the image loads in one place. Also, each slice can be optimized separately, which increases loading speed. Depending on your image, revising a slice or two can be quicker than revising an entire image. Finally, you can selectively assign features, such as rollovers, links, and animation to slices. Have we convinced you yet of the merits of slices? Good. In the next section, we show you how slices work in Illustrator 10.

Creating slices

In Illustrator 10, slices can be applied to objects (vector- or pixel-based or text), groups of objects, or layers. And when any of these are edited, the slices are automatically updated. Read through the following steps for how to create slices. You do need to first create a piece of artwork, however. We recommend using at least one block of text, one group of objects, and one pixel-based image. For this example, we use a mock Web page.

1. **Choose View⇨Show Slices.**

    Now you can see your slices while you create them.

2. **With the Selection tool, select an object on your artboard.**

    In this example, we select the logo. This kind of slice is referred to as an *object- based* slice.

3. **Choose Object⇨Slice⇨Make, and then deselect the object by clicking on the artboard away from the object.**

    After you release the mouse, lines and numbers appear. The red lines and numbers indicate a user-defined slice — one that you made. The pink lines and numbers indicate that the slices were automatically created by Illustrator. Figure 17-12 shows the sliced artwork.

Figure 17-12:
It slices, it
dices, it
darned near
makes
julienne
fries.

4. **Select your group, choose Object⇨Slice⇨Make, and then deselect the group by clicking on the artboard away from the object.**

The group is now assigned a user-defined slice. If you edit any of your objects — scaling the logo, for example — the slices update automatically, as shown in Figure 17-13.

Figure 17-13:
Editing an
object
makes the
slices
update
automati-
cally.

5. **Select the text block and choose Object⇨Slice⇨Make.**

Keep the slice selected.

6. **Choose Object⇨Slice⇨Slice Options.**

The Slice Options dialog box appears.

7. **In the Slice Options dialog box, select HTML Text from the Slice Type pop-up menu.**

The HTML options appear.

8. **Choose your Alignment option and click OK.**

   Now it's time to optimize the slices. *Optimizing* is the process of assigning quality and compression settings to your images.

9. **Choose File⇨Save for Web.**

   For more on the Save for Web dialog box and all its settings, see the section "Creating Web-Specific Pixel Graphics" earlier in this chapter.

10. **In the Save for Web dialog box, select any pixel-based slices with the Slice Select tool and choose JPEG from the file formats pop-up menu.**

    Choose your compression settings. (For the skinny on compression, see the earlier section "Choosing a file format.") We chose High because, in our case, quality is important.

11. **Select your slices that contain vector graphics and then assign a GIF file format to each.**

    Choose your desired palette and other options. You can also assign PNG, SWF, or SVG formats, if so desired.

12. **After you optimize all your slices, click Save to generate an HTML table with your slices. Leave format as HTML and images.**

13. **Click Save.**

    If you don't want to save a file, click the Done button to return to your Artboard.

    Your file is sliced and diced and ready to be incorporated into your Web site.

Here are a few more things you may want to know about slicing:

- ✔ **You can manually slice your image by using the Slice tool.** Just grab the tool and drag around the portion of your artwork that you want the slice to contain. Slice boundaries can be adjusted by using the Selection tool. Manual slices do not update automatically like object-based slices do.

- ✔ **You can apply slices to layers.** These are referred to as layer-based slices. Target a layer in the Layers palette (for more on layers, see Chapter 14), and choose Object⇨Slice⇨Make. The size of the slice is determined by the layer's bounding box.

- ✔ **To eliminate a slice, select it and choose Object⇨Slice⇨Release.**

- ✔ **To delete all slices, choose Object⇨Slice⇨Delete All.**

- ✔ **To show or hide your slice outlines, choose View⇨Show/Hide Slices.**

✔ **You can combine several slices into a single larger one.** Select them all and choose Object➪Slice➪Combine Slices. You can also divide slices into a user-specified number of slices or pixels by choosing Object➪Slice➪Divide Slices.

✔ **To create slices based on a selection of object(s), choose Object➪Slice➪Create from Selection.**

A sliced Illustrator file can be imported into Adobe Photoshop or ImageReady where you can then apply various Photoshop effects or ImageReady animation features to the preserved slices. The same file is also recognized by GoLive, Adobe's HTML authoring application.

Cascading Style Sheet layers

Layer-based slices can also be exported as Cascading Style Sheet (CSS) layers. Using CSS layers enables you to assign (set) a multitude of properties to the elements on your Web page (typefaces, colors, spacing, graphics). They also enable you to create transparent overlapping slices. Use CSS layers to show and hide certain layers on your Web page. For example, you can produce a Web site with text in three languages on three separate layers and then make the layer matching the language of the browser visible while the others remain hidden.

The realm of CSS is fairly advanced but for our purposes here, we show you the very basic steps of how to create a file with CSS Layers:

1. **After your file is created, choose File➪Save for Web.**

   The Save for Web dialog box appears.

2. **Click the Layers tab at the bottom right.**

3. **Check Export as CSS Layers.**

   Select each layer in your file from the Layer pop-up menu. Make sure that either Visible, Hidden, or Do Not Export is selected.

4. **Click Save.**

   An HTML file, which includes CSS layers, is created.

5. **In the Save Optimized As dialog box that appears, specify a name and location for your file.**

6. **Click the Output Settings button.**

7. **In the Output Settings dialog box that appears, make sure that HTML is selected from the second pop-up menu from the top.**

8. **Select Generate CSS from the Slice Output section.**

9. **Click OK and then Save.**

   Your file has been created and saved. Click the Done button to close the Save for Web dialog box.

You can also apply CSS layers to overlapping objects — a logo overlapping a photograph, for example. Place your objects on separate layers and apply slices to those layers. Then choose File⇨Save for Web, and, as we describe in the preceding steps, export as CSS layers. The logo now has a transparent background instead of a background that contains part of the photograph.

Cascading Style Sheets, its versions, and its many facets aren't equally supported by all platforms and all browsers (and their versions). The differences are too great to list here, but you can see them all at the Browser Compatibility Chart on the WebReview.com site (www.webreview.com/browsers/browsers.shtml).

Chapter 18

Moving Files into and out of Illustrator

In This Chapter

▶ Placing different files into an Illustrator document

▶ Managing linked files

▶ Exporting graphics from Illustrator

▶ Working with Photoshop files in Illustrator

*A*lthough you can certainly take a file from concept to final printing using only Illustrator, you probably shouldn't. It's a specialized program, created to be one small (but vitally important) part in a production cycle.

In a typical production cycle, text is created in a word-processing program, such as Microsoft Word; scanned images are edited in an image-editing program, such as Photoshop; and vector graphics are created in Illustrator or Macromedia Freehand. Finally, all these elements are combined in a page-layout program (such as InDesign, PageMaker, or QuarkXPress) or a Web-design application (such as Adobe GoLive or Macromedia Dreamweaver).

Attempting to make Illustrator perform all aspects of the production cycle is like trying to build a house with only a hammer. You may be able to do it, but the task takes you a lot more time to complete, the result looks really awful, and you're a lot more tired and frustrated than if you'd used the right tools for the job in the first place.

Don't get me wrong, Illustrator is a strong link in that production cycle. You can save Illustrator files in nearly *three dozen* different file formats! If you create something in Illustrator and save it properly, you can open your creation in just about any application that ever supported graphics on any platform — even bizarre and forgotten computer platforms, such as Amiga!

The bottom line is that Illustrator is designed to create files for use in other programs as well as receive graphics files created in other programs. Harnessing the full power of Illustrator means making the program work well (and play nicely) with other programs — or in other words, getting files into and out of Illustrator.

In this chapter, you find out how to make Illustrator play well with others — by bringing files that weren't created in Illustrator into your Illustrator document and by moving Illustrator files into other applications.

Bringing Files into Illustrator

You can bring graphics or text into Illustrator in several different ways, but the most straightforward, Joe-Friday way is to use the Place command from the File menu. Every type of graphic or text that can be inserted in Illustrator can be placed with this command, making it the one-stop location for all file importing. The "Getting Files out of Illustrator" section (later in this chapter) contains a list of the most common file formats that Illustrator can both export and import.

When you place artwork into Illustrator, you usually have the option of either *embedding* or *linking* the artwork. Each of these processes has different implications for file size and storage:

- ✔ **Embedding:** Makes the placed artwork part of the Illustrator file, even though the artwork was created elsewhere. That way, you need only the single Illustrator file for your artwork to print properly.

  Embedding can dramatically increase the file size.

- ✔ **Linking:** Creates a link in the Illustrator document to the placed artwork. The file size of the Illustrator document is smaller as a result, and any change to the linked file is automatically reflected in the Illustrator document. Linking also enables the file to be updated outside of Illustrator (while maintaining the link). In order for linked files to print properly, both the Illustrator file and all linked files must be present.

To place a graphic in Illustrator, follow these steps:

1. **Choose File⇨Place.**

   The Place dialog box appears, as shown in Figure 18-1, so that you can choose the file that you want to place.

2. **Select the file that you want to place.**

   If you don't have any files lying around, look in the `Sample Files` folder and pick one of those files.

Figure 18-1:
Select a
document to
embed or
link with the
Place dialog
box.

3. Choose to link or embed the file you want to place.

To create a link between the file you want to place and the Illustrator file (the default setting), make sure that the Link box (lower left) is selected. To embed the file you want to place in the Illustrator file, deselect the Link box.

4. Choose to use the graphic as an artistic element or a template.

If you select the Template check box (lower left), Illustrator creates a special layer for the Photoshop image. (See Chapter 14 for more on layers.) This layer is locked (you can't change anything on the layer), and the graphic is dimmed, making the graphic 50 percent lighter. Template layers also don't print and aren't included in the artwork when you use the Save for Web command. Template layers are especially useful when you plan to use the Photoshop image as a guide for tracing in Illustrator. (See Bonus Chapter 2 on cool techniques on the Web at www.dummies.com/extras/Illustrator10/.)

5. Choose to replace or add the graphic to the rest of the placed graphics (if necessary).

This option is available only after you've already placed a graphic in the file and that graphic is selected. You have the option of replacing that graphic with the graphic that you're about to place or bringing the new graphic in as a separate graphic. Just select the Replace check box to replace the selected graphic, or leave the box unchecked to leave the selected graphic alone.

6. Click the Place button.

Which is better, linking or embedding?

If you're just playing around to see how the program works, it doesn't matter whether you link or embed. But if you're working on a production with tight deadlines and making rapid changes to your document and money is on the line, we recommend that you link whenever possible. Linking makes the chore of changing placed images much easier.

When you embed something, it exists totally within a single Illustrator file: Your artwork is locked down. You can't do anything to it other than move it, scale it (and other such transformations), or run a Photoshop filter on it. That's all, folks — and that isn't much. You can't edit your artwork in another application; because it's embedded in Illustrator, it won't respond to other applications. The term *embedding* is quite literal — it's stuck in there. You can't get your artwork out unless you pry it out with the Export command. (More on that in the section "Getting Files out of Illustrator," later in this chapter).

Here's an example. You recently sent a completed job to your service bureau, but it can't be printed because your five Photoshop images are embedded — two in RGB (red, green, blue) mode and the rest in CMYK (cyan, magenta, yellow, black). The images need to be in CMYK for the job to print properly. Illustrator can't convert pixel data from RGB to CMYK. (Illustrator can only convert vector data.) You need to use Photoshop to convert the pixel images. If the images are linked, however, the folks at your service bureau can change them by opening the image in Photoshop, making the change, and then updating the link — a quick process that takes about a minute on a fast computer.

Because the images are embedded, however, you have two options. You can deliver the original Photoshop graphics over to the service bureau (assuming that your company has one, that you didn't send the job over at the last minute, and that the service bureau is still open). Or you can rack up bad karma if you make the staff at the service bureau do this for you. This entails separating each images into its own layer in Illustrator; exporting the entire document as a Photoshop file; opening the document in Photoshop; deleting all the other layers; cropping the image to the right size; changing the color mode; saving the image; going back to Illustrator; and replacing the graphic. Whew! And this assumes that the service bureau staff actually knows how to do this, which not many people do.

If you know beyond a doubt that your images are perfect, pristine, and final, and never need changing in any way, you can embed them. If your feet touch the earth like the rest of ours do, link your images.

The only hassle that comes with linking is that you have to provide all the linked images with your Illustrator file whenever it leaves your computer because your file won't print properly without them. This procedure is a minor hassle, however, considering the amount of hassle it saves!

Managing links

Whenever you place an image into Illustrator and link it, the image isn't actually in your document — the same way that Dan Rather isn't actually in your house when you watch the news on TV. What you see in Illustrator is a preview of the file — an image of the image, so to speak. Think of the actual file as broadcasting an image of itself to Illustrator while the file itself sits somewhere else on your hard drive. You look at the preview onscreen; when the document prints, the actual file supplies the image for the document. If the actual file gets moved, modified, or deleted, you have a problem — especially if you're printing — because Illustrator uses the preview image instead of the real file. The preview image in Illustrator contains just enough info to be displayed onscreen, but not nearly enough info to print with any quality.

Fortunately, Illustrator provides you with a powerful tool to help you manage links: the Links palette. You can find the Links palette by choosing Window➪ Links. What you get looks remarkably like Figure 18-2, even if you don't have thumbnails of all those people.

Figure 18-2:
Use the
Links palette
for total link
control.

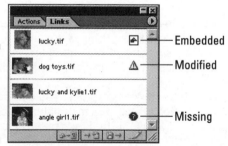

The Links palette shows you all the placed images in your document; alerts you if anything is amiss; and enables you to update, edit, or replace the images — all with the click of a mouse.

The Links palette includes embedded images as well, even though they aren't technically links.

To use the Links palette, you must first understand what the palette is telling you. The Links palette informs you about the status of the graphic through alerts. *Alerts* are tiny icons that appear beside the names of the graphics in the Links palette. They look a little like buttons, but they are strictly informative: Alerts warn you when there is a potential problem with the link. You can fix most problems by clicking the graphic within the Links palette, and then by clicking the Replace Link or Update Link buttons at the bottom of the palette (more on these options in just a second).

The alerts provide the following information:

- **Embedded:** The Embedded icon shows a rectangle overlapping a triangle. This icon indicates that the image data is completely contained within the Illustrator document and not linked to an external file. This situation isn't necessarily a problem, but it can be. See the section "Which is better, linking or embedding?" earlier in this chapter. No "unembed" button exists. The only way to turn this embedded image into a linked file is to click the Relink button at the bottom of the palette, locate the original file on the hard drive, and replace the file with the Link option checked.

- **Missing:** A question mark inside a red octagon (or stop sign) shows that the actual image file is missing. This information is good to know because the image still shows up in Illustrator even if the information that the file needed to print properly is missing. You can fix this image by clicking the Replace Link button. (More about this in a moment.)

- **Modified:** A triangle with an exclamation point (sort of like an emphatic yield sign) indicates that the actual image has been changed outside of Illustrator. This information is also vital because Illustrator still displays the original image.

- **No icon means that everything is okay:** This isn't really an alert. (Yeah, that would be pretty silly — Warning! Everything is normal!) But it's worth noting that when nothing is wrong with a linked image, the palette shows just the filename of the image, its thumbnail, and nothing else.

After you identify the problems with the linked graphics, you can manage them by using the buttons along the bottom of the Links palette (refer to Figure 18-2), by clicking the problem graphic in the Links palette, and then by clicking one of the following four buttons:

- **Replace Link:** This is the first button from the left. Click this button when your image is missing or when you want to swap the selected graphic with another graphic on your hard drive. After you click this button, the Place dialog box opens. Choose a different file or locate the missing file on your hard drive, and then click Place. The new image replaces the old one.

- **Go To Link:** Second from the left, this button is handy for locating and selecting linked graphics. Click the linked graphic in the Links palette and click the Go To Link button. This action selects the graphic in the document as if you clicked it by using the Selection tool. Clicking this button also centers the view on the graphic, making the graphic easy to spot whenever you have a lot of other graphics in the document.

- **Update Link:** Click this third button whenever you see the Modified warning beside a link. This action updates the selected link with the latest information from the original file.

✔ **Edit Original:** This fourth button is available only for linked images — not for embedded images. After you click this option, the selected image opens in the original application that created it.

The Edit Original option is a great way to modify images. After you place a Photoshop image, click this button to launch Photoshop and open the image. In Photoshop, you can make the necessary changes and then save your image. When you go back to Illustrator, it asks whether you want to update your modified image. Click OK to update the information.

Your goal, as you work with placed images, is to avoid all question marks and exclamation points in your Links palette. Fix these problems by using the buttons at the bottom of the palette.

The Links palette offers a few more tidbits through its submenu to help you manage links. Click the triangle in the upper-right corner of the palette (refer to Figure 18-2) to access the Links palette submenu. Here you find Replace, Go To Link, Update Link, and Edit Original commands that duplicate the functions of the buttons along the bottom. You also find various Sort commands, such as Sort by Name, which alphabetizes the linked images within the palette. You can also reorganize the palette by using Show commands, such as Show Embedded, which hides all linked graphics. The Show and Sort commands are useful only when you have several linked images, which is rare in an Illustrator document. The two most useful things in the Links palette submenu are Embed Image and Information. Here's how you use them:

✔ **Embed Image:** Click a linked image in the Links palette and choose Embed Image to embed the image into the Illustrator file.

✔ **Information:** Click an image in the Links palette and choose Information to open the Link Information dialog box. This dialog box is strictly informative. You can't make any changes here, but you find out lots of information about the selected graphic, such as the location of the image on the hard drive, the file size of the image, the image's file type, when the image was created, and a whole lot more. You can also access this dialog box by double-clicking the name of the link.

Getting Files out of Illustrator

Files that are *native* to Illustrator (files saved in the Illustrator format within Illustrator or the Photoshop format within Photoshop) can't be read by every application. However, these files are Portable Document Format- (PDF) based, so any application that can read PDFs generated by Acrobat 5 or a later version (including Acrobat Reader 5.0) can also read Illustrator files. For the applications that can't read Illustrator-native files, Illustrator can export a number of different file formats.

To decide which format to use, consider the eventual use of the file. For instance, if you're posting your artwork on a Web page, you probably want to use either JPEG or GIF formats. (Find out more about these formats in Chapter 17.) If you want to place your file in a Microsoft Word document, you can use EPS, EMF, or BMP formats. (More on those formats in a moment.)

Typically, the manual that accompanies your software describes which file formats it accepts. Illustrator supports the export of 18 different formats, so just choose a format that works in the target application from the list of available formats.

To export your artwork in a certain format, choose File⇨Export from the File menu, choose the format you want from the Format list, and save the file. Some Export formats open an additional dialog box for that specific file format after you click Save. You'll also find various file formats under the Save for Web command, such as PNG, GIF, and SVG as well as JPEG and SWF, which are also found under the Export command.

Not all file formats support vector data! (See Chapter 2 for details.) If you use EPS, PDF, Flash, or SVG, you preserve your paths; but most other formats convert your Illustrator files to pixels.

The following list is a brief summary of the most useful file formats available in Illustrator 10:

- **EPS:** Encapsulated PostScript files are accepted by most software packages. Raster and vector-based data are preserved in EPS files.

  For more information about raster, vector, path, and pixel graphics, see Chapters 2 and 17.

- **GIF:** Graphics Interchange Format files are commonly used on the Web for files with few colors (good for solid-color logos and text).

- **JPEG:** Joint Photographic Experts Group files are highly compressible files that are used on the Web. They're especially good for photographs.

- **PNG:** Portable Network Graphic files are the most flexible of the Web formats, providing support for compression and detail in a single file format.

- **TIFF:** Tagged Image File Format files are the industry standard for pixel-based images for print work.

- **PDF:** Portable Document Format files are designed to keep the look and feel of the original artwork and can be read by anyone with a copy of the free Adobe Acrobat Reader (www.adobe.com).

- **PICT:** PICT files are the built-in Macintosh pixel format. Export any graphics to be viewed on Macintosh screens as PICT.

- **BMP:** BMP files are the built-in pixel format of Windows. Use BMP to export any graphics that will be viewed on Windows screens.

- ✔ **EMF:** Enhanced MetaFile formatted files are perfect for embedding graphics in Microsoft Office applications, such as Word, Excel, and PowerPoint.

- ✔ **PSD:** Photoshop Document files are native Photoshop files, which can contain Photoshop layer information.

- ✔ **Flash:** Flash files are a vector graphic format for the Web.

- ✔ **SVG:** Scaleable Vector Graphics files are the up-and-coming Web standard of vector graphic formats.

Whenever you export files, use the same name as the original document file but with a different extension (the three letters after a filename, traditionally required by Windows and DOS computers). These letters tell you the format of the file just by looking at its name.

Working with Illustrator and Photoshop

Illustrator and Photoshop, both from Adobe, provide unique and useful integration capabilities. You can take files from either application and put them directly into the other application in five ways: dragging and dropping; copying and pasting (almost identical to cutting and pasting); placing; exporting and importing; or opening. Each method produces slightly different results to meet your every need, whim, or desire. (Well, okay, just those desires that center on moving files between graphics applications. You have those all the time, right?)

If you ever bring something from Illustrator into Photoshop (or vice versa) and something weird happens (parts of the image are missing, odd lines streak through the image, nothing happens, or your computer crashes), try saving the file as an earlier version, such as Illustrator 8 or Illustrator 6. Close the file and open it again before you try to copy and paste. Adobe takes great pains to make the two applications as compatible with each other as possible, but whenever a new version of one application comes out, you can usually count on a lag time before the other application is updated to be compatible with the new features. Saving a file in an earlier version enables the application to "understand" the file.

Making life easy: Copy and paste, drag and drop

These methods of getting a file from one program to the other are incredibly easy. Open a file in Photoshop, and then open a file in Illustrator. Make a selection in either program, choose Copy from the Edit menu, and then go to the other application and choose Paste. Or simply click a selection in either program and drag the selection from that one application into an open window in the other application. In Illustrator, you can use any Selection tool to do the dragging. In Photoshop, you need to use the Move tool.

After you move graphics this way, they appear at the height and width that they were when created in the other program. After you drag a graphic from Illustrator to Photoshop, the graphic rasterizes automatically. *Rasterize* is a two-dollar word for the process that converts vector data into pixel data.

Whenever you copy and paste a graphic from Illustrator into Photoshop, the Paste dialog box appears, as shown in Figure 18-3. Choose from the three radio buttons there to select your pasting preference: pixels, paths, or shape layer.

Figure 18-3:
Pasting
Illustrator
data into
Photoshop.

Your first impulse may be to paste the graphic as paths. After all, Illustrator uses paths, not pixels, so you expect this method to preserve your original Illustrator files as they are. Unfortunately, although Photoshop uses paths similar to Illustrator's paths, they work very differently in Photoshop than they do in Illustrator. For example, paths in Photoshop can't have strokes or fills, although paths can be used to fill or stroke an image in Photoshop and to do other important Photoshop-specific things. You just can't use the path to print or display information on the Web.

Your other option is to paste your graphics as a shape layer. Shape layers were first introduced in Photoshop 6 and allow vector data to be retained without rasterization. In order to retain the vector data of shape layers, however, they must reside in a layered file, which limits your file formats to TIFF, PDF, or native PSD. Paste the Illustrator graphic as pixels if your end goal is to create and save a pixel-based Photoshop image.

Copying and pasting or dragging and dropping from Photoshop to Illustrator is easier than going from Illustrator to Photoshop (and that's pretty darn easy). You don't have to worry about the paths-to-pixels issue. Just make your selection and drag it by using the Move tool; or copy the image, go to an open Illustrator document, and paste the image. That's it!

You may assume (quite logically) that because moving Illustrator files into Photoshop rasterizes the files, moving Photoshop files into Illustrator must "vectorize" them. Not true. The pixels in a Photoshop file stay pixels, subject to all the laws and limitations of pixels anywhere else. For example, Illustrator vector data prints out at the highest quality no matter how much you scale, skew, rotate, or distort the data. But pixel data within Illustrator starts to *degrade* (the data gets blurry or worse) if you enlarge it or shrink it. Rotating, skewing, or distorting the pixel data has similar negative effects. Although you don't have to worry about resolution for vector data, you do have to make sure that your pixel data has a high enough resolution: 72 points per inch (ppi) for the Web and anywhere from 150 ppi to 300 ppi or higher for print.

Photoshop graphics that are dragged and dropped or copied and pasted into Illustrator files are always embedded.

Placing files

Placing files into Photoshop or Illustrator is one of the more versatile ways to bring data into the application. Each application provides a variety of options that aren't available by using any other method.

Placing Illustrator files in Photoshop

To place an Illustrator file into Photoshop, open a Photoshop file and choose File➪Place. Select a saved Illustrator file (it doesn't need to be open) from the Place dialog box and click OK. The file opens in Photoshop inside a preview box; see Figure 18-4. We cannot overstate the handiness of this preview box. While inside the preview box, the graphic isn't really "in" Photoshop yet. You can position the graphic, rotate it, and then scale the preview. Then double-click inside the preview box (or press Enter for Windows or Return for Mac), and Photoshop rasterizes the graphic at the best quality possible. If you rotate and scale the image after it's been rasterized, you could blur and otherwise degrade the image. Placing the image into Photoshop requires a couple more steps than copying and pasting or dragging and dropping, but doing so ensures that the image is the highest possible quality.

Placing Photoshop files in Illustrator

Placing Photoshop files into Illustrator is identical to placing any other graphic into Illustrator. See the section "Bringing Files into Illustrator," earlier in this chapter.

Figure 18-4:
The Place
preview box
in Photo-
shop
provides the
highest
quality and
greatest
flexibility for
Illustrator
files brought
into
Photoshop.

100%   Doc: 278K/562K

Now opening in an application near you

Native files can be read by the "opposite" application. In other words, Photoshop can read Illustrator files, and Illustrator can read Photoshop files. One advantage of this capability is that you don't need to have any document already open.

To open a Photoshop file in Illustrator, choose Open from the Illustrator File menu and select the Photoshop file. The Photoshop file opens in a new document within Illustrator, in the color mode of the Photoshop file.

To open an Illustrator file in Photoshop, choose Open from the Photoshop File menu and select the Illustrator file. The Photoshop Rasterize dialog box appears, as shown in Figure 18-5. If you've saved a file as an EPS or if you saved it in an Illustrator 9 or earlier format, this dialog box's name is `Rasterize Generic EPS Format`. If you save the file in Illustrator 10 format, this dialog box is `Rasterize Generic PDF`. Otherwise, these dialog box options are identical, no matter which name you see.

Figure 18-5:
Use the
Rasterize
dialog box
to refine
your graphic
settings.

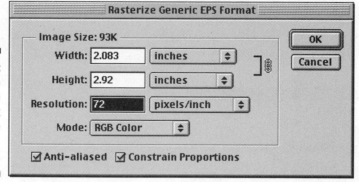

In the Rasterize dialog box, you set the width, height, resolution, and color mode of your graphic. Your exact settings should reflect, as closely as possible, the final purpose of the graphic. You should determine whether the graphic is going to be viewed on screen (Web, multimedia) or if it's going to be printed (desktop or offset). The more you alter these settings after you rasterize the graphic, the more you degrade it.

Exporting a graphic

Exporting is almost the opposite of Placing. Instead of bringing a graphic into an application, you're getting it out of an application. Exporting has two big advantages. First, you don't need a copy of the other application to create the graphic in that format. Second, Illustrator layers export as separate Photoshop layers, instead of as one flattened graphic. (See Chapter 14 for more info on Illustrator layers.) Sadly, Photoshop layers don't export to layers in Illustrator.

You can export any path that you create in Photoshop as an Illustrator file. To export paths from Photoshop, choose File⇨Export⇨Paths to Illustrator. The Export Paths dialog box opens from which you specify those paths to export. Select a path, click Save, and an Illustrator file is created that contains your path.

Exporting from Illustrator is much more powerful than exporting from Photoshop because you can choose to export all your Illustrator layers as separate Photoshop layers. This option provides great versatility in case you want to further edit your graphics in Photoshop.

To export your Illustrator graphic as a Photoshop file, choose File⇨Export. Name the file in the Name field and choose Photoshop (PSD) as your format. After you click OK, the Photoshop Options dialog box appears, as shown in Figure 18-6.

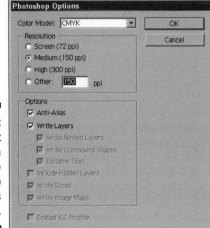

Figure 18-6:
Set
resolution
in the
Photoshop
Options
dialog box.

In the Photoshop Options dialog box, you determine color model, resolution (for more on resolution and which is best for what purpose, see Chapter 2), anti-aliasing, and whether to export the graphic as a single, flattened layer or as multiple layers. Select the Write Layers check box to export the Illustrator layers as Photoshop layers. With this option unchecked, you export the file as a single, flattened layer. With this option checked, your layers will export as separate Photoshop layers.

When in doubt, select the Write Layers option. You can easily delete or flatten the layers in Photoshop (by using the Photoshop Layers palette) if you decide you don't want them.

You also now have the option of exporting your file with slices and image maps for use on the Web. For more on Illustrator and the Web, see Chapter 17. Also, you can export your image with Compound Shapes. When you bring Compound Shapes into Photoshop, they become editable clipping masks. Conversely, your Photoshop clipping masks become editable Compound Shapes when brought into Illustrator 10. For more on Compound Shapes, see Chapter 4.

Using Adobe Illustrator with Nearly Everything Else

Illustrator works great with Photoshop. But what happens when you want to use Illustrator with products made by Adobe's competitors? To make your Illustrator files compatible with as wide a range of applications as possible, you need to go with the standards. Standard file formats are the formats that the majority of applications can use. Whenever you save something using a standard file format, you're almost guaranteed that anyone can open it, regardless of platform or application, just as long as he or she is using an industry standard application, such as QuarkXPress or Macromedia Dreamweaver.

For Web graphics, the standard formats are GIF and JPEG. As of this writing, PNG, Flash, and SVG don't have the universal acceptance needed to declare them standards. Keep an eye on them, however; times change fast. For more information on saving files in these formats, see Chapter 17.

For printing hard copy, the standard format for vector graphics is EPS; the Illustrator options for this format appear in the EPS Format Options dialog box (see Figure 18-7). Virtually all page layout, word processing, and graphics applications accept EPS files. If the application that you're using doesn't accept EPS files, you may seriously want to consider abandoning it for one that does. PageMaker, InDesign, and QuarkXPress all accept EPS files and work well with the file format.

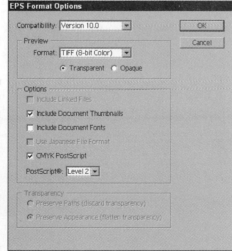

Figure 18-7:
Set compatibility, preview, and other options in the EPS Format Options dialog box.

Fortunately, saving EPS files is vastly more simple than saving for the Web. Choose File⇨Save As, name the file there, and choose Illustrator EPS for the format. Click Save, and the EPS Format Options dialog box opens. (Refer to Figure 18-7.) Typically, running with the defaults (just click OK without changing any settings) works fine. In case you want something different, bone up on the other settings in this dialog box:

✔ **Compatibility:** You can open and edit Illustrator EPS files just as you do any other Illustrator files. Suppose a friend is helping out with a graphics project and doesn't have the latest version of Illustrator. To give an EPS file to this person for editing, set the Compatibility option to match whatever earlier version your friend is using. Otherwise, leave the file set to Version 10.0.

Saving your file to be compatible with an earlier version can alter your graphic. For example, Illustrator 3 doesn't support gradients. If you used gradients, they get broken up into separate objects for every different color in the gradient. The graphic looks the same, but editing can be a problem. The fact that you can save files in the Illustrator 3 format is a testament to Illustrator's compatibility with other applications. Illustrator 3 was outdated almost ten years ago! (That's the computer equivalent of being fluent in ancient Greek.)

✔ **Preview:** Use these options to set how the Preview image displays when linked (Format) and whether the Preview image is transparent or opaque.

• **Format:** This option determines how you create the Preview image, which displays when the graphic is linked to a document in another application. Preview doesn't affect how the image is printed — only how it displays onscreen. Choose TIFF (8-bit Color) for Windows (which most Mac applications can read) or Macintosh (8-bit Color) for Macs (which most Windows applications can read). However, if your PC has problems reading the Mac file, change your preview to TIFF (8-bit color).

• **Transparent** or **Opaque:** This radio button options exists only when you choose TIFF (8-bit color) for your Preview. Choose one to determine how transparent areas in your graphic are handled. Typically, you want to set this option to Transparent, but if you're using the graphic in any Microsoft Office application, you need to select Opaque for full-compatibility.

✔ **Include Linked Files:** Select this check box to embed any linked files in your image.

✔ **Include Document Thumbnails:** In the Open dialog box of some applications, you get a thumbnail picture of the file, which lets you see the picture before you open the file. Select this check box to create one of those thumbnails.

✔ **Include Document Fonts:** Select this check box to build any fonts that you use in your document into the EPS file. Although selecting this option increases file size, it also ensures that your document displays and prints properly if the fonts don't exist on the computer used to open the file.

✔ **CMYK PostScript:** If you use any RGB colors in your document, this option enables them to print on a four-color, CMYK PostScript printer. This check box is a good one to select, just in case.

✔ **PostScript:** Choose levels here to set the PostScript level at which the file prints. PostScript is the language that printers use. You want to use the highest level that the printer is capable of. The latest printers support Level 3, but these files don't print properly on older printers. If the file doesn't print, try using a lower level. Be aware that lower levels can print more slowly and with less quality than Level 3. (But hey, that's better than not printing at all!)

If you save your file with Illustrator 10 compatibility, you can't save it with Level 1 PostScript. Change the compatibility to Illustrator 8 (or an earlier version) to change to Level 1.

Quite frankly, if you have to print at Level 1, you may want to hunt down a better printer. Level 1 printers probably cost you money every time you print to them because they're slow and don't print well.

✔ **Transparency:** This setting appears whenever you set the Compatibility option to any version prior to Illustrator 9. (Transparency was introduced in Illustrator 9. See Chapter 10 for more info.) This feature enables you to make an object semitransparent so that an object beneath it shows through as a blend of the two objects. (Think of a semitransparent red circle overlapping a blue circle, making the overlapped portion appear purple.) Because this is an Illustrator 9 feature, earlier versions don't support it. When you save an Illustrator 10 file as Illustrator 8 or earlier, use a Transparency option to determine how to translate transparent objects into something that earlier versions can understand.

Choose from two radio buttons to either discard or flatten transparency: Preserve Paths and Preserve Appearance, respectively. Preserve Paths discards transparency altogether, keeping the same shapes that you originally created but making the graphic look very different. For example, a red and blue overlapping circle would look just like that, with no purple area where the two overlap. Select Preserve Appearance to create new shapes to maintain the look of the transparency. For instance, new paths are created for the purple area where the two circles overlapped. Preserve Appearance is almost always the way to go; it keeps your artwork looking exactly the way you created it.

If you use the Transparency option when you save an Illustrator document in an older format, you may get some strange and unexpected results. Save in the latest format (Illustrator 10) if you can.

After you complete your settings, click OK. Your Illustrator file is saved as an EPS file, ready to use just about anywhere!

After you master saving your Illustrator artwork as an EPS, you can create graphics that are compatible with every major print publishing application available. Saving graphics as GIFs or JPEGs (which we cover in Chapter 17) enables you to make artwork that can be displayed in nearly every Web browser in existence. Add the ability to move files back and forth between Illustrator and Photoshop, as well as the many Export options, and you can create graphics that work anywhere.

Part V
The Part of Tens

The 5th Wave   By Rich Tennant

In this part . . .

This section is a mishmash of things so specialized that they need special attention. Find tips on how to increase your productivity and customize Illustrator just the way you want. The info you find here ranges from nuts-and-bolts kind of stuff to downright silly toys. From hidden goodies to obscure trivia to quality-enhancing production techniques, this part has something for everyone!

Chapter 19

Ten Production-Enhancing Tips

- -

In This Chapter

▶ Making holes in objects

▶ Avoiding using Photoshop filters in Illustrator, and why

▶ Getting gradients to print properly

▶ Making complex graphics simpler

▶ Hiding elements you aren't using

▶ Using the Tool Tips

▶ Changing your units of measurement on a whim

▶ Moving brushes, swatches, and styles between documents

▶ Placing documents within documents within documents

▶ Making type easier to select

- -

*I*f you can picture something, you can probably create it in Illustrator. The only trick is knowing how to create it. People who use Illustrator rely on thousands of little tricks to make their lives easier, make production faster, avoid unnecessary hassle and expense, and generally make their world a better place to live. Well, those thousands of tricks may not all fit in one book, but here are ten simple ways to jazz up your use of Illustrator.

Punching Holes

Take a close look at the two pictures in Figure 19-1. In the image on the left, the hole in the center is actually a white circle that makes the life preserver appear to have a hole in its center. In Illustrator, white is a color that is really "there" — and it blocks anything behind it. In the second picture, the hole in the center really is a hole, revealing whatever is behind it (in this case, an alarmed passenger noticing just how few life preservers his ship has).

Figure 19-1:
A life
preserver
without a
hole (left)
and with a
hole (right).
Similar but
not the
same. (Just
ask the guy
on the right.)

How is this remarkable feat accomplished? If you set the Fill color for the white circle to None, just that circle becomes transparent, revealing the gray circle behind it — so that won't work. The trick is to use Compound Paths. The Compound Paths command joins two or more paths in such a way that wherever the paths overlap, you get a hole revealing whatever is lurking behind the paths. Incidentally, this is how the holes in letters, such as O and P, are created, so that when you run type over an object, you see the object through the holes.

All you need to create a compound path is two objects — one to serve as a cutting tool and one to serve as a place to put the hole. Then follow these handy do-it-yourself steps (no safety goggles required):

1. **Place the object that you'll be using to make a hole in front of the object in which you want to cut the hole.**

2. **Select both objects with any Selection tool.**

3. **Choose Object⇨Compound Path⇨Make.**

    Where the paths overlap, you get a see-through area — you know, a hole.

To make the paths behave normally again, select the objects and choose Object⇨Compound Path⇨Release.

Perform the same feat by using the Pathfinder palette and selecting the Subtract From Shape Area command from Shape Modes. For more details, see Chapter 4.

Whoa! Don't Use That Photoshop Filter!

In the beginning, Adobe gave us Photoshop filters, which you could use to manipulate pixel information in ways you never could before. You could take a scanned photograph and make it look like a fresco painting or a reflection on rippling water. You could easily create things nobody had ever seen before, all using filters. And everybody thought Photoshop filters were so cool when they came out. Especially the folks at Adobe, who decided to make it possible to use Photoshop filters in just about every application they made (including Illustrator) in an effort to make everything else seem as cool as Photoshop. This was a bad idea for a multitude of reasons:

- ✔ Photoshop filters are designed to work in Photoshop, so they run at a fraction of their normal speed when you use them outside Photoshop.

- ✔ Photoshop filters work only on pixels, not vectors (see Chapter 2) so most of the time, the filters aren't usable in Illustrator.

- ✔ Whenever you apply a Photoshop filter to an image, Illustrator automatically embeds the image, even if you don't want to embed it.

- ✔ Most importantly, you have very little control over a Photoshop filter in Illustrator. In Photoshop, you can target the filter so it affects only a small part of the image. You can run the filter on different parts of the image with different intensities. In Illustrator, however, you can't target a small area and tell the filter to "change *that*, and only that." The tame, controllable Photoshop filter runs amok — slathering the same intensity over the entire image. You can't fade the filter back after you apply it (as you can in Photoshop). Nope. Subtlety is not an option.

Unless you're doing a radical experiment in artistic frustration, leave those Photoshop filters in Photoshop. Of course, if you've made a wonderful mountain out of a molehill in Illustrator, you can bring that image into Photoshop and tweak it there. In the long run, you spend far less time if you open your Illustrator image in Photoshop, run your filter there, save the image, and then plunk it back into Illustrator.

This rather quirky workaround (quirkaround?) should not dissuade you from applying filters to your paths by using the Effect menu. These filters have all the coolness of the Photoshop filters, but they apply to vectors instead of pixels (and offer you a whole lot more control and flexibility than the Photoshop filters). The filters in the top half of the Filter menu are also fine to use because they apply to paths, not to pixels. Just don't use the ones in the bottom of the Filter menu (everything below Artistic, as shown in Figure 19-2) on pixel-based images (unless you want a mess). For more information on using Photoshop with Illustrator, see Chapter 18.

Filter

Apply Neon Glow	⌘E
Neon Glow...	⌥⌘E

Colors	▶
Create	▶
Distort	▶
Pen and Ink	▶
Stylize	▶

Artistic	▶
Blur	▶
Brush Strokes	▶
Distort	▶
Pixelate	▶
Sharpen	▶
Sketch	▶
Stylize	▶
Texture	▶
Video	▶

Figure 19-2:
The Photoshop filters (from the Filter menu) to avoid using on placed pixels.

When White Isn't Nothing

Double negatives aside, here's a little tip that can save you *beaucoup* bucks whenever you use gradients and spot colors in artwork you're creating for print.

If you work with print publishing, you come to think of the color white as being *nothing*. In most of the familiar printing techniques, specifying the color white means *don't put down any ink* (or toner, or dye, or any of the methods for putting color on paper) for anything colored white. White ink doesn't exist (except in rare situations) — and no, correction fluid doesn't count. The white that you see in print publications is just the white of the paper.

This approach depends on an actual, tangible piece of paper to provide the white for the image. To save yourself untold woe, don't use the technique we describe here if your artwork is destined to live on the Web. It's strictly a hard-copy issue.

Suppose you're creating a two-color publication using black ink and a nice blue Pantone 273 ink. The publication may be pretty dull in only two colors, but that's all you have a budget for, so you decide to spice things up by using gradients. You create lovely gradients by blending Pantone 273 into white (assuming that white means *no ink*). Unfortunately, in terms of gradients, Illustrator thinks of a blend as a whole new CMYK (cyan, magenta, yellow, black) color (see Chapter 1) — so the blend between white and a spot color, such as Pantone 273, involves much more complicated instructions to the computer than you may have intended.

Sure, your graphics look perfect, but unbeknownst to you, your job has mutated from a two-color job to a five-color job. Usually, you discover this after your job is already at the printer, and then you have to pay hundreds of extra dollars for a mistake you didn't even know you made.

The trick is to use the same Pantone color for all steps of the gradient (see Figure 19-3). Just follow these steps:

1. **Choose Window➪Gradient.**

   The Gradient palette appears.

2. **Choose Window➪Swatch Libraries➪Pantone Coated (or another swatch library of your choice).**

   The Pantone swatch library opens.

3. **Click the color of your choice in the Pantone library and drag the color from the library onto a color stop in the Gradient palette.**

   A *color stop* is the icon that looks like a little house; it represents a color in the gradient.

   Repeat this until all color stops in the Gradient palette are the same color. (See Chapter 10 for more information on Gradients.)

   At this point, the gradient is one solid color. Not a gradient at all, really. But wait!

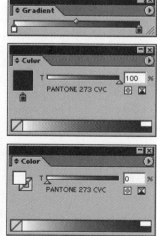

Figure 19-3:
The same color is used at two different tint percentages, specified in the Color palette.

4. **Double-click a color stop in the Gradient palette.**

   The Color palette opens, showing the Pantone color set to 100%.

5. **Set the tint of the Pantone color to 0%.**

This action gives you true, one-ink spot-color gradients that use the paper as "white" in that good old traditional way. See Chapter 10 for more info on gradients.

Expanding for Simplicity

Sometimes you try to create fancy artwork, and it just doesn't work out the way you planned; for example, it doesn't print, or after you choose File⇨Save for Web, parts of your graphics are missing or displaying improperly. This kind of failure can lead to feelings of low self-esteem and low aesthetic self-worth. But don't blame yourself. Blame your computer. It rarely provides you with any warning or indication that what you're doing may not work. Worse yet, your computer almost never tells you what to do if your efforts don't succeed.

Fortunately, when your efforts don't work in Illustrator (including problems with printing and copying between applications, or a selected object that contains an element you can't work with), the difficulties are almost always caused by the same culprits. Many of the features of Illustrator — such as gradients, patterns, custom brushes, and object blends — are very mathematically intensive. This situation can make the computer or printer choke at inopportune moments. Fortunately, the Expand command applies the Heimlich maneuver to the most complex graphics.

Expanding turns complex objects into simpler objects — making the objects easier for the computer or printer to understand — by making every color a separate, basic object. Expanding also makes the objects less editable, so make a copy of any graphic that you expand!

To expand an object, follow these steps and examine Figure 19-4:

1. **Select the object with any selection tool.**

2. **Choose Object⇨Expand.**

    The Expand dialog box opens.

3. **In the Expand dialog box, choose to expand the Fill, the Stroke, and the Object (if you selected an object blend) by selecting those check boxes.**

    Select Fill to expand the fill and simplify gradients. Select Stroke to create custom brushes, and select Fill or Stroke to create patterns — or just leave all three selected to cover all your bases.

After you expand a gradient, you need to specify the number of objects that the gradient is broken into. Choose the smallest number that doesn't produce visible banding. The default value of 255 objects (in the Objects field of the Expand dialog box) is too large for all but absolutely huge gradients! Click OK, and your graphic is reduced to its basic components. Visually, the graphic looks almost identical, except that it now has many more paths. The graphic may seem more complex because it has more paths — but it just looks more complicated because you can actually see those paths. In reality, when the object isn't expanded, all those paths have to be created anyway whenever you print the graphic or save the graphic for the Web. Expanding is a way of doing this work up front. Although visually more complex (because of all the extra paths), the graphic becomes much simpler mathematically, and you should be able to work with it.

Figure 19-4:
The original object with a gradient fill (top left) is expanded (bottom left) to 20 objects (with paths showing) and the final object (bottom right).

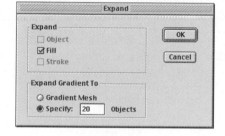

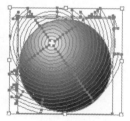

Quick! Hide!

Simply hiding things can greatly improve your productivity in Illustrator. Otherwise, you may have a hard time seeing your current creation with all the floating palettes and interface elements in the way.

You can hide all open palettes and the Toolbox by pressing the Tab key (unless the Type tool is selected and a blinking I-beam cursor is on your page — then you just insert a Tab into your text). Press the Tab key again to bring everything back.

If you're creating exclusively for the Web, hide the Artboard and Page Tiling. These features show you the size of the page you're printing to and the printable area on that page. This information is useless if you're never going to print! Choose View⇨Hide Artboard and View⇨Hide Page Tiling to make them go away.

Have you ever made an object that contains so many points that after you select it you can't tell what the object *is* anymore for all the highlighted points and lines? You can hide these, too, while keeping the object selected. Choose View⇨Hide Edges to make the highlights disappear.

You can hide everything you have open on your computer (including your desktop) except for the current Illustrator document by clicking the Full Screen Mode with Menu Bar button in the Toolbox, as shown in Figure 19-5. To hide everything *including* the Menu bar, click the Full Screen Mode button. (You can toggle through these modes by pressing the F key on your keyboard; this works for both PCs and Macs.) To get a completely unobscured view of your artwork, switch to Full Screen Mode and press the Tab key to hide your palettes. Real power-users work this way, using keyboard shortcuts to access all their tools and menu items.

Figure 19-5:
The View Mode buttons enable you to view your graphic in a variety of ways.

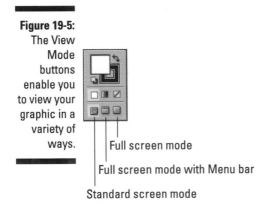

Full screen mode

Full screen mode with Menu bar

Standard screen mode

Taking a Tip from Illustrator

Illustrator has a helpful feature: *Tool Tips.* If you hover your cursor over a tool for a moment, a little yellow box of text pops up telling you what the tool is. If the tool has a keyboard shortcut, that shortcut appears in parentheses after the name.

Tool Tips, despite their name, don't work with tools alone. (And they don't give you tips — just the names of things. Go figure.) They work just about anywhere in Illustrator that you can position a cursor. Tool Tips give you information about whatever the cursor is over. Hover over a color swatch, and the Tool Tip tells you the name of that color. Hover over a brush, and it tells you the name of the brush. Not sure what a cryptic icon in the Pathfinder palette means? Just let the Tool Tip tell you.

Tool Tips are invaluable whenever you're using the program because there are just too many things to remember. With Tool Tips, you don't have to!

To turn Tool Tips off or on, choose Edit⇨Preferences⇨General and select (check) or clear (uncheck) the Show Tool Tips check box.

Changing Your Units Whenever You Want

Do you feel that no matter what you do, your units of measure seem to be wrong? Are they always set to points, for example, when you really want inches? (Sometimes centimeters are easier to work with.) Fortunately, Illustrator lets you change your mind on-the-fly.

To see your measurement options, choose View⇨Show Rulers and then right-click in Windows (Ctrl+click on the Mac) any location on the rulers at the top and side of your screen. You get a pop-up menu that shows all the units of measurement that Illustrator understands. Choose the unit you desire, and from that moment on, Illustrator uses that unit of measurement.

You can reposition rulers by right-clicking in Windows (clicking on the Mac) where the rulers meet at the upper-left corner. To reset them, double-click that corner.

However, you don't have to change your unit of measurement to use a different one. In any field where you specify an amount (such as the Height and Width options in the Rectangle dialog box), just type in the amount you want, followed by the abbreviation of the unit of measurement that you want to use. If you don't know the abbreviation, just use the whole name. Illustrator makes the conversions for you.

Reusing Your Brushes, Swatches, and Libraries

Has this ever happened to you? You go through the trouble to create custom brushes, beautiful colors, and outstanding appearances, save them in the Styles palette, and later discover that they're all specific to the document that you created them in. Rats! To prevent that from happening to you again, you can open the swatches, brushes, and styles that you created in one document in any other document.

For example, to get the brushes from another document, choose Window➪Brush Libraries➪Other Library. An Open dialog box appears. Choose the document with the brushes that you want to add to the current document, as if you were going to open it. Click Open. Instead of opening that document, Illustrator opens the custom brushes in their own palette, ready for you to use. Follow the same steps, choosing Window➪Swatch Libraries➪ Other Library or Window➪Style Libraries➪Other Library to add your swatches or styles.

Avoiding Russian Dolls

Have you ever seen those cute Russian dolls? You know, the hollow doll that you open to find another smaller doll inside? And then you open that one to find an even smaller doll inside? And then you open *that* doll. . . .

Illustrator enables you to create the digital equivalent of those Russian dolls. You place a Photoshop image into Illustrator, rotate the image, add text over the image, and save the whole thing as an Illustrator file. To add more, create a new document in Illustrator, placing the previously created Illustrator graphic (which also contains within it a Photoshop file) into the new document by using the File➪Place command. You save this Photoshop file within an Illustrator file within another Illustrator file as an EPS file and place it within a page-layout document. You have a Photoshop fill now embedded four layers deep within the page-layout document. (Dizzy yet?)

Although nothing prevents you from creating the digital equivalent of a Russian doll, the computer prevents you from ever using such files. Each time that you place one file into another, you add a level of complexity to the file. Every time that you rotate or scale that placed file, you keep adding levels of complexity until you finally create a file that can never print or go on the Web successfully.

Subscribe to the KISS method: Keep It Simple, Sillygoose! Avoid going more than three places from the original file (such as a Photoshop file placed inside an Illustrator file, placed inside an InDesign document, with scaling happening in only one of those places). Two places are even better if you can limit yourself. If you need to bring Illustrator data from one Illustrator document to another, open both documents and copy and paste the info rather than place it.

Selecting Type When You Want

If you work with type and objects, you may discover how annoying it is to select an object that's lurking behind type. Even when you click where there's obviously no type, you still select the type instead of the object behind it. This happens because one of Illustrator's most annoying features is turned on. Type Area Select automatically selects type when you click anywhere in its area — not just when you click directly on the type or its path.

Turn off this (ahem) feature by choosing Edit⇨Preferences⇨Type & Auto Tracing. In the Type & Auto Tracing Preferences dialog box, remove the check mark from the Type Area Select check box. Click OK. Breathe easier. Henceforth, Type shall be selected whenever you click directly on a letter or on its path, and at no other time, by royal proclamation of the user.

Chapter 20

Ten (Or So) Ways to Customize Illustrator

In This Chapter

▶ Telling palettes where to go

▶ Setting up custom keyboard shortcuts

▶ Getting easier access to tools

▶ Changing the startup documents

▶ Tweaking the default settings

▶ Editing preferences

▶ Creating Actions

Keyboard commands are great shortcuts — you gotta love 'em, finger cramps and all — but what if you could make them easier to use? Or maybe you have some styles that you use all the time and you want them to be (gasp) available all the time. And how about that quirky default page size that each new document shows up wearing? Well, if you itch to tinker, adjust, and fine-tune (but you've misplaced your ball-peen hammer), you've come to the right place. This chapter shows you how to adjust, redefine, and yes, customize the way Illustrator works for you.

Before you go on a feature-tweaking rampage, consider this: You're changing the way Illustrator works. So a word to the wise: Read first. Then, if you like what you see, make a change and try it out for awhile before you change anything else. Return to default settings if you make a mistake.

Positioning Palettes

Illustrator saves all palette positions just as they are when you quit Illustrator. The next time that you use Illustrator, the palettes appear right where you left them. This structure is handy most of the time, but your palettes can get a bit disorganized if you move them all over the place while chasing a creative inspiration. If you want to get them back to Square One with no fuss, read on.

Because Illustrator saves the palette positions in the Preference file, you can save a set or sets of palette positions for later use by saving a copy of the Preference file. Whenever you need to reset the palettes to their convenient locations, replace the active Preference file with the saved version.

Keep in mind that this shuffling of files may zap other Preference settings, such as your units of measurement or your Pencil Tool preferences (see Chapter 8) that you may have changed.

On the Mac, the Preferences file is inside the System folder, tucked inside a folder named (surprise) `Preferences` that is tucked inside the `Adobe Illustrator 10` folder. Hey, sometimes obvious is nice. In Windows 2000, this Preferences file is called `AI Prefs` and is located in the `Documents and Settings/(your name)/Application Data/Adobe/Adobe Illustrator 10` folder.

Changing the Items on the Menu

You can customize all the Illustrator menu commands by using the Keyboard Shortcuts dialog box (shown in Figure 20-1). Go to this dialog box by choosing Edit⇨Keyboard Shortcuts.

You can redefine even the most common commands, such as Open and New, with different keyboard shortcuts. To add a new keyboard shortcut, follow these steps:

1. **Choose Edit⇨Keyboard Shortcuts.**

   The Keyboard Shortcuts dialog box opens.

2. **Choose Menu Commands from the pop-up menu at the top left of the dialog box (the default name is Tools).**

   A list of all Illustrator menus appears. Click the arrow beside the menu name to open the complete list of items under that menu. If the item already has a keyboard shortcut, you find it listed to the right of the menu item, in the Shortcut column.

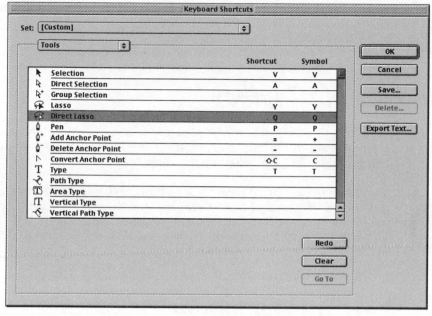

Figure 20-1:
Use the
Keyboard
Shortcuts
dialog box
to customize
menu
commands.

3. **Change the keyboard shortcuts by highlighting the current keyboard shortcut, typing a new shortcut, and pressing Enter.**

If the item has no keyboard shortcut assigned to it, you can give it one. To highlight the empty space, click in the Shortcut column (to the right of the menu item) and type in your shortcut there.

You can also print out a big sheet of all the keyboard shortcuts, even if you haven't changed any of them. To print out all the keyboard shortcuts, follow these steps:

1. **Choose Edit➪Keyboard Shortcuts.**

   The Keyboard Shortcuts dialog box opens.

2. **Click the Export Text button in the lower right of the Keyboard Shortcuts dialog box.**

   A Save dialog box opens.

3. **Name the text file that you want to contain your keyboard shortcuts, specify a location for it on your hard drive, and then click OK to save the text file.**

4. **Open any word processing program on your computer, choose File➪Open, open the text file you just created, and then print it as you would any word processing document.**

You can always return to the original keyboard commands by choosing Illustrator Factory Defaults from the Set pop-up menu in the upper-left corner of the Keyboard Shortcuts dialog box.

The Flexible Toolbox

Give each tool its own keyboard shortcut to access any tool by pressing a key on the keyboard. For example, pressing the V key brings up the Selection tool and pressing the Z key brings up the Zoom tool.

To change the keyboard shortcut for a tool (or to add shortcuts for tools that don't have any), choose Edit⇨Keyboard Shortcuts. In the Keyboard Shortcuts dialog box, find the tool you want to change (or add) and then highlight the current command. Type a new shortcut, and then click OK to make the new shortcut available.

The Start-up Document

You may notice that whenever you open a new document in Illustrator, the new document always appears the same way. For example, the Artboard and Page Tiling are always visible, the Swatches palette always has the same contents, and so on. The appearance of a new document doesn't happen by random chance but is determined by the start-up document file. This document controls the way that each new document is created, and you can change it to make each new document open the way that you want it to. Here are some items that you can change in this document:

- **Number of layers:** If you only need three, this option makes it so.
- **Zoom percentage:** If you find the best balance of detail and readability at a 63% zoom, that zoom is yours.
- **Artboard** and **Page Tiling:** You can show or hide these to suit your needs.
- **Window size:** This option is especially handy if you're working on several images at once.
- **Styles:** Add the styles you want and delete the ones you don't — the result is exactly what you'll have for your new documents.
- **Swatches:** You can make the Swatches palette open with exactly the swatches you want — no more, no less.
- **Brushes:** New documents open with the brushes you have in the Brushes palette at the time you save the start-up document. (How about leopard spots?)

To change the start-up document, follow these steps:

1. **Open the start-up document in Illustrator.**

   Illustrator has two of these: Adobe Illustrator Startup_CMYK and Adobe Illustrator Startup_RGB. You can find them inside your `Plug-Ins` folder (located in your Illustrator `Application` folder).

   CMYK (cyan, magenta, yellow, black) documents and RGB (red, green, blue) documents (see Chapter 1) have separate start-up documents. This arrangement enables you to tailor each start-up document to the specific work environment. For instance, RGB files are often used for Web graphics and CMYK is used for print graphics. In the RGB start-up file, you can hide the Artboard and Page Tiling (which are print-specific features); you can also turn on Pixel Preview. In the CMYK file, you can add color swatches that represent your company's corporate colors to the Swatches palette.

2. **Make changes to any of the items on the handy list that precedes these steps.**

   For example, if you want new documents to have three layers instead of one, put three layers in the Layers palette. The layers don't need any artwork in them; just the act of adding layers in the Layers palette is enough. If you want Pixel Preview turned on automatically, choose it from the View menu. Add or delete swatches from the Swatches palette, and so forth.

3. **Save the document and close it.**

Henceforth, each new document that you create reflects the items that you change in the start-up document.

The start-up document does *not* change existing documents.

Changing the Default Settings

Don't stop with the start-up document — you can change the way the entire Illustrator application works. Assuming that you have a plan (handy to have at a time like this), choose Edit➪Preferences➪General. Behold: The General Preferences dialog box appears, as shown in Figure 20-2.

The General Preferences dialog box is just the first of several preferences dialog boxes containing a multitude of options for you to change. Each change affects the way that the application works, and Illustrator saves these changes when you quit the program, regardless of the documents that you're working in.

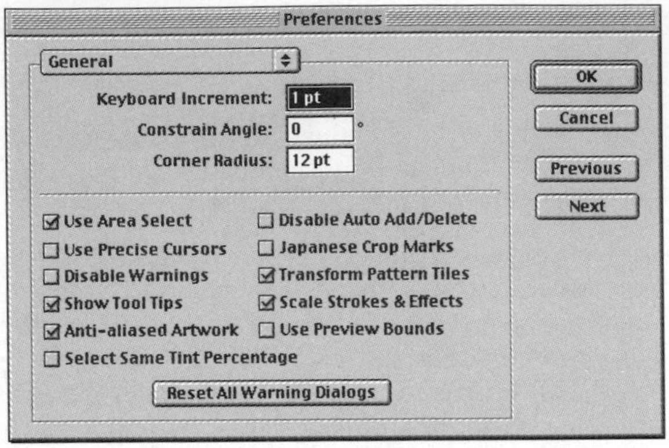

Preferences

General

Keyboard Increment: 1 pt
Constrain Angle: 0 °
Corner Radius: 12 pt

OK
Cancel
Previous
Next

☑ Use Area Select   ☐ Disable Auto Add/Delete
☐ Use Precise Cursors ☐ Japanese Crop Marks
☐ Disable Warnings   ☑ Transform Pattern Tiles
☑ Show Tool Tips   ☑ Scale Strokes & Effects
☑ Anti-aliased Artwork ☐ Use Preview Bounds
☐ Select Same Tint Percentage

Reset All Warning Dialogs

Figure 20-2:
The General
Preferences
dialog box.

Don't start changing preference settings all helter-skelter when you first stumble across this dialog box. Doing so may cause unexpected behaviors in the application. Illustrator may start printing your letterhead in hieroglyphics. A better idea is to look at the list of items and only change one at a time, testing each item after you change it, even writing down what you did so you can remember the changes. If the results of a change aren't up to snuff, then be sure to change the preference back to its original setting.

Changing Hidden Commands You Never Knew About

In addition to those nice, respectable, visible menu commands and tool shortcuts, all sorts of nifty shortcuts just hang around in Illustrator without a single menu item or tool associated with them. These shortcuts are handy commands, such as Increase Type Size: Ctrl+Shift (Windows) ⌘+Shift (Mac). Even better, every one of these commands can be customized. Simply scroll through the Keyboard Shortcuts dialog box to find every command that exists in Illustrator. If you find one that looks as though it may be useful to you, give it a new shortcut.

Using a Master Document

Although the start-up document enables you to customize certain items in your new documents, you're limited to one start-up document (well, two actually: one for RGB and one for CMYK). If you're really clever (and of course you are), you can simply use multiple documents as your start-up documents, without having to swap them in and out of the Plug-Ins folder.

Try keeping a folder full of seemingly empty documents that contain special sets of styles, swatches, brushes, and layers. When you open one that has the stuff you want, choose Save As. In effect, you get a custom document, without the process of loading or creating any of the styles, swatches, brushes, or layers that you're using.

Action Jackson

Have you ever found yourself doing things again and again (such as typing the word *redundant* dozens of times)? Have you ever wished that your computer could do some of this tedious work for you? Well, that's where Actions come in. Actions make Illustrator do the grunt work while you get to do all the fun stuff.

Illustrator comes with hundreds of Actions, although only a dozen are installed with the software. You can find the rest on your Illustrator application CD-ROM. Better yet — you can make your own Actions! *Actions* can be virtually any series of Illustrator activities, such as scaling, rotating, changing colors, or bringing selections to the front. You can even use Actions to select objects if they have specific names.

One of the handiest uses for Actions is creating compound keyboard shortcuts. For example, you can perform a set of procedures, such as Create New Layer, Place, and Scale at the same time, without even wrenching your back. Instead of performing all three keyboard commands individually, you can easily set up an Action to do all three simultaneously. Result: One keyboard command does three tasks! You just smile and watch. Choose Window⇨Actions, and meet the friendly Actions palette in Figure 20-3.

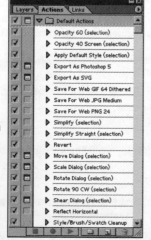

Figure 20-3:
The Actions Palette puts power at your virtual fingertips.

To use any Action, click it in the Actions palette and then click the Play Current Selection button (the right-pointing arrow) at the bottom of the palette.

Creating your own Action feels something like taping your voice or image and then playing it back. When you record an Action, Illustrator watches what you do and records every step as closely as possible. (This procedure is a lot like creating a macro in Word.)

Computers have no imagination; you have to tell them exactly what to do. Therefore, your recorded Actions must use precise values. Anything that requires a level of human interaction does not get recorded. In effect, Illustrator says, "That's not my department. So there." For example, creating a one-inch rectangle is a precise action. Drawing a squiggly line is not. You can't always know in advance whether Illustrator can record all the actions you perform — but you know for certain after you play it back. Hey, it's not a program; it's an adventure.

To create your own Action, just follow these steps:

1. **Open a new document in Illustrator and choose Window⇨Actions.**

   The Actions palette opens.

2. **Click the Create New Action button.**

   The New Action dialog box opens.

3. **Name the Action and click Record.**

   For example, type the name **Red Rectangle** for the Action. After you click Record, the Action records everything you do, tapping your phone, and transmitting that information back to Adobe where they're keeping a file on you. Just kidding. Honest.

4. **Perform a series of actions with the keyboard or the mouse.**

   For the example, select the Rectangle tool and drag out a rectangle in the document. Then choose a red swatch from the Swatches palette for the Fill color.

5. **Click the Stop Playing/Recording button.**

   The Action shows up on the Actions palette, ready for, um, *action*. Great gung-ho attitude, eh? But hold on a minute. . . .

6. **Prepare to test your Action.**

   In this case, delete your original rectangle. This finishing touch prevents the Action from creating another rectangle of the exact same size, shape, color, and position.

7. **Test your Action by clicking the name of the Action and then clicking the Play Current Selection button.**

   If the Action does exactly what you planned, it's ready for duty.

The preceding example is a simple Action. With a bit of practice, you can create infinitely more complex Actions. This wonder results from a simple fact: An Action records (nearly) everything you do from the time you start recording to the time you click Stop. The Action can be a simple menu command or something as complex as the creation of some amazing artwork, as if by magic.

Sticky Settings

Some of the things that you do in Illustrator remain "sticky" until you quit the application. For example, if you create a rectangle that's 1 x 2 inches, the next time that you click with the Rectangle tool, the values are automatically set to 1 x 2 inches. All the dialog boxes in Illustrator remember what you did last during your current Illustrator session. (But don't worry; they won't tell a soul.)

Between sessions, the entries in the Preferences dialog box and the positions of the palettes are all that remain constant. Oh, well. At least *something* does.

Index

• A •

absolute measurements, Transform palette, 213
Acrobat Reader, PDF files, 60
Actions, 347–349
adaptive color, GIF files, 287
Add Anchor Point tool, 115–116
adding/subtracting points, 115–116
Adobe Acrobat Reader, PDF files, 60
Adobe GoLive, 10
Adobe InDesign, 10
Adobe PageMaker, 10
aliasing, printing, 268
Align palette, 248
alignment, 244–245, 248. *See also* grid
  constraining via shift, 245
  grid, 245–246
  Paragraph palette, 264–266
  Polar Grid tool, 245–246
  rulers, 247
  Smart Guides, 246–247
  Snap to Point, 244
anchor points, 41–42
  combination-corner anchor points, 121–122, 131
  converting, 114–115
  corner points, 114–115
  curve transitions, 129
  curved-corner anchor points, 120–121, 130–131
  cusp points, 120–121
  direction points, 118
  Liquify tools, 226
  m-curve anchor points, 120–121
  one-third rule, 128
  paths, 118
  Pen tool and, 118
  smooth anchor points, 118–119
  smooth points, 114–115
  straight-corner, 119–120

angles
  Calligraphic brushes, 167
  constraining, 128
  Pen tool, 124
  Reflect dialog box, 211
anti-aliasing
  printing, 268
  rasterization and, 185
Appearance palette, 188
  effects and, 183–184
  fill effects, 194
  fills, 189, 190–192
  global effects, 189
  groups, 192–194
  layers, 192–194
  positioning items, 190
  reading, 188–190
  removing appearances, 195–196
  stroke effects, 190, 194
  strokes, 189, 190–192
  styles, 188–196
  target, 189, 193
  transparency, 189
Arc tool, 147–148
Arrange command, 236–237
arrow keys, nudging and, 48, 113
Art Brush Options dialog box, 155, 156
Art brushes, 150, 155–157
  flipping, 157
  naming, 157
Artboard, 21–23
artistic elements, placing graphics as, 311
Artistic Sample brush palette, 151
artwork, Pattern brushes, 162
  positioning, 163–166

• B •

Back position, stacking and, 236
background, rasterization and, 185
banding, color, 281

baseline, type spacing, 261–262
baseline shift, type, 264
Bevel Join, strokes, 179
Bézier curves, 10, 40, 147
black and white printing, 15
Blend modes, 175–176
Blend Options dialog box, 218–219
Blend tool, 217–219
blends, 52–53, 217–219
Bloat tool, liquification, 224
Blur setting, JPEG files, 291
BMP file format, 316
bounding box, scaling and, 208
Bring Forward command, 237
Bring to Front command, 50–51, 237
Brush options, Liquify tools, 225–226
brush strokes, Object submenu, 112
brushes, 149–151
   art abilities and, 151
   Art brushes, 150, 155–157
   Artistic Sample palette, 151
   Calligraphic brushes, 150, 167–168
   Chalk Art brushes, 152
   moving to other documents, 338
   new, 153–155
   Pattern brushes, 150, 159–166
   Scatter brushes, 150, 158–159
   size, Liquify tools, 226
Brushes palette, 150–151
Butt Cap, strokes, 178

• C •

Calligraphic brushes, 150, 167–168
caps, strokes, 176, 177, 178
   dashes and, 180
Cascading Style Sheets. See CSS
centimeters, 13
Chalk Art brush, 152
Character palette, 17, 252, 254–255
   Font Style box, 256–257
   point size, 261
circles
   drawing, 67–68
   Ellipse tool, 132
   Pen tool, 132–133
clipping masks, 54, 185–186
   Object submenu, 112
   rasterization and, 185

closed paths, 125
closing
   documents, 30
   palettes, 17
CMYK color, 13–14, 92–94
   embedded files, 312
   printing, 14
   when to use, 15
color
   banding, 281
   Blend modes, 175–176
   CMYK, 13–14, 92–94
   complementary, 94
   display, printing, 268
   fills and, 82
   generation by screen, 14
   gradient fill, 99–100
   layer highlighting, 243
   Line Segment tool, 146–147
   math and, 175–176
   new, Color palette, 91–92
   None, 87
   out-of-gamut warnings, 91
   paths, 83–84
   printing, 14
   Process color, 87
   process printing, 93–94, 274
   Registration, 87
   RGB, 13–14, 92–94
   saving new, 92
   separations, printing, 271, 273–276
   spot color, 274
   strokes and, 82–84
   Swatches palette, 86–88
   total number, GIF files, 288
   Web publishing, 278–279
   Web Snap, 289
   white, 332–334
color mode, 92–94
color models, 92–94
   rasterization and, 184
   Rasterization dialog box, 185
Color palette, 17, 90–92
   Swatches palette, 86
color sliders, Color palette, 91
color table, Save for Web dialog box, 285

colorization
   Art brushes, 157
   Pattern brushes, 163
combination-corner anchor
      points, 121–123
   Pen tool, 131
commands
   keyboard, 20, 341
   menus, customizing, 342–344
   unavailable, 20
compatibility
   Illustrator and other programs, 323–326
   Web publishing graphics, 284
complementary color, 94
composite proofs, 271
compound paths, 54–56
compound shapes, 71–72, 73–75
Concentric Divides, Polar Grid tool, 245
constraining
   angles, 128
   mirror images, 211
context menus
   Ctrl+click, 21
   right-clicking, 21
context-sensitivity, Pattern brushes, 162
control handles, 118. *See also* direction
      points
   lines, constraining, 128
Convert Anchor Point tool, 115
converting anchor points, 114–15
copies, number to print, 272
copying
   layers, 241
   Photoshop to Illustrator, 317–319
   transformations and, 213, 214
corner points, 114–115
corners, joins, 179
Create Gradient Mesh dialog box, 172
Create Outlines command, 54
crescent moon shape, 77–78
Crop command, Pathfinder, 76
crossed paths, filling, 85–86
Crystallize tool, liquification, 224
CSS (Cascading Style Sheets)
   layer-based slices, 307–308
   SVG files, 297
Ctrl+click in context menus, 21

cursor, Text tool, 254
curve transitions, 129
curved lines
   direction points, 127
   dragging, 124, 126–128
   overcompensation, 129
   Pen tool, 125–131
curved-corner anchor points, 120–121
   Pen tool, 130–131
curves
   Arc tool, 147–148
   Bézier, 147
   smooth, Pen tool, 145
cusp points, 120–121

● *D* ●

dashes, strokes, 177, 179–181
defaults
   customizing, 345–346
   printing, 268
Delete Anchor Point tool, 115–116
descenders, type, 260
deselecting, 105, 111
diameter, calligraphic brushes, 168
digital photographs, pixel-based
      images, 33–36
dimming images, layers, 243
Direct Lasso tool, 104
Direct Select Lasso tool, 46
   freeform selection, 108–109
Direct Selection tool, 43, 46, 47, 104,
      105–106, 128
   mesh points, 171
   points, 113
   transformations, 205
direction, Art brushes, 157
direction handles, Object submenu, 112
direction line, points and, 113
direction points, 41–42, 113–114, 118
   curved lines, 127
   handles, 42
   lengths, one-third rule and, 129
direction-changing points, 114–115
Distort menu, 49–50
distorting paths, 48–50
Distortion Filters, 49–50

distortions. *See also* live distortions
  Envelope, 228–231
  Free Distort filter, 223
  Pucker & Bloat filter, 221–222
  Roughen filter, 222
  Scribble & Tweak filter, 222
  Twist filter, 223
  warps, 232–233
  Zig Zag, 223
dithering, 94
  color, Web publishing, 278–279, 281
  GIF files, 287–288
Divide command, Pathfinder, 75–76
docking palettes, 17–18
document area, 21–23
  Artboard, 21–22
  Scratch area, 21–22
documents
  closing, 30
  naming, 12
  opening, 23
  saving, 28–29
  scrolling, 25–26
  Untitled, 12
download time
  interlacing, 288
  Save for Web dialog box, 285
dragging
  curved lines, 124, 126–128
  marquees and, 104–105
  one-third rule, 128, 129–130
  Photoshop to Illustrator, 317–319
  straight lines, 124
drawing, 44. *See also* shape creation
drawing programs, 10
  painting programs comparison, 149
Dreamweaver, 10
duration, gradients, 98

• E •

editing. *See also* image editing
  blends, 218–219
  paths, Pencil tool and, 143
  styles, 197-199
  symbols, 301–302
  warps, 232

effects
  editing, 195
  fills, 194
  graphic styles, 200
  live effects, objects, 181–186
  removing/changing, 183–184
  RGB color, 15
  strokes, 194
  warps, 232–233
Effects menu, 181
  commands on other menus, 182
  grayed-out options, 183
  Roughen command, 181
Ellipse tool, 66, 67–68
  circles, 132
ellipses, drawing, 67–68
ellipsis (. . .) in menus, 20
embedding files, 310–312
EMF (Enhanced MetaFile) format, 317
encoding, SVG files, 297
endpoints, 125
Envelope, 10
Envelope distortions, 228–231
EPS (Encapsulated PostScript) files, 22, 316
Eraser tool, 144
  Pencil tool and, 138
Exit command, 30
Expand Compound Shape command, 73
Expand dialog box, 334–335
Export command, 61
Export dialog box, 292
exporting
  as Flash graphics, 59
  Illustrator to Photoshop, 321–322
  as PDF format, 315–317
  Photoshop to Illustrator, 321–322
  as SVG vector graphics, 59
extensions, filenames, 20–21

• F •

fading, transparency and, 52
fidelity
  Pencil tool, 139–140
  Smooth tool, 144
file formats, Web publishing, 281–283
  compatibility, 284
  JPEG, 282

Macromedia Flash files, 283
PNG, 282
Save for Web dialog box, 285
selecting, 283–284
SVG, 283
SWF files, 283
file size
  embedded files, 310
  Save for Web dialog box, 285
filename extensions, 20
files, multiple, 192
Fill, 109–110
Fill box, 82–83
  Color palette, 90
fills, 81–83, 169
  Appearance palette, 189, 190–192
  color and, 82
  effects, 189, 194
  gradients and, 82, 96–97
  graphic styles, 200
  hiding, 82
  holes, 329–330
  imaginary paths, 85–86
  Line Segment tool, 146–147
  meshes, 171
  Paintbrush tool, 153
  paths, 82, 85–86
  patterns and, 82, 94
  Pencil tool, 138
  textures, 94
filter-based distortions, 49–50
filters
  Distortion, 49–50
  Free Distort, 223
  Photoshop filters, 331–332
  Pucker & Bloat, 221–222
  Roughen, 222
  Scribble & Tweak, 222
  Twist, 223
  Zig Zag, 223
fit, Pattern brushes, 163
Fit in Window, Zoom tool, 26
Fixed method
  Calligraphic brushes, 168
  Scatter brushes, 158
Flare Options palette, 58
Flare tool, 56–58, 66

flares, 56–58
Flash format, 284, 317
  exporting as, 59
flipping
  Art brushes, 157
  mirror images, Reflect command, 210–211
  paths, 33
  Pattern brushes, 163
font families, type, 256–258
fonts, type, 256–259
  SVG files, 296
Free Distort filter, 223
freeform selections, 108–109
front end, 10
Front position, stacking and, 236

• **G** •

GIF (Graphics Interchange Format) files, 281–282, 284, 316
  color, total number of, 288
  Color Reduction Algorithm, 287
  dithering, 287–288
  interlacing, 288
  JPEG file comparison, 282
  lossy compression, 288
  saving as, 286–289
  transparency, 287–288
  Web Snap (color), 289
global effects, Appearance palette, 189
glyphs, 297
GoLive, 10
gradient fill, 96–101
Gradient Mesh tool, 171
Gradient Meshes, 39, 169–173
Gradient palette, 17, 98–99
gradient sliders, 99
Gradient tool, 98
gradients
  duration, 98
  fills and, 82
  linear, 100–101
  radial, 100–101
  strokes and, 82
  Swatches palette, 87
graphic styles, 200–201

graphics. *See also* images
  as artistic elements, 311
  path-based, 32
  pixel graphics, Web publishing, 284–291
  placing, 310–311
  Save for Web command, 284–285
  saving as GIF file, 286–289
  saving as JPEG files, 289–291
  saving as PNG files, 291
  slices, 304–308
  as templates, 311
  vector, 32, 41
grayed-out options, Effects menu, 183
grayscale color, 93
Grayscale color model, 185
grayscale printing, 15
grid, 245–247. *See also* alignment
Group Selection tool, 46, 47, 104, 106–108
grouping objects, 51
groups, 244
  appearance, 192–194
  grouping, 244
  layers, 244
  options, 242–243
  relationships, 244
  selecting, 104
  subgroups, 106
  ungrouping, 244
  viewing in layers, 241–242
guides, 247–248
Guides and Grid Preferences
    dialog box, 245

• *H* •

Hand tool, 26–27
handles, 118. *See also* direction points
  direction handles, Object submenu, 112
  Liquify tools, 226
  moving, 43, 114
  paths, 42
heart shape, 133–134
hidden commands, customizing, 346
hidden tools, 16
hiding/showing, 335–336
  Artboard, 22
  Color palette, 94
  Toolbox, 17

high smoothness, 142
Highlight option, Gradient Meshes, 173
highlighting, Type tool and, 254
history of Illustrator, 9–10
holes, paths, 54, 329–330
horizontal measurements
    Reflect dialog box, 211
    scaling, 209
HSB color, 93
HTML (HyperText Markup Language),
    SVG files, 283

• *I* •

Illustrator, history of, 9–10
image editing, 10–11
images. *See also* graphics
  pixel-based, 31, 33–36
imaginary paths, fills, 85–86
importing files. *See* embedding files;
    linking files
inches, 13
indent setting, 265–266
InDesign, 10
inkjet printers, RGB color and, 15
insertion point, Type tool, 253
instances, symbols, 299
Intensity option, Liquify tools, 226
interlacing, downloading and, 288
interpolation, 34
Intersect Shape Areas, Shape Modes, 73
Inverse command, 111

• *J* •

jagged edges, path-based graphics, 37
joins, strokes, 176, 177, 179
JPEG (Joint Photographic Experts Group)
    files, 284, 285, 316
  Progressive setting, 290
  Quality settings, 289–290
  saving as, 289–291

• *K* •

Keep Selected Paths, Pencil tool, 142
kerning, type spacing, 262
keyboard arrow keys, nudging and, 48

keyboard commands
  menus, 20, 341
  palette position, 342
Keyboard Shortcuts dialog box, 342–344

• L •

Lasso tool, 46, 47, 104
  freeform selection, 108
Layer Options dialog box, 242–243
layer-based slices, CSS, 307–308
layers, 51, 235–236
  appearance, 192–194
  copying, 241
  creating, 239–240
  dimming images, 243
  grouped objects, 244
  groups, viewing, 241–242
  highlight color, 243
  locking/unlocking, 51, 241, 243
  moving in stacking order, 237
  multiple, 239–240
  naming, 242
  objects, viewing, 241–242
  options, 242–243
  Photoshop, 318
  previewing, 243
  printing, 243
  Save for Web dialog box, 285
  selecting all, 111
  stacking order, 236–237, 240
  templates, 243
  viewing/hiding, 241, 243
Layers palette, 51, 238
  active layer, 50
  thumbnails, 238–239
leading, type spacing, 261–262
lens flare, 57–58
libraries
  moving to other documents, 338
  Pantone, 89
  swatch libraries, 86, 89–90
line drawing, paths and, 33
Line Segment tool, 146–147
line segments, 118
  controlling direction, 127
  direction points, 118

one-third rule, 129
open paths, 125
linear gradients, 100–101
lines
  constraining, 128
  Line Segment tool, 146–147
lining up. *See* alignment
link management, 313–315
linking files, 310–312
links, styles, 198
Links palette, 313–315
Liquify tools, 10, 224–225
  Bloat options, 224, 226
  Brush options, 225–226
  brush size, 226
  Crystallize options, 224, 226
  outlines and, 228
  pressure-sensitive tables, 224, 226
  Pucker options, 224, 226
  Scallop options, 224, 226
  Twirl options, 224, 226
  Twirl Rate options, 226
  Warp options, 224, 226
  Wrinkle options, 224, 226
live distortions, 223–225
live effects, objects, 181–186
  removing, 196
locking layers, 51, 241, 243
lossless compression, Flash files, 294
lossy compression, GIF files, 288
low smoothness, 142

• M •

Macintosh/Windows, moving
    between, 20–21
Macromedia Dreamweaver, 10
  Flash files, 291–294
Macromedia Flash files (SWF), 283
Macromedia Flash (SWF) Format Options
    dialog box, 293–294
Magic Wand palette, 46, 109–110
Magic Wand tool, 46, 47, 104, 109–110
marquees, selection and, 47, 105
masks, 54
  clipping masks, 185–186
master documents, 346–347
math, color and, 175–176

Matte setting
  GIF files, 288
  JPEG files, 291
m-curve anchor points, 120–121
measurement units, 337
  moving objects and, 207
  Transform palette, 213–214
menus, 19–20
  context, 21
  customizing commands, 342–344
  ellipsis (...), 20
  keyboard commands, 20
  palettes, 18–19
  submenus, 20
  unavailable commands, 20
mesh points, 171
meshes, 169–173
  Envelope distortion, 229
  fills, 171
mirror images, Reflect command, 210–211
Miter Join, strokes, 179
monitors, resolution, 31
morphing, 52–53
mouse, Pencil tool drawing and, 140
mouse pointer, tool names and, 17
Move dialog box, 206–207
moving
  handles, 43, 114
  objects, 206–207
  objects, behind others, 50–51
  points, 113
  selected objects, 48
  within stacking order, 237
multiple selections, 108
Multiply option, Blend modes, 175

naming
  Art brushes, 157
  documents, 12
  files, extension, 20
  layers, 242
  template layers, 243
Navigator palette, 27
New Brush dialog box, 155, 164
New Document dialog box, 11–15

Next Object Above command, 111
Next Object Below command, 111
None, Swatches palette, 87
Non-Uniform scale changes, 209
nudging, arrow keys, 48
  points, 113

Object submenu, 111–112
object-based slicing, 59, 304
objects
  constraining, 245
  cropping, 76
  grouping, 51, 244
  layers, 51
  live effects, 181–186, 196
  merging, 76
  Minus Back command, 76
  options, 242–243
  organization, 50–51
  outlining, 76
  overlapping, breaking up, 75–76
  Pathfinder palette, 77–79
  selecting, moving selection, 48
  stacking, 72, 235–236
  styles, applying, 197
  transformed duplicates, 214
  transforming, 48
  transparency, 52
  trimming, 76
  ungrouping, 244
  viewing in layers, 241–242
one-third rule of dragging, 128–130
opacity, transparency and, 174
Open dialog box, 23
open paths, 125
  dashes, 177
  fills, 85–86
  Pen tool, 125
opening documents, 23
organization, 50–51
orientation, 12–13
  printing, 270
origin point
  Rotate tool and, 210
  scaling and, 209

Outline command, Pathfinder, 76
Outline mode, 28
outlines, Liquify tools and, 228
output, printing, 272
overlapping objects
  breaking up, 75–76
  stacking order and, 237
overlapping paths, 55

• P •

page orientation, 12–13
page setup, printing, 268–269
Page Setup dialog box, 269–270
page size, 12–13
Page Tiling, 22–23
PageMaker, 10
Paintbrush tool, 149, 153
painting programs, 10
  drawing programs comparison, 149
  meshes and, 170
palettes, 17–19
  Align, 248
  Brushes, 150–151
  Character, 17, 252, 254
  closing, 17
  Color, 17, 90–95
  combining, 18
  docking, 17–18
  Flare Options, 58
  Gradient, 17, 98–99
  Layers, 51, 238–243
  Links, 313–315
  Magic Wand, 46, 109–110
  menus, 18–19
  Navigator, 27
  Paragraph, 254–255, 264–266
  Pathfinder, 71, 75–77
  positioning, shortcuts, 342
  Stroke, 85, 176–177
  Styles, 18
  Swatches, 84, 86–90
  Symbols, 299–304
  tabbing, 17–18
  Transform, 213–214
  Transparency, 173–176
  Web color, 278

Pantone libraries, 89
paper size, printing, 270
Paragraph palette, 254–255
  alignment, 264–265
paragraphs, spacing around, 265–266
Pasteboard, 22
pasting Photoshop graphics to
      Illustrator, 317–319
path-based graphics, 32
  flexibility, 33
  limitations, 38–39
  pixel-based comparison, 32, 36–38
  PostScript and, 40–41
  print speed, 40
  when to use, 39
Pathfinder commands, 75–76
Pathfinder palette, 71, 75–79
paths. See also transformations
  anchor points, 118
  blending and, 217–219
  closed, 125
  closing, Pencil tool, 138
  color, 83–84
  combination-corner anchor
      points, 122–123
  compound, 54–56
  continuing, Pencil tool, 137
  crossed, filling, 85–86
  direction points, 114
  distoring, 48–50
  Edit Selected setting, Pencil tool, 142
  editing existing, Pencil tool, 137
  editing with Pencil tool, 143
  Envelope distortion, 229–231
  fills, 82
  guides, changing to, 247–248
  handles, 42
  holes, 54
  Keep Selected setting, Pencil tool, 142
  moving, 48
  one-third rule, 129
  open, 125
  overlapping, 55
  patterns, applying, 95
  patterns from, 95–96
  Pen tool and, 118

paths *(continued)*
  Photoshop, 318
  points, 41–42
  strokes, 82, 176
  text, 53–54
Pattern Brush Options dialog box, 162–163
Pattern brushes, 150, 159–166
  artwork, 162–166
  colorization, 163
  context-sensitivity, 162
  fit, 163
  flipping, 163
  Side pattern, 161
  size, 163
  testing new, 166
  tiling, 162, 163
patterns
  creating from paths, 95–96
  fills and, 82, 94
  paths, 95
  strokes and, 82
PDF (Portable Document Format), 316
  exporting as, 315–317
  saving as, 60
Pen tool, 10, 117
  anchor points, 118
  angles, 124
  circles, 132–133
  combination-corner anchor points, 131
  curved lines, 125–131
  curved-corner anchor points, 130–131
  heart shape, 133–134
  line segments, 118
  open paths, 125
  paths and, 118
  Pencil tool, switching between, 145
  precision, 145
  right angles, 124
  shape creation, 131–134
  shapes best drawn with, 145
  smooth curves, 145
  straight lines, 123–124
  tracing items, 145
Pencil tool, 135
  accuracy, 137
  ease of use, 136–137
  Edit Selected Paths, 142

Eraser tool and, 138
  fidelity, 139–140
  fills, 138
  Keep Selected Paths, 142
  mouse use, 140
  multipurpose use, 138–144
  overview, 136–138
  paths, closing, 138
  paths, continuing, 137
  paths, editing, 137, 143
  Pen tool, switching between, 145
  precision, 145
  preferences, 139–143
  shapes best drawn with, 146
  sketching, 146
  Smooth tool and, 138
  smoothness, 141–142
  strokes, 138
  tweaking and, 142–143
perceptual color, GIF files, 287
Photoshop, Illustrator and, 317
  exporting to/from, 321–322
  moving files between, 319–320
  opening files in each, 320–321
Photoshop filters, 331–332
PICT file format, 316
pixel graphics, Web-specific, 284–291
Pixel Preview mode, 59
  Web publishing, 280
pixel-based images, 31–36
  limitations, 38–39
  path-based comparison, 32, 36–38
  previewing as, 59
  print speed, 40
  resolution and, 37
  Web graphics, 59
  when to use, 39
pixels
  fidelity and, 140
  interpolation, 34
  numeric values, 185
  page size and, 13
  rasterization and, 184
  resampling, 35
  resolution and, 31
  size, 141
Place dialog box, 310–311

placing files
  Illustrator to Photoshop, 319
  Photoshop to Illustrator, 319–320
placing graphics, 310–311
PNG (Portable Network Graphics) files,
    282, 284, 316
  saving as, 291
point type, 253
points, 13, 112, 114. *See also* anchor points;
    direction points
  adding/subtracting, 115–116
  direction-changing, 114–115
  handles, 42
  moving, 113
  paths, 41–42
  Pucker & Bloat filter, 222
  smoothness settings, 141
  stray points, Object submenu, 112
  type size, 260–261
Polar Grid tool, 245–246
Polygon tool, 66, 68–69
polygons, drawing, 68–69
positioning palettes, shortcut, 342
PostScript
  Bézier curves and, 40
  Illustrator history and, 10
  paths and, 40–41
  Print dialog box option, 272
PPD (Printer Prep Document), 275
precision
  Pen tool vs Pencil tool, 145–146
  scaling, 209
preferences
  Arc tool, 147–148
  Pencil tool, 139–143
  Smooth tool, 144
pressure, Calligraphic brushes, 168
Pressure method, Scatter brushes, 159
pressure-sensitive tablets, Liquify tools
    and, 224, 226
Preview mode, 28
previewing
  Art brushes, 157
  layers, 243
  Pixel Preview, type, 259
  Pixel Preview mode, 59
Print dialog box, 30, 267–268, 271–273

Print Setup dialog box, 269–270
printable area, 22–23
printer name, 270
printers, 269–270
  Print dialog box, 272
printing, 30, 267
  aliasing, 268
  black and white, 15
  CMYK color, 14
  color, 14
  color display, 268
  composite proofs, 271
  copies, number of, 272
  grayscale, 15
  layers, 243
  orientation, 270
  page setup, 268–271
  paper size, 270
  PPD, 275
  print range, 272
  printer name, 270
  printer type, 269–270
  process printing, 274
  quickly, 267–268
  resolution, 268
  running with the defaults, 268
  scaling, 270
  Scratch area elements, 22
  separations, 271, 273–276
  speed, path-based graphics, 40
  template layers, 243
Process color, 87
process printing, color, 93–94, 274
proportion, scaling and, 208
PSD (Photoshop Document) files, 317
publishing to Web. *See* Web publishing
Pucker & Bloat effect, 182
Pucker & Bloat filter, 49–50, 221–222
Pucker options, Liquify tools, 224, 226

QuarkXPress, 10
quick-retract method, point
    conversion, 115
Quit command, 30

• R •

Radial Dividers, Polar Grid tool, 245
radial gradients, 100–101
Random method
  Calligraphic brushes, 168
  Scatter brushes, 158
rasterization, 184–185
  Photoshop to Illustrator moves, 318
  pixel numeric values, 185
  SVG files, 298
Rasterization dialog box, 184–185
Rectangle tool, 66
rectangle type, 253
Rectangular Grid tool, 245–246
Redo command, 29–30
Reflect command,
    transformations, 210–211
Reflect dialog box, 211
reflecting
  paths, 33
  Transform palette, 213
Registration, color, 87
  separations, 274
relationships, groups, 244
Release Compound Shapes command, 74
repeating transformations, 213
replacing links, 314
resampling, 35
Reselect command, 111
resolution
  Flash files, 294
  monitor, 31
  pixel-based images and, 37
  pixels and, 31
  printing and, 268
  rasterization and, 185
  Web graphics and, 58
RGB color, 13–15, 92–94
  embedded files, 312
  rasterization and, 185
Rotate tool, 208, 210
rotating, 208, 210
  paths, 33
  Scatter brushes, 159
Roughen command, 181
Roughen filter, 222

Round Cap, strokes, 178
Round Join, strokes, 179
Rounded Rectangle tool, 66, 67
rulers, 13, 247
Russian doll phenomenon, 338–339

• S •

Save a Copy command, 60
Save As command, 60
Save As dialog box, 29
Save command, 59–60
Save dialog box, 29
Save for Web command, 59, 61, 279
  graphics, 284–285
Save Selection command, 111
saving
  colors, 92
  documents, 28–29
  Export command, 61
  graphics, as GIF files, 286–289
Scale dialog box, 207–210
Scale tool, 207–210
scaling, 207–210
  bounding box and, 208
  horizontal measurement, 209
  origin point, 209
  precision, 209
  printing, 270
  proporation and, 208
  vertical measurement, 209
Scallop tool, liquification, 224
Scatter brushes, 150, 158–159
Scratch area, 21–22
Scribble & Tweak filter, 222
scrolling, 26
Select menu, 47, 110–112
selecting, 45–46
  deselecting, 105, 111
  freeform, 108–109
  groups, 104
  Inverse command, 111
  layers, all, 111
  marquees, 47, 105
  methods, 103–104
  moving selected objects, 48
  multiple selections, 108

Next Object Above command, 111
Next Object Below command, 111
  reselecting, 111
  Save Selection command, 111
  specialized functions, 111–112
  text, 254
  transforming selected objects, 48
  type around objects, 339
Selection tool, 46, 104–105
  transformations, 205
Selection tools
  Direct Lasso tool, 104
  Direct Select Lasso tool, 46
  Direct Selection tool, 46–47, 104–106
  Group Selection tool, 46–47, 104–108
  Lasso tool, 46–47, 104
  Magic Wand tool, 46, 47, 104, 109–110
  Selection tool, 46, 104–105
selective color, GIF files, 287
Send Backward command, 237
Send to Back command, 50–51, 237
  transparency and, 52
Send to Current Layer command,
    50–51, 237
Separation Setup dialog box, 275–276
separations, printing, 271, 273–276
shadows, 214
shape creation, 65–66
  circles, 67–68
  compound shapes, 71–75
  Ellipse tool, 66–68
  Flare tool, 66
  Pen tool, 131–134, 145
  Pencil tool, 146
  Polygon tool, 66, 68–69
  Rectangle tool, 66–67
  Rounded Rectangle tool, 66, 67
  Spiral tool, 66, 68–71
  squares, 66–67
  Star tool, 66, 68–70
Shape Modes, 73–75
Shear tool, 212, 214
shearing paths, 33
shortcuts. *See also* keyboard commands
  palette position, 342
  tools, 344

size. *See also* scaling
  Art brushes, 157
  brushes, Liquify tools, 225–226
  embedded files, 310
  files, Save for Web dialog box, 285
  Pattern brushes, 163
  Scatter brushes, 159
  thumbnails, layers, 239
  type, 259–264
sketching, Pencil tool, 146
skew, 212
skin tones, 169
Slice Options dialog box, 305
slices, 304–307
  layer-based, CSS, 307–308
  object-based, 59
  Save for Web dialog box, 285
Smart Guides, 246–247
smooth anchor points, 118–119
smooth curves, Pen tool, 145
smooth paths, combination-corner anchor
    points, 122–123
smooth points, 114–115
Smooth tool, 144
  Pencil tool and, 138
smoothness
  Pencil tool settings, 141–142
  points and, 141
  Smooth tool, 144
Snap to Point, alignment and, 244
snapping to position, 244–246
spacing
  baseline, 261–262
  kerning, 262
  leading, 261–262
  paragraphs, 265–266
  Scatter brushes, 159
  tracking, 262
  type, 261–262
Spiral tool, 66, 68, 70–71
spot colors, 274
squares, drawing, 66–67
stacking, 235–237
stacking order, 72, 236–237, 240
Star tool, 66, 69–70

startup, 11–12
start-up document, customizing, 344–345
sticky settings, 349
straight lines
    Line Segment tool, 146–147
    Pen tool, 123–124, 145
    Pencil tool, 138
straight paths, combination-corner anchor
        points, 123
straight-corner anchor points, 119–120
stray points, Object submenu, 112
Stroke box, Color palette, 82–83, 90
Stroke palette, 85, 176–177
strokes, 81–83, 169, 176–177
    Appearance palette, 189, 190–192
    attributes, 176
    Bevel Join, 179
    caps, 176, 177, 178
    color, 82–84
    dashes, 177, 179–181
    effects, 189, 194
    gradients, 82
    graphic styles, 200
    hiding, 82
    joins, 176–177, 179
    Magic Wand tool, 109–110
    multiple, 192
    Object submenu, 112
    paths, 82, 176
    patterns, 82
    Pencil tool, 138
    weight, 176
    width, 84–85
styles, 188, 196–200
Styles palette, 18, 197–199
subgroups, 106
submenus, 20
    fonts, 258
    Links palette, 315
    Object, 111–112
Subtract from Shape Area, Shape
        modes, 73
subtracting points. *See* adding/
        subtracting points
sunrise shape, 78–79

SVG (Scalable Vector Graphics) format,
        283, 284, 317
    exporting as, 59
SVG Options dialog box, 296–298
swatch libraries, 86, 89–90
    moving to other documents, 338
Swatch Options dialog box, 88–89
Swatches palette, 84, 86–87
SWF (Shockwave Files) files, 283
Symbol Sprayer, 299–300
symbolism, 10
Symbolism tools, 299–304
symbols
    custom, 301
    editing, 301–302
    instances, 299
Symbols palette, 299–301

• *T* •

tabbing palettes, 17–18
tangent handles, Liquify tools, 226
target feature, Appearance palette, 189, 193
Target Layer Appearance button, 193
templates
    layers, 243
    placing graphics as, 311
text. *See also* type
    bold, 257
    graphic styles, applying, 200–201
    highlighting, 254
    italic, 257
    Paragraph palette, 254–255
    paths, 53–54
    point type, 253
    rectangle type, 253
    selecting, 254
text styles, 200
Text tool, cursor, 254
textures, fills, 94
thumbnails, Layers palette, 238–239
TIFF (Tagged Image File Format) files, 316
tiling
    Page Tiling, 22–23
    Pattern brushes, 162, 163

pixels and, 34
printing and, 267
Tool Tips, 336–337
Toolbox, 16–17
toolslots, 16
tracking, type spacing, 262
Transform Again dialog box, 215–216
Transform Each dialog box, 213, 215
Transform palette, 213–214
transformations, 205
  blending, 217–219
  copying, 213
  copying during, 214
  Direct Selection tool, 205
  duplicate objects, 214
  moving, 206–207
  partial, 216–217
  path portions, 213
  Reflect command, 210–211
  repeating, 213
  rotating, 208, 210
  scaling, 207–210
  Selection tool, 205
transforming objects, 48
transitions, curves, 129
transparency, 52
  Appearance palette, 189
  GIF files, 287–288
  graphic styles, 200
  stacking and, 236
  thumbnail layers, 238
Transparency palette, 173, 187
  Blend modes, 175–176
  opacity, 174
Trim command, Pathfinder, 76
trimming objects, 76
tweaking, Pencil tool and, 142–143
Twirl options, Liquify tools, 226
Twirl Rate options, Liquify tools, 226
Twirl tool, liquification, 224
Twist filter, 223
type, 251. *See also* text
  ascenders, 260
  baseline shift, 264
  bold, 257
  descenders, 260

font overuse, 259
fonts, 256–258
Horizontal Scale, 262–263
italic, 257
Paragraph palette, 254–255
Pixel Preview, 259
point size, 260–261
point type, 253
rectangle type, 253
reshaping, 262–263
selecting around objects, 339
size, 259–260
spacing, 261–262
typefaces, 256–258
Vertical Scale, 262–263
Type menu, 252
Type tool, 252–254
typefaces, type, 256–258

• *U* •

UI (user interface), 15
  menus, 19–20
  palettes, 17–19
  Toolbox, 16–17
  Windows/Macintosh, 20–21
Undo command, 29–30, 124
ungrouping objects, 244
Uniform scale changes, 209
units of measure, 12–13, 337
  moving objects and, 207
  points, 13
  rulers, 13
  Transform palette, 213–214
Untitled documents, 12

• *V* •

vector-based graphics, 32, 41
  Web-specific, creating, 291–298
vertical measurements
  Reflect dialog box, 211
  scaling, 209
Vertical Scale boxes, type, 262–263
View/Hide button, layers, 241

• *W* •

Warp, 10
warp distortions, 232–233
Warp options, Liquify tools, 226
Warp Options dialog box, 228–229
Warp tool, liquification, 224
Web color palette, 278, 279
Web color reduction algorithm, 287
Web graphics
  pixel-based images, 59
  resolution, 58
  Save for Web command, 59
Web options, 58–59
Web publishing, 277–278
  banding, color, 281
  color, 278–279
  dithering, color, 278–279, 281
  file compatibility, 284
  file formats, 281–284
  GIF files, 281–282
  JPEG files, 282
  Macromedia Flash files, 283
  pixel graphics, 284–291
  Pixel Preview mode, 280
  PNG files, 282
  RGB color, 14
  SVG files, 283
  SWF files, 283
  Web palette, 278
Web Safe RGB, 94
Web Snap, color, 289
Web-safe color space, 278, 279
Web-specific vector graphics
  Macromedia Flash files, 291–294
  SVG files, 294–298
weight, strokes, 176
white as cover, 332–334
Windows/Macintosh, moving
    between, 20–21
workspace. *See* UI
Wrinkle options, Liquify tools, 226
Wrinkle tool, liquification, 224

XML (eXtensible Markup Language),
    SVG files and, 283

Zig Zag filter, 223
Zoom tool, 24–26